Sparks   (62-11738)   2-3-44

Commanders of the Army of the Potomac

Commanders
of the
Army of the Potomac

WARREN W. HASSLER, JR.

Louisiana State University Press
Baton Rouge

For Libby

Copyright 1962 by
Louisiana State University Press
Manufactured in the United States of America by
Kingsport Press, Inc.
Library of Congress Catalogue Card Number: 62-11738
Design: Ernst A. Seemann

Preface

TO POSSESS SOME KNOWLEDGE OF THE SEVEN UNION GENERALS
who commanded the Army of the Potomac from 1861 to 1865 is
to start oneself well on the road toward a comprehension of the
main Federal military effort in the East. Much of the Lincoln government's war activities centered around the support of this magnificent military machine and its leaders. These seven men with
stars on their shoulders differed greatly in character traits and in
ability. In fact, it would be difficult for the military historian to
find a more diverse and challenging group. Several of these soldiers were incompetent; several were skillful but not completely
successful; none was perfect, by any means.

This study attempts to assay the stewardship of these men as
commanders of the Army of the Potomac; to examine their handling of the army on campaign, and to look at their administrative
and organizing talents; to delineate their more significant characteristics of a personal nature; to investigate their military-political
relations with the President, the Secretary of War, and the Congress, as well as their rapport with the General-in-Chief at Washington. The work is based on primary sources as well as on standard secondary studies. While the earlier and later careers of these
seven generals are not ignored, the chief emphasis is placed upon
the months in which they held tenure as leaders of the main Union
army in the East.

Up to now, no book has quite done what the present author has
undertaken. Such works as Gamaliel Bradford's *Union Portraits*,
R. M. Johnston's *Leading American Soldiers*, and the book edited
by Theodore F. Dwight, *Critical Sketches of Some of the Federal
and Confederate Commanders*, concern themselves with only a

few of the commanders of the Army of the Potomac, and none of them really comes to grips with any of these generals. It is hoped that this present study will be at least an introduction to and a primer for any further, more exhaustive research and writing pertaining to Lincoln's lieutenants in the East. It is the author's intention not to reach his evaluations and assessments of these seven commanders too quickly, or without having prepared the reader for them by giving at least a sufficient amount of material pertaining to the actual handling of the army by the general under discussion.

The present writer's debt of gratitude is extended to George T. Ness, E. T. Crowson, Francis F. Wilshin, Frederick Tilberg, C. Percy Powell, and a host of other kind and helpful people. The maps were drawn by Robert W. Kramer. For permission to use pictures and maps, special thanks are given to the National Archives and to the National Park Service, Department of the Interior. The bibliographical essay is selective only, and the student wishing reference to additional sources or books should consult the footnotes.

WARREN W. HASSLER, JR.

The Pennsylvania State University
University Park, Pennsylvania

Contents

Illustrations

Maps

Introduction

> It is the managerial class, the commanders and their staffs who are supposed to see the big picture and perhaps even do something about it, who are in the most difficult position and have the greatest opportunities of becoming confused.
>
> —*James A. Field, Jr.*

THE PARADE OF SECESSION BEGAN WITH THE PALMETTO STATE. South Carolina withdrew from the Union after Abraham Lincoln's election by "mounting the Blue Cockade" on December 20, 1860. A few days later President James Buchanan called the General-in-Chief of the United States Army, Brevet Lieutenant General Winfield Scott, to Washington from New York City, where "Old Fuss and Feathers" had been maintaining army headquarters since the early 1850's.[1]

Scott was then seventy-five years of age—older than the capital itself—and was a soldier of world renown. Certainly he was the most masterly that the Republic had produced up to that time. His military services in the War of 1812 and in the Mexican War had been truly superb, and he had been successful also on a number of sensitive diplomatic missions. He was possessed of a few petty foibles, but these were on the surface and were essentially insignificant. Besides being a gourmet, Scott was also a dress parade in himself, being seen usually resplendent in a fine uniform which included

---

[1] Robert Underwood Johnson and Clarence Clough Buel (eds.), *Battles and Leaders of the Civil War* (New York, 1884), I, 167, cited hereinafter as *B. & L.*

sash, sword, and large gold epaulets. In 1861, however, the old "Giant of Three Wars" was practically incapacitated by dropsy, gout, and vertigo, and by two British bullets which he still carried in his six-foot-five-inch frame of some 350 pounds. He was unable to ride a horse, and a derrick was required to hoist him onto the back of an animal to enable him to witness reviews. He was obliged to lie down a great deal of the time on a sofa, while his active moments were spent sitting in an oversized armchair. At times he fell asleep with visitors present.[2]

Scott arrived in the Federal capital late in December, 1860. He immediately persuaded Buchanan to appoint as colonel, on January 1, 1861, Charles P. Stone, a retired army officer of Mexican War service, and to place him on his staff. From that time until April 16, Stone was inspector general of the District of Columbia Volunteers, and was in charge of organizing and disciplining these private military companies. He organized also various trade groups into military units: two troops of cavalry and thirty-three companies of infantry—some 3,000 men in all.[3]

On March 4, 1861, Lincoln was inaugurated President after a stealthy and secret rail trip into Washington. As Commander-in-Chief of the Army and Navy of the Union, Lincoln, unlike a number of his predecessors in that high office, was lacking in any real military background or training. He had been elected captain of a company of Illinois militiamen in 1832 in the Black Hawk War, but he had found it difficult to maintain discipline. When some of his men went off on a drinking binge, Lincoln had been directed to wear a wooden sword for two days. He had been arrested also at another time for shooting off a weapon in camp. At no time had he seen action. The Confederate president, Jefferson Davis, on the other hand, had an extensive military background. He was a gradu-

[2] William H. Russell, *My Diary, North and South* (Boston, 1863), 148; Charles W. Elliott, *Winfield Scott: The Soldier and the Man* (New York, 1937), *passim.*

[3] George W. Cullum, *Biographical Register of the Officers and Graduates of the United States Military Academy . . .* (New York, 1868), II, 118.

ate of West Point, a hero of the Mexican War, and a former Secretary of War under Franklin Pierce.[4]

When he became President, Lincoln tried to inform himself on military matters. He took from the Library of Congress a book on military art and science, written by Henry W. Halleck, and studied it. However, despite his outstanding abilities in most other areas of statecraft, Lincoln was weakest in the field of military affairs. Until approximately the middle of the war, he was not a great Commander-in-Chief, being especially ineffective as a strategist and tactician. However, as will be noted in these pages, by early 1864, when U. S. Grant came East, Lincoln had, by trial and error, brought himself to a high plane as the supreme chief of military activities. In short, during the last year of the war, he was to become a consummate war director.

Lincoln's first Secretary of War was Simon Cameron, an elderly and somewhat corrupt czar of politics in the Keystone State. Cameron was named to the War Department post as part of a political deal made by Lincoln's managers at the Republican convention at the Wigwam in Chicago—the Pennsylvania politico to get an important cabinet post if he threw his delegates to the man from Springfield. Despite his reluctance to appoint to the cabinet a man with such a record, Lincoln felt obliged to keep the pledge of his political assistants at Chicago, and named him Secretary of War. The War Department, under this man, soon became a seat of corruption for which the Secretary himself was chiefly responsible.[5]

Then, on April 12, 1861, Union-held Fort Sumter, in the harbor of Charleston, South Carolina, was bombarded and forced soon to surrender. On the 15th Lincoln called for 75,000 militia. Due to the fact that some states did not fill their quotas, the President got actually less than 45,000 men. These hastily assembled amateurs, who were to fight hard at Bull Run, were very deficient in training,

[4] Benjamin P. Thomas, *Abraham Lincoln: A Biography* (New York, 1952), 31–33.

[5] See J. G. Randall, *The Civil War and Reconstruction* (Boston, 1937), 227; A. Howard Meneely, *The War Department in 1861* (New York, 1928), *passim*.

being especially untutored in such things as tactical evolutions, loading, and firing. So far as the regulars were concerned, it was not until the end of June, 1861, that there were assembled at Washington, D. C., one provisional battalion of infantry, 300 Marine recruits in one battalion, a provisional cavalry regiment plus a squadron of dragoons, and nine artillery batteries.[6]

The terrain over which military operations were to be waged in the East was far from being ideal from the Union (offensive) point of view. Practically the whole countryside was covered with heavy forests. Roads were few and poor, thereby making the waterways, and especially the railroads, important as avenues of supply and communication. With Washington as the Union capital, and with Richmond about to become the Confederate capital, an offensive southward from the former toward the latter could be reasonably expected. Here, however, the Southerners had a defensive advantage; for, besides the narrow, forest-lined roads, most of the important rivers ran in a west-to-east direction, perpendicular to the Federal line of advance. West of the Blue Ridge Mountains, the Shenandoah River flowed almost due northward and watered a fabulously rich valley which was to be used by one side or the other to outflank the main contending armies to the east. The Potomac River, of course, formed the chief west-to-east Federal defensive barrier. And at the point where the Shenandoah joined the Potomac stood Harper's Ferry, gateway to the Confederacy's wealthy Shenandoah Valley and to Pennsylvania's lush Cumberland Valley. If, as was expected, the Union was to assume the offensive to reconquer the seceded states, Harper's Ferry, like Washington, would undoubtedly be a prominent site and base for a southward Federal thrust.[7]

Four days after Fort Sumter was bombarded, Stone was named commander of the District of Columbia Volunteers (which title he kept until July 23). With the eight companies of regulars that

[6] R. M. Johnston, *Bull Run, Its Strategy and Tactics* (Boston, 1913), 2–4, 5, 7.
[7] *Ibid.*, 15.

THE EASTERN
THEATER OF
OPERATIONS

Scale in Miles

0 10 20 30 40 50

Scott had assembled, these volunteer companies protected the capital until state troops from the North could be collected and forwarded to Washington. Also, during July, Stone's tiny force was engaged in guarding the important Baltimore and Ohio Railroad, and other outposts. On April 18 a force of Virginia troops seized Harper's Ferry and the United States arsenal there. This force, at first under the command of Colonel Thomas J. Jackson, reached a total of approximately 7,000 effectives by the end of May. Jackson fortified the heights overlooking the ferry with a view to holding the place. On the twentieth of April, Virginia forces seized Norfolk and the important Federal navy yard there.[8]

Meanwhile, preparations were being made by Scott to receive and accommodate at Washington the expected levees from the loyal states. A Major Irvin McDowell, assistant adjutant general on Scott's staff, had been engaged in "inspecting troops at Washington, D. C.," since February, and was to continue in that capacity into April. On April 26 McDowell was assigned to the command of the few troops stationed on Capitol Hill, as well as of the Capitol itself. He continued in this assignment, and in "organizing and mustering D. C. Volunteers into the service at Washington," into May. On May 14 McDowell was promoted to the rank of brigadier general in the regular army. As Lieutenant Colonel E. D. Townsend, Scott's chief of staff, reports it, "McDowell so commended himself to Secretary Cameron, by his skilful management of these new troops [on Capitol Hill], that a little later, with the influence of Mr. [Salmon P.] Chase, Secretary of the Treasury—like himself an Ohio man—he was selected to receive the commission of brigadier general in the regular army." [9]

[8] Cullum, *Biographical Register,* II, 118; Johnston, *Bull Run,* 44–45, 47.

[9] Cullum, *Biographical Register,* I, 559; *The War of the Rebellion: A Compilation of the Official Records of the Union and Confederate Armies* (Washington, 1880–1901), Series I, Volume II, 603, cited hereinafter as *O.R.* (see under Government Publications, in Bibliography, for table converting the cumbersome official designations of series, volumes, and parts of this source into simple Arabic designations); E. D. Townsend, *Anecdotes of the Civil War . . .* (New York, 1884), 13–14.

In an effort to establish a more unified command, Scott, on April 27, in General Orders No. 12, created the Military Department of Washington, to be commanded by fifty-eight-year-old Colonel Joseph K. F. Mansfield, veteran of the Mexican War. Then, Lincoln issued a call on May 3 for 42,034 three-years volunteers, 22,714 additional regulars, and 18,000 seamen. On the same day, in a message to Major General George B. McClellan at Columbus, Ohio, Scott enunciated what came to be known as his "Anaconda" plan—a scheme expanded somewhat in another message to McClellan on May 21. Scott's design called for a complete naval blockade of the Confederacy and for a powerful thrust down the Mississippi River. It was also the view of the General-in-Chief that it would take some 300,000 men, three years of grim fighting, and a general of the capacity of James Wolfe to defeat the determined foe.[10]

Washington had need of all the soldiers it could receive at this time, for, on May 6, General Robert E. Lee, in command of all Virginia forces and adviser to Jefferson Davis in Richmond, ordered Colonel Philip St. George Cocke, at Culpeper Court House, to move a force of troops to the railroad hub of Manassas (known also as Manassas Junction). In approximately two weeks, Cocke had at Manassas a force which was steadily reinforced.[11]

Then, on May 17, the Department of Northeastern Virginia was created. McDowell was placed in command of it "and of the defenses of Washington south of the Potomac." When Lincoln offered him two stars to go with the new promotion, the General declined them, saying that he would not accept a major generalcy until he really earned it by deeds. McDowell was fearful also that if he accepted the two stars his action would lead to much jealousy and would work against him in the long run. As to the Confederate reaction to this appointment, the later Lieutenant General James Longstreet states, "Most of us knew [McDowell] and of his attainments, as well as those of [General P.G.T.] Beauregard, to the

[10] 2 O.R., 607; 107 O.R., 369–70, 386–87.
[11] Johnston, Bull Run, 19, 23–24, 133; 2 O.R., 806, 847.

credit of the latter, so on that point we were quite satisfied." [12]

Meantime, to command the hodgepodge of Union forces which was gathering in Pennsylvania and western Maryland for the purpose of moving against the Confederates at Harper's Ferry, the officials at Washington scraped the bottom of the barrel and came up with incompetent old Major General (of Pennsylvania militia) Robert Patterson, who had participated in the War of 1812. His opponent in gray at the ferry—named to that command on May 15 —was one of the ablest of the Southern officers, General Joseph E. Johnston.[13]

Until May 24 all the Federal troops were kept on the north bank of the Potomac. But on that date some 8,000 soldiers, under the immediate command of Mansfield's inspector general, Colonel Samuel P. Heintzelman, occupied Arlington and Alexandria without any fighting, the Confederates pulling back toward Fairfax Court House. Then, on May 27, in General Orders No. 26, McDowell was named commander of the Army of Northeastern Virginia, and of a "new military geographical department" (known as the Department of Northeastern Virginia), which included all of Virginia east of the Alleghenies, except for the area around Fortress Monroe. Scott had been asked, again, to choose between McDowell and Mansfield. Despite his reluctance, he selected the former, although he advised McDowell to seek a means of declining the job. McDowell, however, refused to reject the command. Henceforth, a slight coolness developed between the General-in-Chief and McDowell, according to Lieutenant Colonel James B. Fry, which did not promise well for the trying days ahead. Also, Mansfield was miffed at not being selected to this important active command, and friction arose between him and McDowell. Cer-

[12] Cullum, *Biographical Register,* I, 559; John G. Nicolay and John Hay, *Abraham Lincoln: A History* (New York, 1890), IV, 323–24; James Longstreet, *From Manassas to Appomattox* . . . (Philadelphia, 1896), 36.

[13] Johnston, *Bull Run,* 45–47.

tainly this was not the most auspicious beginning for the new
Union field commander, who would have need of every ounce
of sympathy, aid, and co-operation which was in the power of
his brother officers to give him.[14]

[14] B. & L., I, 171; 2 O.R., 37–41; Johnston, Bull Run, 19; Cullum, Biographical Register, I, 559; James B. Fry, McDowell and Tyler (New York,
1884), 9, 10; Report of the Committee on the Conduct of the War
(Washington, 1863), II, 37, cited hereinafter as C.C.W.

Commanders of the Army of the Potomac

CHAPTER ONE

Irvin McDowell

> Whoever makes the first aggressive
> move will be beaten.
> —*Sylvanus Thayer*

THE MAIN STRIKING FORCE OF THE UNION BORE A SOMEWHAT
ostentatious name: The Grand Army of the United States; and its
first field commander was himself somewhat pompous and punctilious. Picture a huge, bulky man, forty-two years old, "square
and powerfully built, but with rather a stout and clumsy figure
and limbs, a good head covered with close-cut thick dark hair,
small light-blue eyes, short nose, large cheeks and jaws, relieved
by an iron-grey tuft somewhat of the French type." Of great physical strength, Irvin McDowell was possessed also with energy that
seemed limitless. Said one who saw him in the late spring of
1861: "McDowell . . . made a deep impression upon me. . . .
He was at that time in the full flush of mature manhood, fully
six feet tall, deep-chested . . . and in every respect a fine and impressive soldier."[1]

The career of the new Federal commander had been a varied one
before Sumter. McDowell first saw the light of day on October 15,
1818, in Columbus, Ohio. His forebears were Scotch-Irish. Young
Irvin received a part of his early education at the Collège de
Troyes, in France. In 1834 he entered West Point, and graduated
twenty-third in a class of forty-five in 1838. His first service was
as a lieutenant of artillery. He was, for a time, an instructor and
adjutant at the Military Academy. During the Mexican War Mc-
Dowell served on Brigadier General John E. Wool's staff, and

[1] William Swinton, *Campaigns of the Army of the Potomac* . . .
(New York, 1866), 41; Russell, *My Diary*, 145; B. & L., I, 171; James
Harrison Wilson, *Under the Old Flag* . . . (New York, 1912), I, 66.

was brevetted captain in 1847 for gallant and meritorious conduct at the battle of Buena Vista. Although engaged from time to time in several other minor assignments, he was usually on duty as General-in-Chief Winfield Scott's assistant adjutant general at the headquarters of the army. McDowell had been married in 1849 to a rather plain-looking woman, Helen Burden, of Troy, New York, and the union had been blessed with four children. For one year, 1858–1859, he had been on leave of absence in Europe, studying foreign military institutions and practices. When the Civil War broke out, McDowell was still serving on Scott's staff, and had attained only the rank of brevet major.[2]

The patriotic and intensely pro-Union McDowell had personal characteristics that were wide-ranging. He was "always a close student," and "was well informed outside as well as inside his profession." His chief hobbies were architecture and landscape gardening, and he was a lover of music. Although he was later viciously accused of being drunk on the field of battle, McDowell was "of unexceptionable habits," and not only shunned the use of any alcoholic beverage but actually refrained from drinking tea or coffee. He was soon to become famous for his use of odd headpieces, one of these being a basket-shaped bamboo hat, and another "an immense Japanese wash-bowl, which he wore on his head." A less winning quality, however, was the General's gluttony. "At dinner," states cavalryman James H. Wilson, "he was such a Gargantuan feeder and so absorbed in the dishes before him that he had but little time for conversation. While he drank neither wine nor spirits, he fairly gobbled the larger part of every dish within reach, and wound up with an entire watermelon, which he said was 'monstrous fine!' "[3]

[2] Cullum, *Biographical Register*, I, 559; Dumas Malone (ed.), *Dictionary of American Biography* (New York, 1933), XII, 29–30, cited hereinafter as *D.A.B.*

[3] *B. & L.*, I, 171; Copy of Extract from Journal of Col. W. A. Roebling, aide to McDowell, Aug. 22, 1862, in Fitz John Porter Papers, Division of Manuscripts, Library of Congress; Wilson, *Under the Old Flag*, I, 66.

While he was "outspoken in his opinions," McDowell was reserved in his personal relations with his subordinate officers; and this, combined with his poor memory for faces and names, and his absent-minded habit of losing himself in his own thoughts while others were speaking to him, tended to make him unpopular. As one veteran of the war phrased it, "McDowell had none of those traits of personal magnetism which have often made inferior generals very popular with the rank and file." He was humorless, and had a violent temper which showed itself "on several trying occasions." Once, the General almost knocked off the head of a Wisconsin private "because he straggled," and the troops witnessing this incident were angered. At other times he received officers in the rudest manner. Perhaps Salmon Chase—one of McDowell's staunchest supporters and admirers—summed up the commander's traits in the most balanced way:

McDowell . . . is a loyal, brave, truthful, capable officer. He is a disciplinarian. . . . He never drinks, or smokes, or chews, or indulges in any kind of license. He is serious and earnest. He resorts to no arts for popularity. He is attended by no clacquers and puffers. He has no political aims. . . . He is too indifferent in manner, and his officers are sometimes alienated by it. He is too purely military in his intercourse with his soldiers. There is an apparent *hauteur:* no, that is not the word—rough indifference expresses better the idea—in his way toward them, that makes it hard for them to feel any very warm personal sentiments toward him.

But many in the Confederacy regarded the National commander quite highly.[4]

Finally, as to experience and qualifications for important field command, McDowell had several grave shortcomings. "Although," writes Major General George B. McClellan of him, "in some respects a very good bureau officer and a fair disciplinarian and drill officer for a school of instruction, he lacked the qualities necessary for a commander in the field." Before May 27, 1861, his highest

---

[4] Roebling's Journal, Aug. 27, 28, 1862; Jacob W. Schuckers, *The Life . . . of Salmon Portland Chase.* (New York, 1874), 450.

actual command rank had been that of lieutenant of artillery. And, unfortunately for the Federals, McDowell lacked real confidence in himself and in his ability to win. Before beginning his Bull Run campaign, he said, "half in jest, half seriously," to William Howard Russell, famous London *Times* war correspondent, "I declare I am not quite easy at the idea of having your eye on me, for you have seen so much of European armies, you will, very naturally, think little of us, generals and all." On another occasion, asserts Russell, "he did not hesitate to speak with great openness of the difficulties he had to contend with, and the imperfection of all the arrangements of the army." The General's chief of staff, Captain James B. Fry, mentions a further trait that could become harmful if allowed to go beyond bounds: "McDowell was dominated by the feeling of subordination and deference to General Scott which at that time pervaded the whole army." Henry Villard, war reporter with the army, observed that "in my frequent intercourse with him, I gained the impression that he lacked the resolute determination which alone could insure success in his trying task of organizing an effective army for aggressive war out of the raw material gathering under his command. With his evident want of confidence in himself, he appeared to be full of misgivings from the start. This self-distrust showed itself in his constant talk of the difficulties surrounding him and of the doubts he felt of the possibility of overcoming them." Such were the characteristics and background of the man upon whose shoulders now rested the hopes of the North.[5]

As soon as he was named to the command of the Grand Army, "McDowell entered on his duties with great alacrity, working night and day to prepare his command for the approaching conflict." When Alexandria and Arlington Heights were occupied on the night of May 23–24, the Union commander was for pressing on at

[5] Charles A. Davis, *Three Years in the Army* . . . (Boston, 1894), 120; Russell, *My Diary*, 145, 164; *B. & L.*, I, 181; Henry Villard, *Memoirs of Henry Villard* (Boston, 1904), I, 179–80.

once toward Manassas; but, for reasons not stated, this difficult endeavor was not permitted. So the General established his head-quarters at Robert E. Lee's fine estate and mansion, Arlington, which high ground commanded a magnificent view overlooking the Potomac River and the city of Washington.[6]

As a defensive step, almost immediately after the Potomac had been crossed, McDowell began the construction of a few earth-work fortifications at the southern bridgeheads of the Long Bridge and Aqueduct Bridge, as well as the construction of similar works covering the approaches to Alexandria and Arlington. Not until near June 14, however, were artillery pieces emplaced in these forts.[7]

Perceiving a certain lack of organization, McDowell, by May 29, formed his regiments into three brigades, while his supplications for badly needed staff officers yielded him several competent engi-neers. But when the Union commander gathered together eight regiments to deploy them for a review—"the only instance previous to the battle that even that number of troops were manoeuvred in one body"—he was sharply criticized for trying to "make a show." [8]

Meanwhile, the Confederates were not idle. The com-mander of all Virginia forces, General Robert E. Lee, visited Manassas on May 29; and as a result, the Confederates established a defensive line along Bull Run, a small stream running in a gen-eral northwest-to-southeast direction, some five miles east of Manassas. A few days later the capital of the Confederacy was shifted from Montgomery, Alabama, to Richmond, and Mc-Dowell's old West Point classmate, P. G. T. Beauregard, arrived at Manassas to take command of the Southern forces gathering there. "Old Bory," the Creole of Fort Sumter fame, felt then that the Federals would most likely attack at Bull Run with approxi-

[6] J. H. Stine, *History of the Army of the Potomac* (Washington, 1893), 7; *C.C.W.*, I, 129, 134; 2 *O.R.*, 655.

[7] J. G. Barnard's report, Swinton, *Army of the Potomac*, 30; 2 *O.R.*, 653–54.

[8] 2 *O.R.*, 653–54; Johnston, *Bull Run*, 22; *C.C.W.* (1863), II, 3.

mately 20,000 men, and that he would need 10,000 to 15,000 men to resist such a move.[9]

In the meantime, at Harpers Ferry, Johnston received authority on June 13 to act as he deemed best, and he began immediately to pull his Confederate troops out of the town and to move back toward Winchester. However, Patterson's Federal soldiers were advancing through western Maryland to the Potomac at only a snail's pace, and did not cross the river until June 17. Patterson had at least 18,000 men as compared to Johnston's 8,000 to 12,000. Of course, to keep Johnston from joining Beauregard at Bull Run, Patterson's only course was to *attack* Johnston. "If Patterson was not in condition to do this," observes William Swinton, New York *Times* war correspondent, "his force should immediately have been withdrawn to the front of Washington and united with McDowell's." [10]

McDowell's own army numbered on June 21 approximately 14,400 men. He was asked on this day to expound a plan of his own for uniting his force and that of Patterson. McDowell replied that, because of the distance between these two Federal armies, and because of the danger of exposing a flank if one of them marched to join the other, "the force to move from each position should be constituted without reference to material support from the other." A movement of his own force further west than Vienna was opposed by McDowell. The General-in-Chief decided that the main advance should be against Manassas, and verbally asked McDowell on June 24 to draw up a plan of operations. Since the scheme which McDowell presented on this date was very close to the one actually used, it requires some examination.[11]

First of all, McDowell assumed, correctly, that the Confederates at Bull Run numbered about 25,000, and that they would probably

[9] Johnston, *Bull Run*, 33–34; 2 *O.R.*, 894, 902.

[10] 2 *O.R.*, 925; Johnston, *Bull Run*, 29–30; Robert Patterson, *A Narrative of the Campaign in the Valley of the Shenandoah in 1861* (Philadelphia, 1865), 63; Swinton, *Army of the Potomac*, 45.

[11] 2 *O.R.*, 718, 726.

be reinforced by an additional 10,000 men. He also assumed, this time incorrectly, that Patterson would contain Johnston's army at Winchester. McDowell called for a movable column of his own of 30,000 men, with 10,000 in reserve (some of whom apparently would be left in the works near Washington). His main line of supply and communication would be the Orange and Alexandria Railroad. He had received intelligence that Beauregard had some guns in position along Bull Run, and that there were probably some fieldworks along the Run and at Manassas. McDowell asserted that Bull Run was "fordable at almost any place." He proposed, therefore, by a turning movement, to outflank the Confederate position along Bull Run and, by seizing or threatening Beauregard's communications, to force him to abandon the field and retreat. McDowell would advance his main force of 30,000 simultaneously by three routes: one was to move along the railroad; another from Vienna or Falls Church was to march between Fairfax Court House and Centreville; while the third would advance via the Little River Turnpike. His three columns were to be united before reaching Bull Run, and then the turning attack would be made. The tenor of his words indicated McDowell's belief that victory would be attained by this plan.[12]

The Union commander immediately presented his plan to the Lieutenant General. According to Scott's military secretary, Lieutenant Colonel Schuyler Hamilton, the old general, after listening to the presentation, said, "General McDowell, that is as good a plan of battle as I ever saw upon paper." But Scott indicated, prophetically, that it would all be hopeless if McDowell's plan depended upon Patterson's holding Johnston in the Valley. Although grasping the situation, McDowell, in his plan of operations, did not concern himself with Johnston's army, although this enemy force was part and parcel of the operation toward Manassas. In tone, McDowell remained a subordinate commander and not the commanding general of a sizeable army of over 30,000 men. Consequently, an unfortunate Union command structure resulted.

[12] *Ibid.*, 720–21; *B. & L.*, I, 174–75.

Scott himself was partially to blame, for he drifted rather than really coming to grips with the problem of the big picture on the military chessboard. For his part, McDowell shifted to Scott the responsibility of considerations of actions taking place just a short distance to the west. He was unwise in assuming that his movement on Bull Run was being covered completely by Scott.[13]

Another weakness of McDowell's ambitious plan of operations was that it involved a main stroke, a secondary effort, plus an additional feint. Three converging forces would have to concentrate simultaneously upon the battlefield for success to be gained. Even well-trained soldiers, with able commanders and smooth-functioning staffs, would have found it a difficult enterprise to master. It was, in reality, beyond the capabilities of a hastily gathered, untrained aggregation going into its maiden battle. McDowell correctly assumed that "leaks" in information from Washington would forewarn the Confederates and enable them, in a short time, to augment their force at Bull Run. To counterbalance this, in part, rapidity in moving was essential; but McDowell, even allowing for the rawness of his soldiers, was painfully lacking in this asset. When the General spoke to his superiors of the greenness of his troops, and begged for a little more time to organize them, he was told, "You are green, it is true; but *they* are green also; you are all green alike." This attitude by the administration showed a lack of appreciation of the greater difficulties of the offensive.[14]

As to transportation, McDowell wanted only the smallest possible number of supply wagons; but had he had a sizeable wagon train, he would have been less dependent upon the brittle Orange & Alexandria Railroad, and would have thus been given greater mobility. Unfortunately, his troops had an oversupply of such encumbering items as packs, overcoats, tents, and other baggage. McDowell should have realized that, in his short advance against Bull

---

[13] Stine, *Army of the Potomac*, 9–10; *B. & L.*, I, 181; Johnston, *Bull Run*, 62–63.

[14] Johnston, *Bull Run*, 63–64; *C.C.W.* (1863), I, 38; Swinton, *Army of the Potomac*, 40, 42–43; Stine, *Army of the Potomac*, 7.

Run, the railroad was then not a safe or practicable line of supply and communication (although it might become so if Manassas Junction could be seized). He should have used the roads for supply, and sent forward every possible man to augment his main striking force, instead of stringing many of them out as a reserve along the railroad.[15]

A final council of war was called by Lincoln on June 29. Scott at once announced his opposition to a major advance against the Confederates at Bull Run. Then, writes Lieutenant Colonel E. D. Townsend, Scott's chief of staff, "General McDowell spread his maps on the table, and demonstrated his plan with . . . clearness and precision. . . ." The scheme was approved, and Scott loyally accepted his superiors' decision and strove valiantly to make a success of it.[16]

McDowell had many qualms about his army prior to moving it toward Bull Run. "I had no opportunity," he said, "to test my machinery; to move it around and see whether it would work smoothly or not. There was not a man there who had ever maneuvered troops in large bodies. . . . I wanted very much, a little time; all of us wanted it, we did not have a bit of it." There exists a description of McDowell at this time—and it shows his lack of sufficient staff officers and the absence of discipline of the troops—walking alone through the crowded streets of Washington, unnoticed and unsaluted by the ill-trained soldiery. When a friend, John Bigelow, visited the National commander at his headquarters at Arlington Heights, he found the General very distressed. "This is not an army," McDowell said to him; "it will take a long time to make an army." Bigelow pitied him as he had never pitied any man.[17]

[15] Johnston, *Bull Run,* 64, 65–66; William T. Sherman, *Memoirs of General W. T. Sherman* (New York, 1875), I, 178.

[16] *C.C.W.* (1863), I, 36, 37, 62; Townsend, *Anecdotes of the Civil War,* 55–57; *Congressional Globe,* July 24, 1861, p. 246.

[17] Theodore B. Gates, *The Ulster Guard . . .* (New York, 1879), 112; John Bigelow, *Retrospections of an Active Life* (New York, 1909), I, 360.

Meantime, Patterson was floundering to the west. He finally crossed the Potomac on July 3, and occupied Martinsburg, West Virginia. Despite Scott's urgings that he move via Leesburg toward Alexandria, Patterson halted at Martinsburg. He telegraphed Washington that he would attack Johnston only when he heard that McDowell had made his attack! "If the enemy retires I shall not pursue," trumpeted the muddle-headed old militiaman. Then came more specific instructions from Scott on the thirteenth: ". . . if not strong enough to beat the enemy early next week [i.e., on the sixteenth], make demonstrations so as to detain him in the Valley of Winchester." Nothing could be clearer—yet Patterson's reactions were pathetic. He declared blatantly on July 14 that he would not attack Johnston "unless I can rout him." Swinton terms Patterson's conduct at this time "ridiculous"; and R. M. Johnston asserts, "A critique of Patterson's generalship belongs less to the domain of military art than to that of musical comedy." [18]

On July 17 the General-in-Chief wired Patterson as follows: "Do not let the enemy amuse and delay you with a small force in front, whilst he reenforces [Manassas] Junction with his main body." But on that very day, Patterson had withdrawn his army to Charlestown, thereby enabling the enterprising Johnston, on the eighteenth, to put 9,000 men in motion by rail for Manassas. Most of this force joined Beauregard on the twentieth and twenty-first, in time to be of decisive help in the Bull Run battle.[19] Around Manassas, Beauregard had under his command approximately 24,000 men—styled the Confederate Army of the Potomac—and thirty-five guns. His line along Bull Run, stretching southward from the Stone Bridge to the Manassas Railroad, was some seven miles in length.[20]

[18] 2 O.R., 157–66; Swinton, Army of the Potomac, 46; Johnston, Bull Run, 74.

[19] 2 O.R., 167, 168; C.C.W. (1863), II, 5.

[20] Alfred Roman, The Military Operations of General Beauregard. . . (New York, 1884), I, 83; Johnston, Bull Run, 82, 88–89, 109–10.

McDowell's Grand Army, or Army of Northeastern Virginia, as it was sometimes called, aggregated 35,732 men, although his total number of effectives was probably about 28,452. His main column of operations was composed of the following divisions: First Division, commanded by Brigadier General Daniel Tyler; Second Division, commanded by Brigadier General David Hunter; Third Division, commanded by Heintzelman; and Fifth Division, commanded by Colonel Dixon S. Miles. The Fourth Division, commanded by Brigadier General (of New York militia) Theodore Runyon, was left behind at Alexandria by McDowell, although it was brought forward as far as Centreville during the battle. The army had also fifty-five guns—chiefly regular army batteries—including twenty-six smoothbores and twenty-nine rifled pieces, which equalled almost two guns per thousand infantrymen. There was little cavalry with the Federal army.[21]

While the staff and command arrangements were poor, McDowell's infantry organization was not too bad. However, the hurried way in which it was arrived at, and the inexperience prevalent, led to breakdowns in combat. The artillery was the strong point in the Union army, and McDowell was trained primarily as an artillery officer. Yet it was poorly organized, the batteries having been crudely doled out to the brigades, some brigades having two batteries and some having none. Several artillery changes were actually made on the march and in battle. A grouping by divisions would have been a much better arrangement. The division and brigade commanders were, on the whole, men of fair ability. Their staffs (and McDowell's), however, were small, and were composed of inexperienced young officers—although many of the latter were regulars. Actually, there was no systematized command. Some of the brigades were formed just a few hours before the advance began. Most of the regimental colonels were poor; but even worse were the lower-ranking officers. "The Quartermaster, Commissary, and Ordnance departments," says Wil-

[21] 2 *O.R.*, 309; Thomas L. Livermore, *Numbers and Losses in the Civil War* . . . (Boston, 1900), 77; Johnston, *Bull Run*, 90–97, 98–99.

liam A. Ganoe, "had neither means of supply nor subordinate officers who knew their duties. The few trained higher officers could not impart their knowledge to a multitude in a short time." The engineer department played but a small role in the campaign. Only about 800 of McDowell's troops were really trained. Another weakness was that, at McDowell's headquarters, there was an "absence of maps and reliable guides," and the General himself did not know the country well, although there was little real excuse for this. Adding to McDowell's handicaps was the fact that during the battle he "was accompanied by only two aides-de-camp." [22]

Finally, on July 16, McDowell issued his marching orders for the general advance. Showing the influence of the "masked battery" bogey, the General stated that three things would be considered unpardonable: "*First.* To come upon a battery or a breastwork without a knowledge of its position. *Second.* To be surprised. *Third.* To fall back." The troops marched out of the Alexandria area promptly on the sixteenth, carrying three days' rations in their haversacks. The food supply wagons were to move out on the seventeenth. Near 5:00 P.M. on the sixteenth, McDowell arrived at Alexandria to join the march of Heintzelman's division. When the guides were delayed in arriving by lack of horses, the army commander returned to Washington. Later that evening, at the Washington railroad station, W. H. Russell was astonished to see McDowell, alone on the platform, anxiously looking into the box cars. It turned out that the General was seeking two artillery batteries that could not be accounted for, and was obliged to perform this sleuthing chore himself because his few staff officers were busy at headquarters. Although McDowell did not appear to Russell to be in good spirits, he nonetheless spoke confidently of his army's advance. [23]

[22] Johnston, *Bull Run*, 9, 100–103; William A. Ganoe, *The History of the United States Army* (New York, 1942), 256, 258.

[23] 2 *O.R.*, 303–305; Journal of Samuel P. Heintzelman, July 18, 1861, Div. of MSS, Library of Congress.

McDowell's marching orders showed a painstaking concern with detail. He hoped that the Confederates would tarry in their advanced positions near Fairfax, and his orders were well drawn up to give the Federals an initial success in that eventuality. In elucidating certain concepts of his circumspect, feeling-out type of march, McDowell caused his division commanders to overdo this cautious policy by scouting and deploying to an excess. This consequently delayed and somewhat demoralized his green troops, who had to march and wait under a blistering July sun. McDowell should have sent some cavalry forward ahead of the army on the sixteenth, and his order should have been issued for just one day's work, not two. Also, apparently, the General forgot that his brigades had been grouped into divisions. Then, too, if the enemy did not choose to remain at Fairfax, McDowell's night marches were useless and unwise. Finally, three of his divisions were concentrated on the Warrenton-Little River pike, where delays in the long column would be inevitable.[24]

July 16—the day on which McDowell's army jumped off—was clear and warm, but not stifling. By July 18 it was seen that all the Federal units would reach Centreville on this day, after a leisurely march which Colonel William T. Sherman contends "demonstrated little save the general laxity of discipline." After glancing at the evacuated Confederate camps and fieldworks at Fairfax Court House, McDowell sent this overly optimistic message to Scott in Washington: "Their retreat must have a damaging effect upon them."[25]

McDowell was unaware, on July 18, that Johnston had left the Valley and was in the process of joining Beauregard; so, in his mind, in order to prevent a possible later movement by Johnston from the Valley, the Union commander determined to seize a vital point (Gainesville) on the railroad from the Valley, and thus pre-

[24] Johnston, *Bull Run,* 116–18, 118 n–19 n.
[25] Heintzelman's Journal, July 16, 17, 1861; 2 *O.R.,* 306, 743–44; Sherman, *Memoirs,* I, 181.

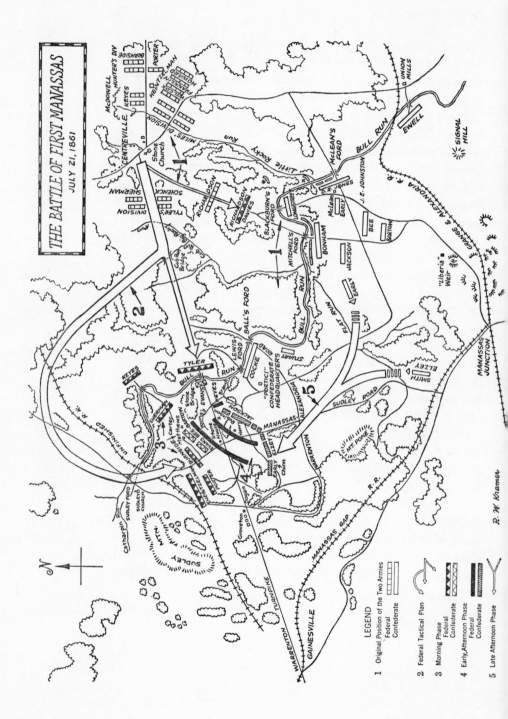

THE BATTLE OF FIRST MANASSAS

JULY 21, 1861

LEGEND

1 Original Position of the Two Armies
　　Federal
　　Confederate

2 Federal Tactical Plan

3 Morning Phase
　　Federal
　　Confederate

4 Early Afternoon Phase
　　Federal
　　Confederate

5 Late Afternoon Phase

R. W. Kramer

vent the junction of the two main enemy armies—a junction which was, of course, already about to take place. At 8:15 on the morning of the eighteenth, McDowell sent this positive order to division commander Tyler at Centreville: "Observe well the roads to Bull Run and to Warrenton. Do not bring on an engagement, but keep up the impression that we are moving on Manassas." Despite these clear directions, and despite warnings from Captain James B. Fry, McDowell's chief of staff, and from Major John G. Barnard, Tyler, at 2:00 P.M. on the eighteenth, deliberately provoked a combat at Blackburn's Ford—on one of the roads from Centreville to Manassas—where enemy troops and guns were plainly seen. The result was a sharp clash and repulse, one Union regiment breaking and fleeing to the rear, after which Tyler withdrew the entire force toward Centreville. Arriving in the late afternoon at Centreville, in time to witness the end of Tyler's withdrawal from Blackburn's, McDowell engaged in a torrid and unseemly public wrangle with Tyler—a set-to which led to a lifelong feud between the two generals.[26]

"The operations on the 18th," writes Fry, "confirmed McDowell in his opinion that with his raw troops the Confederate position should be turned instead of attacked in front." McDowell believed also that Stone Bridge was mined and covered by guns and abatis. Unfortunately, the Federal setback at Blackburn's Ford made McDowell gun-shy about launching at least a holding attack on the Confederate right-center at Mitchell's Ford or especially at Blackburn's Ford, although this action would have been most desirable in conjunction with his turning movement against Beauregard's left.[27]

Having once decided on a plan of attack, speed was of the essence. Most authorities, including Joe Johnston, agree that McDowell would probably have been victorious had he been able to bring himself to attack on either July 19 or 20. But both of these

[26] Nicolay and Hay, *Abraham Lincoln,* IV, 346; *B. & L.,* I, 178, 183, 187; 2 *O.R.,* 312, 329; *C.C.W.* (1863), II, 20.
[27] *B. & L.,* I, 179; 2 *O.R.,* 307, 318; Johnston, *Bull Run,* 136–37.

days—days on which Beauregard was being reinforced by Johnston—were spent by the Federal commander in reconnoitering the
Confederate line. McDowell stated on the twentieth that he wanted
to make the reconnaissance in force, but that he "deferred to the
better judgment of others" and tried to get information of the
enemy's position "by observation and stealth." Showing his lack of
decision and confidence in his own judgment, McDowell, on the
same day, was *again* talked out of doing what he wanted to do—
something that would have been a wise move; namely, to advance
his right wing on the twentieth so it would have less distance to
move on the twenty-first in its swing around the Confederate
left flank.[28]

Finally, on the afternoon of July 20, McDowell was ready to discuss his plan of battle with his top officers. The council of war at
Centreville lasted from the afternoon until 10:30 P.M., during
which time possible movements were debated, although McDowell
refrained from asking for definite opinions. "I noticed no want of
confidence in our commander," wrote Erasmus D. Keyes after
the war. The final plan—issued apparently just before midnight on
the twentieth—called for a wide-sweeping turning movement by the
Union right wing, composed of Hunter's and Heintzelman's divisions (about 12,000 men) and five batteries, all under Mc-
Dowell's personal command. This force would begin its circuitous
march two hours after midnight, cross Bull Run at Sudley Ford,
swing down upon Beauregard's left flank, open up Stone Bridge to
the Federals on the Warrenton pike, and then roll up the whole
Confederate line and press it back some seven or eight miles to
Manassas. While the Union right wing was striking the enemy's
left, Tyler's division, with four batteries, was to make a secondary
holding attack or demonstration at Stone Bridge. The two separated National forces were then to join on the southwest bank of
Bull Run at Stone Bridge. Miles's division was to remain near
Centreville, and make a feint toward Blackburn's Ford. If he won

[28] *B. & L.,* I, 180, 182, 183; 2 *O.R.,* 308, 317, 328–31.

the battle at Bull Run, McDowell planned to march westward along the Manassas Gap Railroad, tearing up communications, and "interpos[ing] between the forces under Beauregard and those under Johnston," whom McDowell still believed to be in the Valley.[29]

McDowell's battle order was weak in several respects. First, it ignored the probable presence of Johnston at Masassas. Then, McDowell's scattering out of his army might well invite a menacing counterattack from Beauregard's right and center against the weakly held Federal base and line of communications. Also, a night march with such raw troops—who had proved their lack of discipline and marching qualities in the advance from Alexandria—and a turning movement over such a great distance (about ten miles) would tire his men so as to weaken them for the decisive part of the fight. The plan depended upon the close co-operation of the Union center and right, and called for greater skill on the part of his inexperienced officers than they possessed. Colonel Matthew F. Steele states that "it further involved the hazard of forming his line of battle parallel to the Warrenton Pike, his line of retreat; or with his back to the stream; or with his face to the rear." It is always dangerous in war to have an army split by such an obstacle as a stream like Bull Run. Beauregard felt that, for McDowell, "it would . . . have been much better if, with more dash, the flank attack had been made by the Stone Bridge itself and the ford immediately above it." Certainly, had the Federals used the farm ford, or even Poplar Ford (much closer to the bridge than to Sudley Ford), they would have been able to attack earlier and with troops less fatigued. However, while the turning movement to the north was undoubtedly risky, it was, for green troops, far less dangerous than a direct frontal attack on the strong enemy position along Bull Run. In summation, McDowell's plan of battle was perhaps the only one plausible, considering all fac-

[29] Heintzelman's Journal, Sept. 1, 1861; Erasmus D. Keyes, *Fifty Years' Observation of Men and Events* (New York, 1884), 432; 2 *O.R.*, 325, 326.

tors. Most authorities consider it to have been, in essence, a skillful one.[30]

During the night of July 20–21, McDowell once again showed doubt in his own judgment. "It had been my intention," he states in his report, "to move the several columns out on the road a few miles on the evening of the 20th, so that they would have a shorter march in the morning; but I deferred to those who had the greatest distance to go, and who preferred starting early in the morning and making but one move." He further asserts that "could we have fought a day—yes, a few hours—sooner, there is everything to show that we should have continued successful."[31]

Adding to the Federal problem was the fact that McDowell became ill on the night of July 20–21 because of having eaten some bad canned fruit which resulted in a choleraic attack. This, combined with the extremely hot weather on this clear day, caused the Union commander at times during the battle to transfer from horseback to a light carriage. Owing to a delay in the leading division—Tyler's—which did not break camp as ordered at 2:30 A.M., the other divisions were two or three hours behind schedule. Not until approximately 6:00 A.M. did Tyler deploy along Bull Run near Stone Bridge, and his demonstrations there were so feeble that they were contained by small Confederate forces. Instead of having his turning force—the divisions of Hunter and Heintzelman—at Sudley Ford at 6:00 A.M., it was not until approximately 9:30 that this force of McDowell's arrived there, thus giving the enemy time to shift troops northwestward to meet the threat. Also, the National force which had moved from Centreville to near Mitchell's Ford opened an artillery fire at 8:00 A.M. which was so weak as to indicate to the alert Confederates that this was merely a demonstration.[32]

[30] Johnston, *Bull Run,* 145 ff; Matthew F. Steele, *American Campaigns* (Washington, 1935), 145; *B. & L.,* I, 218; John C. Ropes, *The Story of the Civil War* (New York, 1899), I, 158–59; Sherman, *Memoirs,* I, 181.

[31] 2 *O.R.,* 317, 325.

[32] *C.C.W.* (1863), II, 41; 2 *O.R.,* 318; Joseph E. Johnston, *Narrative of Military Operations . . .* (New York, 1874), 41.

McDowell himself rode out of Centreville at 4:00 A.M., and by 6:45 he was near Stone Bridge. He then retraced his steps eastward along the pike, and rode northward along the circuitous route to Sudley Ford taken by his turning column. The battle had opened between Sudley Church and the Stone House—located at the intersection of the Warrenton pike and the Manassas-Sudley road—at approximately 10:30 A.M. McDowell arrived at the firing line at about 10:45. Several military writers have criticized McDowell for going himself into the fray—where he actually exercised very little control of the battle—and suggest that he should have set up his command post somewhere in the center-rear of his army, where he could direct the whole operation and feed in his ample reserves at the proper time, as Johnston did on the Confederate side.[33]

With the engaged Union line facing southward, McDowell desired the arriving troops from Sudley Ford to deploy on the *left* (east) of those engaged; but, despite his presence, he permitted the men coming up to form on the *right* (west) of Hunter. This began a continual and unwise shift to the right during the whole combat of the Federal forces, *away* from Tyler's men at Stone Bridge. However, had McDowell thrown forward at once all his available men, he would probably have carried the day. As it was, his timidity permitted Evans, Bee, and Bartow to hold on north of Young's Branch until about 11:30 A.M., before falling back to Henry Hill, south of the pike.[34]

In the early afternoon McDowell, in personal command, began his assaults on Henry Hill, his total available force there numbering 10,000 to 13,000 men. "The attack," writes Colonel Steele, "was badly made from every tactical point of view. . . . The assaults were all straight to the front; there was no real effort to make a flank attack." "Moreover," declares Colonel G. F. R. Henderson, "instead of massing the troops for a determined onslaught, driven home by sheer weight of numbers, the attack was made by suc-

[33] Johnston, *Bull Run,* 182–89; *B. & L.,* I, 185.
[34] Johnston, *Bull Run,* 186–89; 2 *O.R.,* 408.

cessive brigades, those in the rear waiting till those in front had been defeated; and in the same manner, the brigades attacked by successive regiments. Such tactics were inexcusable." Nonetheless, at first, in the early afternoon, McDowell seemed to have the better of it. The Confederates were forced to fall back into the pine woods to the rear of the Henry plateau to rally. The high-water-mark for McDowell came when he unwisely ordered the fine batteries of Charles Griffin and James B. Ricketts forward to the edge of the plateau, where, after a gallant fight, they were cut to pieces by close musketry fire. The Union commander had climbed to the top of the Henry house at this time to observe the sway of battle.[35]

Now, however, exhausted by the dryness and great heat, and having been on their feet since 2:00 A.M., many Federal soldiers began to drift away. The arrival of Edmund Kirby Smith's Confederate brigade, and later of Jubal Early's, on McDowell's right flank, led, at 4:00 or 4:30 P.M., to the disintegration and retreat of the National forces. The Federals who had fought in the Henry Hill area retired the way they had come, by way of Sudley Spring back to the Warrenton pike east of Stone Bridge. The fine rear-guard performance of the regulars at Buck Hill, under McDowell's direction, enabled the withdrawing soldiers to extricate themselves safely. Then, the General himself rode via Sudley's back to the pike east of Bull Run. Before leaving the fighting arena, Mc-Dowell moved a force from near Centreville toward Blackburn's Ford to check any enemy pressure there against his line of retreat. On the Centreville heights the General encountered excited civilians, including ladies and politicians, caught up in the maelstrom of the retreat which had now become a rout.[36]

The tide of refugee Federal soldiers had passed through Centre-

[35] 2 O.R., 345–46, 394, 494–95, 496; Steele, *American Campaigns,* 146–47; G.F.R. Henderson, *Stonewall Jackson and the American Civil War* (London, 1898), I, 181.

[36] B. & L., I, 190–91; 2 O.R., 320–21; Johnston, *Bull Run,* 230–33, 236; Russell, *My Diary,* 168–74.

ville by 7:30 P.M. After darkness had fallen, McDowell himself reached Fairfax Court House. He "was so tired," reports Fry, "that while sitting on the ground writing a dispatch he fell asleep, pencil in hand, in the middle of a sentence," and had to be aroused by a staff officer. He wired Washington, reporting honestly the demoralization and rout of his army. At 2:30 A.M., on July 22, the Union rear guard pulled out of Centreville. Later that morning, in a downpour of rain, with his troops thronging into Washington, the unfortunate National commander dismounted at Arlington, after thirty-two hours in the saddle, his disastrous six-day campaign having come to an end. However, as Confederate E. P. Alexander notes, "Never did an enemy make a cleaner escape out of such an exposed position, after such an utter rout." Perhaps the angels had not deserted McDowell altogether.[37]

Of the approximately 35,000 men comprising his army, McDowell had, at Bull Run, probably some 28,500 effectives. He took about 18,000 men across the stream to the west side, but it is doubtful if he ever had more than 8,000 men engaged at any one time. While the Confederates had a total force aggregating approximately 32,000, it is unlikely that they had more than 18,000 engaged. Each side had some 48 artillery pieces available, and the Federals lost 27 of theirs. McDowell lost also, in captured equipment, 4,500 muskets, almost 500,000 cartridges, 11 flags, 64 horses, 26 wagons, and much clothing and camp baggage.[38]

As to casualties, those reported officially by both sides are quite probably too low. The best available figures are those cited by Colonel Thomas L. Livermore: the Union forces lost 481 killed; 1,011 wounded; 1,216 missing (including prisoners)—a total loss of 2,708 men. The Confederates lost 387 killed; 1,582 wounded; twelve missing—a total loss of 1,981 men.[39]

[37] 2 O.R., 316–21; E. P. Alexander, *Military Memoirs* . . . (New York, 1907), 50; *B. & L.,* I, 193.

[38] 2 O.R., 309; Johnston, *Bull Run*, 266, 267; Johnston, *Narrative,* 55–56.

[39] Johnston, *Bull Run*, 260–62; Livermore, *Numbers and Losses*, 77.

Shortly after the battle, while quietly working at his desk at Arlington in an endeavor to reorganize his confused mass of soldiery, McDowell was visited by President Lincoln. When the Chief Executive said to him, "I have not lost a particle of confidence in you," the General replied, "I don't see why you should, Mr. President." However, throughout the remainder of the year, McDowell remained quite sensitive and defensive in his views regarding the defeat at First Bull Run, blaming the politicians for forcing him into a premature campaign. On July 25 he was superseded in command of the army by McClellan, and was left in command of but fifteen regiments on the south bank of the Potomac.[40]

"The issue of this hard-fought battle," asserted McDowell in his report, "in which our troops lost no credit in their conflict on the field . . . should not prevent full credit being given to those officers and corps [sic] whose services merited success if they did not attain it." "The work of the Union army," declares J. G. Randall, "was not as badly done as has often been inferred." Actually, as Townsend notes, "it is rather a matter of wonder that an army should have done even so well, under such circumstances, as this one did at the outset." "As things were," says Edward Channing, "a little greater efficiency on the part of the Northern officers would have given the decision to the North." [41]

When McClellan superseded him in command of the main Union army in the East, McDowell remained as a division and then as a corps commander under "Little Mac" until August, 1862. At that time he was named head of the short-lived Department of the Rappahannock. Later that month he was a corps and wing commander under Major General John Pope, and participated with the

[40] Margaret Leech, *Reveille in Washington* . . . (New York, 1941), 107; 2 *O.R.*, 758, 763; Russell, *My Diary*, 507; Allan Nevins and Milton Halsey Thomas (eds.), *The Diary of George Templeton Strong* . . . (New York, 1952), III, 174, 179, 188, 195; Nicolay and Hay, *Abraham Lincoln*, IV, 356.

[41] 2 *O.R.*, 322; J. G. Randall, *Lincoln the President* . . . (New York, 1945), I, 385; Townsend, *Anecdotes of the Civil War*, 60; Edward Channing, *History of the United States* (New York, 1925), VI, 329.

latter's Army of Virginia in the battles of Cedar Mountain and Second Manassas. This was the last important combat command he ever held. Unjustifiably, he became most unpopular with his troops after the Federal defeat at Second Manassas—again being falsely accused of drunkenness on the battlefield—and spent the year 1863 serving on various army boards in Washington. From 1864 to 1868 McDowell commanded a territorial department on the West Coast; from 1868 to 1872 he headed the Department of the East; and for the next four years he commanded the Department of the South. In 1872 he was promoted to major general in the regular army, and four years later returned to San Francisco as department commander. He held that post until his retirement from the army in 1882. Residing in San Francisco, McDowell—whose hobby, it will be recalled, was landscape gardening and architecture—served as city park commissioner until his death on May 4, 1885.[42]

[42] Cullum, *Biographical Register,* I, 559–60; *D.A.B.,* XII, 29–30.

CHAPTER TWO

George B. McClellan

> While the Confederacy was young
> and fresh and rich, and its armies were
> numerous, McClellan fought a good,
> wary, damaging, respectable fight
> against it.
> —*General Francis W. Palfrey*

EXCITEMENT BORDERING ON NEAR-PANIC WAS STILL EVIDENT in the streets of distraught Washington on the afternoon of July 26, 1861, when the "Young Napoleon of the West" stepped off the train. Major General George Brinton McClellan set up his headquarters on Fifteenth Street near Pennsylvania Avenue, at the eastern end of Lafayette Square. On July 27 he "assumed command of the division of the Potomac, comprising the troops in and around Washington, on both banks of the river."[1]

Washingtonians soon grew accustomed to seeing the dashing thirty-four-year-old general riding madly down the avenue, mounted on his big black charger Dan Webster, with his panting staff officers hard-pressed to keep pace. McClellan, despite his five-feet-eight-inch height, was always an inspiring-looking soldier. His stockiness and fully developed chest made him appear shorter than he actually was. He was a handsome blue-eyed man, broad-shouldered and muscular, with very dark auburn hair, mustache, and touch of a goatee. He had a well-shaped head, a straight nose, and regular features. "Little Mac," as his soldiers called him, carried himself well, and was a magnificent horseman. He was al-

[1] George B. McClellan, . . . *Report on the . . . Army of the Potomac . . .* (Washington, 1864), 2.

ways impeccably dressed, and wore the popular kepi-type cap instead of the regulation black felt hat with the wide brim and high crown.[2]

If McDowell's pre-Civil War career had been a solid one, McClellan's was spectacular. He was born in Philadelphia on December 3, 1826, the son of a prominent surgeon of Scottish ancestry. Young George graduated second in the class of 1846 at West Point. Serving with Scott's army in Mexico, McClellan won two brevets (and declined one for Molino del Rey). After routine assignments, he was sent as an observer to the Crimean War, and his report on European military institutions and techniques won for him a high reputation. McClellan retired from the service in 1857 and became a high railroad official. His marriage to Ellen Mary Marcy was rewarded with two children.[3]

Soon after the outbreak of civil war, McClellan accepted Ohio Governor William Dennison's offer to command the volunteer troops of Ohio, Indiana, and Illinois, with the rank of major general. While striving to organize these raw levees, McClellan drew up and sent to Scott a comprehensive plan of grand strategy to defeat the Confederacy which foreshadowed in some ways Scott's "Anaconda."[4]

Seeing that Confederate forces were gathering in western Virginia and threatening the important Baltimore and Ohio Railroad, McClellan dropped his training and organizing activities at Cincinnati, and vigorously moved his men against the enemy. His forces launched a surprise attack on Confederate troops at Philippi on June 3, in the first land battle of the war, and drove the enemy from the field so rapidly that the affair became known as the "Philippi races." And when Lee sent reinforcements to western Virginia to try to keep that pro-Union part of the state from seceding

[2] B. & L., I, 89; Oliver Otis Howard, Autobiography . . . (New York, 1908), I, 167.

[3] Cullum, Biographical Register, II, 140–41; D.A.B., XI, 581, 582.

[4] George B. McClellan, McClellan's Own Story . . . (New York, 1887), 29, 43, cited hereinafter as M.O.S.; 107 O.R., 228–29.

from secession, McClellan himself moved against them decisively. Although hesitating at one point, he defeated the graycoats at Rich Mountain on July 11 and at Carrick's Ford two days later. To all intents and purposes, these miniature but essentially able victories sealed the doom of the Confederates in western Virginia. His successes elicited from Scott on July 13 this encomium: "The General-in-Chief . . . the Cabinet, including the President, are charmed with your activity, valor, and consequent success. . . . We do not doubt that you will in due time sweep the rebels from Virginia, but we do not mean to precipitate you as you are fast enough." Three days later McClellan received the official thanks of Congress for his triumphs. On July 22, the day after the defeat of McDowell at Bull Run, McClellan was urgently called to Washington, and arrived there four days later.[5]

McClellan's personal traits were baffling to many. U. S. Grant onced owned that "McClellan is to me one of the mysteries of the war." While perhaps the most popular general ever to command American troops, McClellan was at the same time "reserved and retiring" in manner when dealing with the masses. But with closer associates the General could open up more. "His whole appearance," writes Major General Jacob D. Cox, "was quiet and modest, but when drawn out he showed no lack of confidence in himself." He was ever the Christian gentleman—courtly, dignified, God-fearing, sometimes boyish. He was a hearty eater, consumed moderate quantities of wines and liquors, smoked cigars, and occasionally chewed tobacco in the typical American manner. The General believed that he was the chosen instrument of the Almighty to save the Union, and acted accordingly.[6]

Well versed in large-scale enterprises since his railroad days, McClellan, in the custom of generals and civilians of the time, did not hesitate to press upon his superiors his own views of political as

[5] *B. & L.,* I, 126–28; 2 *O.R.,* 64 ff., 204, 215–16, 236, 753.
[6] John Russell Young, *Around the World with General Grant* . . . (New York, 1879), II, 216; *B. & L.,* I, 89; Russell, *My Diary,* 479–80, 520–21; *M.O.S.,* 57, 82–83, 172.

well as military matters, whether solicited or not. And it must not be thought that McClellan was always unaware of the interrelationship between the civil and military authority. Among other similar statements, the General once said during the war, "I regard the civil or political questions as inseparable from the military in this contest." He was not afraid to assume the responsibility, on his own, of initiating courses of action. He was generally deferential and proper in his intercourse with his superiors, although, if he believed an error or injustice was being committed, he could lash out strongly against any one. At times he showed obtuseness and a lack of tact in dealing with Lincoln. But he was basically a kind and just man, as careful of the integrity of the individual as of the law. Nonetheless, McClellan was a political partisan, and this was, unfortunately, a handicap in his case. He was a conservative Democrat and a gradual emancipationist, and favored compensating the slave owners if their human property was taken away from them against their wishes.[7]

One of McClellan's greatest talents was in appealing to the better qualities of his soldiers and in flattering them to the extent that most of them revered him. His flowery manifestoes, while sounding bombastic and Napoleonic today, were, in 1861, most effective. Yet it must not be thought that McClellan was a "soft" general; on the contrary, he was a firm disciplinarian of iron will and authority. However, at other times, McClellan could be warm and gentle, as in his almost daily letters to his wife. The General's only recreation seemed to be in confiding all things to his loving spouse, and his letters home were often written in a breezy, light-hearted style. Also, his concern for the well-being of his soldiers was genuine. He preferred to gain an objective, if possible, by dexterous maneuvering rather than by a frontal attack.[8]

[7] 4 *O.R.*, 627; McClellan to Cameron, Aug. 1, 1862, George B. McClellan Papers, Div. of MSS, Library of Congress; Warren W. Hassler, Jr., *General George B. McClellan: Shield of the Union* (Baton Rouge, 1957), 5, 7.
[8] McClellan's *Report* (New York, 1864), 36; 2 *O.R.*, 208–209, 236.

One of McClellan's faults was his tendency to be a perfectionist. As Colonel Oliver L. Spaulding asserts, "He was never satisfied with what he had, nor willing to make the best of an imperfect tool. He could always see wherein he might make improvements, given time; and he took time, at the expense of losing his opportunities. He could not be content with a plan that took into account all apparent factors, and trust to the inspiration of the moment to take care of the unforeseen; his plan must be complete. His reasoning powers carried him up to contact with the enemy; at that moment, when an independent will entered the problem, he became hesitating." He was usually a circumspect man, seldom willing to take chances unnecessarily. Yet some of his finest actions came when, against his will, he was forced to undertake some extremely hazardous gambles, as in the Seven Days battle. Given the critical situation he faced when taking the command of the Army of the Potomac—if it may be called that now—he was perhaps the man then best qualified and suited by temperament and talents to accept what Grant termed the "vast and cruel responsibility," the "terrible test" which was thrust upon him in the summer of 1861.[9]

Having arrived in Washington in the critical week after Bull Run, McClellan's relations with his superiors were of vital consequence. He got along, on the whole, amicably with Secretary of War Simon Cameron and, when face to face, with Lincoln. However, it was not long before McClellan and his immediate superior, the General-in-Chief, were at loggerheads. Perhaps Scott was a trifle jealous of the vigor and great popularity of the young general. On McClellan's part, while it was impossible for him to clear everything through his punctilious superior, it must be said that at times he did treat the old general in a somewhat cavalier fashion, although ever being courteous and proper to him when they were together.[10]

[9] *D.A.B.*, XI, 584; Young, *Around the World with General Grant*, II, 216.
[10] Russell, *My Diary*, 480; *M.O.S.*, 136–37.

The situation faced by McClellan in July of 1861 when he arrived in the capital was appalling. "I found no army to command," the General stated; "a mere collection of regiments cowering on the banks of the Potomac, some perfectly raw, others dispirited by the recent defeat." It was "rather a mob than an army," declares Swinton. McClellan quickly established an efficacious provost marshal department which rounded up stragglers and enforced a rigorous discipline. Reviewing boards were set up which soon cashiered several hundred incompetent officers. Alcohol was forbidden in the camps. The total force about the capital of some 50,000 men soon learned to respect their new commander as a strict and brilliant organizer and drillmaster. The General constructed also some thirty-three miles of interlocking fortifications about Washington.[11]

In all of these activities McClellan was given practically a free hand by his superiors in the administration and by Congress. Toward the end of July the General was writing his wife, Ellen, as follows: "I find myself in a new and strange position here: President, cabinet, Gen. Scott, and all deferring to me. By some strange operation of magic I seem to have become the power of the land. . . . Oh! how sincerely I pray to God that I may be endowed with the wisdom and courage necessary to accomplish the work." He even got along well, at first, with the Radical Republicans, although later, when the notorious Joint Committee on the Conduct of the War was formed, McClellan, because of his politics, was to become its chief target for slander, abuse, and interference.[12]

By August 2, 1861, McClellan's army numbered 65,000 effectives, as compared with Johnston's 41,000. On this date, in response to the President's request to submit a comprehensive plan of operations for the Union armies, McClellan urged that his own Army of the Potomac should number no less than 273,000, with

[11] McClellan's *Report*, 9–10, 44; Swinton, *Army of the Potomac*, 66 n; B. & L., II, 112–13.

[12] See T. Harry Williams, *Lincoln and the Radicals* (Madison, 1941), especially Ch. II–VII; *M.O.S.*, 67 n.

20,000 men for the defensive works of Washington. He recommended that the Federals attack the Confederates from the Mississippi River, Virginia, and Kentucky and Tennessee, using their superior naval power to assist the army movements. However, his idea of repeated landings on the Atlantic coast was unrealistic. McClellan was handicapped, moreover, by the grossly erroneous estimates of the enemy's numbers made for him by Allan Pinkerton, the famous detective who headed the General's secret service. Pinkerton—calling himself "E. J. Allen"—and his operatives insisted, for example, that in October, 1861, the Confederate forces in Virginia numbered no less than 118,000 men. These almost daily reports from Pinkerton did not tend to make the already cautious commander any more likely to embark on a premature campaign if he could help it.[13]

By October 15 McClellan felt that his drilling and organizing activities had progressed to a point where he could amalgamate his many brigades into divisions. The commanders of these new units were to be Irvin McDowell, Nathaniel P. Banks, Samuel P. Heintzelman, Charles P. Stone, William B. Franklin, Joseph Hooker, William F. Smith, Louis Blenker, Fitz John Porter, Don Carlos Buell, and George A. McCall. Nonetheless, the men in the ranks themselves had a long way to go. "Soldiers they are not in any sense of the word," declared George G. Meade at this time. Then, on October 21, with the cry of "On to Richmond" reappearing in the Northern newspapers, a brigade of Stone's division, led by a friend of Lincoln's—the inexperienced political Colonel Edward Baker—blundered into a military deathtrap at Ball's Bluff, a few miles up the Potomac from Washington, and was badly cut up, with the loss of 921 men. In this minor military debacle, Baker was killed, and, although McClellan himself suffered little loss of prestige, Stone was persecuted by the Radicals

[13] McClellan's "Memorandum for the President," Aug. 2, 1861, "E. J. Allen" to McClellan, Oct. 4, 28, Nov. 15, 26, 1861, McClellan Papers; 4 O.R., 601.

on the Committee on the Conduct of the War. Nonetheless, by the end of October McClellan reported that he had present for duty in his whole department a grand total of 134,285 men, of which, however, only 76,285 were available for actual fighting.[14]

Then, on November 1, 1861, Scott retired from the service, and McClellan was named to succeed him, at the age of thirty-four, as General-in-Chief of all the Union armies. He was to retain also personal command of the Army of the Potomac. McClellan drew up a nicely worded tribute to the old soldier, and saw him off on November 3 at the railroad station. The parting scene moved the young general. He wrote to his wife, "The old man said that his sensations were very peculiar in leaving Washington and active life. I can easily understand them; and it may be that some distant day I, too, shall totter away from Washington, a worn-out soldier, with naught to do but make my peace with God. The sight of this morning was a lesson to me which I hope not soon to forget." [15]

When he took over as General-in-Chief, McClellan perceived that all the National armies were stationary, including those in the West. However, it was the army directly under the noses of the politicians—the Army of the Potomac—that was soon to be censured, along with its commander, for remaining immobile. In the period immediately after his promotion to the chief command, McClellan wrote lengthy dispatches to his other army commanders—Benjamin F. Butler, Thomas W. Sherman, Don C. Buell, and Henry W. Halleck—seeking to synchronize and co-ordinate their future movements so as to have them advance simultaneously. "If this plan was wise," said McClellan, "then it is unnecessary to defend any delay which would have enabled the army of the Potomac to perform its share in the execution of the whole work." He declared further that "even if the Army of the Potomac had

[14] George Meade, *Life and Letters of George Gordon Meade* (New York, 1913), I, 223; McClellan's *Report*, 10, 14–17; *B. & L.*, II, 123–34.
[15] *M.O.S.*, 173–74; 122 *O.R.*, 613–14.

been in condition to undertake a campaign in the autumn of 1861, the backward state of affairs in the West would have made it unwise to do so. . . ." [16]

On December 20 McCall's Pennsylvania Reserve division won a small but smart victory over the Confederates at Dranesville. But the General-in-Chief was not up and about to enjoy it fully; McClellan was stricken on this date with a near-fatal case of typhoid fever, which incapacitated him for almost a month. So the anxious President, pathetically eager for an advance by the Army of the Potomac, regardless of strategy or weather conditions or of other matters regarding preparation and organization, called a series of councils of war at the White House on January 10–13. Present were Lincoln, McDowell, Franklin, and a number of cabinet members (but not Cameron). Salmon P. Chase and William H. Seward (although unversed in military matters), and McDowell, favored an early overland advance through Manassas—a plan which was reluctantly acquiesced in by Franklin. Although still quite ill with a disease which had long-lingering after-effects, McClellan mustered enough strength on the twelfth and thirteenth to arise from his sick bed and attend these conferences—appearances, relates the General, which "caused very much the effect of a shell in a powder-magazine." When badgered by Chase, who wanted him to divulge his campaign plans to the large group assembled, McClellan, stating that there were too many leaks in top-secret data, refused to reveal his strategy, and was backed by Lincoln in this decision.[17]

A few days after these war councils at the White House, Edwin M. Stanton, a former Democrat and Attorney General in Buchanan's cabinet, succeeded Cameron as Secretary of War. Be-

[16] B. & L., II, 436; McClellan, Report, 10, 37–42; C.C.W. (1863), II, 422.
[17] A. K. McClure (ed.), The Annals of the War . . . (Philadelphia, 1879), 76–79; Swinton, Army of the Potomac, 79–85; M.O.S., 156–58; Diary of Montgomery C. Meigs, Jan. 13, 1862, Div. of MSS, Library of Congress.

fore his appointment, Stanton had been a violent and caustic critic of Lincoln and his administration. He had been also a professed warm friend and supporter of McClellan, as well as a legal counsellor, ever since the summer of 1861. But the General found to his consternation that his former comrade had suddenly, upon his accession to office, turned into a frigid opponent who was now not even available for an interview. Although devoid of military training or knowledge of any kind, Stanton, along with the congressional Radicals, became suddenly obsessed with a belief that McClellan should begin his grand offensive against Johnston's army at once, and began applying great pressure on the President to order it. The new Secretary quickly moved all telegraph lines from army headquarters into his own office, and even went so far as to take a public slap at McClellan and his policies in the New York *Tribune*.[18]

Stanton brought to the War Department great energy and industriousness—characteristics not possessed by his inept predecessor. He could at infrequent times be companionable and entertaining, and no one could doubt his intense patriotism to the Union and abolition causes. It is believed that Stanton never knowingly permitted any graft or corruption to stain the War Department, and he died a comparatively poor man. Delay in anything even remotely pertaining to his office would find "Old Mars," as Lincoln called him, swinging into action immediately to discover and eliminate the obstruction. It seems that he had no personal ambition then to succeed Lincoln in the presidency. An indefatigable worker, the Secretary often spent as many as eighteen hours a day standing at his high desk transacting business concerned with the war office, as well as taking all his meals and sleeping at the War Department building. It is probable that his great exertions during the war years

[18] Biographical sketch, Edwin M. Stanton Papers, Div. of MSS, Library of Congress; William D. Kelley, *Lincoln and Stanton* . . . (New York, 1885), 17; *C.C.W.* (1863), I, 75; *M.O.S.*, 152, 154; *B. & L.*, II, 120; Gideon Welles, *Lincoln and Seward* (New York, 1874), 190, 191, 193; George W. Julian, *Political Recollections* . . . (Chicago, 1882), 204; New York *Tribune*, Feb. 20, 1862.

weakened his health and led to his relatively early demise in 1869.[19]

These admirable characteristics, however, were perhaps more than balanced by certain extremely weak and disagreeable traits, many of which hindered greatly the Union military effort. Secretary Stanton was completely untutored in military science and was contemptuous of it. He had a hatred and distrust of educated army officers, especially if they were graduates of West Point. The "Black Terrier," as he was known, was arrogant, irascible, and impatient, and formed snap judgments which were adhered to with grim tenacity even when shown to be wrong. He loved contention and antagonism, and was frequently coarse and discourteous in his relations with the patient and forebearing President, as well as with others. By nature an intriguer, Stanton made friends easily with the rabid Radicals of the Committee on the Conduct of the War. Blustering and browbeating, he was, however, basically a timid man; and whenever confronted by men who would not bow and bend to his bullying tactics—men like McClellan, Gideon Welles, E. A. Hitchcock, and Montgomery Blair—Stanton would usually back down. A sensationalist, the Secretary was seized frequently with alarms and panics. A man of greater deviousness and duplicity it would be difficult to find. He was capable of monstrous injustices, and knew not how to apologize for his errors and unfairness. His disposition to assume vast and often unnecessary powers was insatiable. A more self-righteous and militarily inefficient superior to the new General-in-Chief and to the commanders in the field would be almost impossible to discover; yet Lincoln backed him throughout the war.[20]

[19] Noah Brooks, *Washington in Lincoln's Time* (New York, 1895), 28–29; Charles A. Dana, *Lincoln and His Cabinet* (Cleveland, 1896), 20, 26–27; Hugh McCulloch, *Men and Measures* . . . (New York, 1889), 301; A. K. McClure, *Abraham Lincoln and Men of War-Times* . . . (Philadelphia, 1892), 155–62; John T. Morse, Jr. (ed.), *Diary of Gideon Welles* . . . (Boston, 1911), I, 55, 56, 67–69, 127–29.

[20] Stanton to Lincoln, Feb. 14, 1862, Stanton Papers; Theodore C. Pease and James G. Randall (eds.), *The Diary of Orville Hickman Browning* . . . (Springfield, 1925), I, 533, 538–39; Howard K. Beale (ed.), *Diary of Edward Bates* . . . (Washington, 1933), 228, 280, 381, 391; U. S.

Then, in late January, and in early March, 1862, perhaps as a result of the increasing pressure being placed upon him by Stanton, the Radicals, the press, and the public, Lincoln issued to McClellan, without even consulting him, a series of five general and special war orders. Although not believing so at the time of promulgating them, Lincoln, by the end of the war, was to come to realize that "they were all wrong," and so acknowledged to Grant. The first two of these orders, handed to McClellan on January 27 and 31, ordered a forward movement of all Union armies on February 22, with the Army of the Potomac instructed to advance against Johnston by way of Manassas. Permitted to reply to these directives, McClellan pointed out the many disadvantages of the overland route through Manassas desired by the administration. He contrasted these with the numerous advantages to be gained if he moved his army down the Chesapeake Bay to Urbanna on the Rappahannock River, or to Mobjack Bay or Fortress Monroe, from which points there would be but a short land march to Richmond, with few perpendicular rivers to cross, and with easy land communications to maintain. The General's views prevailed, and he was permitted, reluctantly, to advance as he desired—the course of action which the Confederates feared most.[21]

However, relations between the President and his top general came to a critical pass on March 8, when McClellan was summoned to the White House. As the General relates it, Lincoln said he had "a very ugly matter" to discuss with him. It was that the President had heard, in such a way as to believe it, that McClellan had come up with the scheme of moving the Army of the Potomac down the coast with the traitorous intention of deliberately exposing Washington to capture by the enemy. Lincoln concluded his little speech,

Grant, *Personal Memoirs of U. S. Grant* (New York, 1886), II, 105, 123, 506, 536, 537; McClure, *Abraham Lincoln and Men of War-Times*, 155–62; Morse (ed.), *Welles's Diary*, I, 55–69, 127–29, 148–49, 203, 234.

[21] Morse (ed.), *Welles's Diary*, I, 95; Grant, *Memoirs*, II, 122; 5 *O.R.*, 41; McClellan to Stanton, Jan. 31, 1862, McClellan Papers; Swinton, *Army of the Potomac*, 94.

McClellan writes, "with the remark that it did look to him much like treason." The General-in-Chief jumped to his feet and insisted hotly that the President retract his remark and apologize at once for such a base charge. The Chief Executive complied immediately, asserting that he had meant to say that such statements were abroad but that he personally did not believe them. Still angry, McClellan insisted that his coastal plan be submitted to the unusual procedure of having it voted upon by his twelve division commanders. In the ballot which followed, McClellan's plan was sustained, eight to four—the four "nay's" coming from McDowell, Heintzelman, Barnard, and Edwin V. Sumner, all so-called "Radical generals." [22]

Two other orders from the President were given to McClellan on March 8. One of them compelled the General, against his wishes, to organize his divisions into four corps, to be commanded by the Radical generals McDowell, Sumner, Heintzelman, and Keyes, each of whom, except Keyes, had voted against McClellan's coastal plan. The second presidential directive instructed McClellan to begin his advance not later than March 18; in addition it told him how many units to employ, instructed him in timing the movement of different bodies of troops, and stressed the necessity of clearing the lower Potomac of Confederate batteries (installations which would automatically fall anyway once the Army of the Potomac started down the bay). Like the others, these presidential orders played unwittingly into the hands of the Confederates. [23]

On March 8 the Confederate ironclad *Virginia* (ex-*Merrimac*) went on her spree, only to be contained on the following day by the *Monitor*. While McClellan, Welles, and others remained cool, the President, and especially Stanton, panicked. But McClellan received assurances that the Federal navy could handle the Confederate ironclad monster, and that the great amphibious enterprise could proceed. On the same day—March 9—Johnston suddenly

[22] *M.O.S.*, 195–96, 236–37; McClellan, *Report*, 49; *B. & L.*, II, 166; Heintzelman's Journal, Mar. 8, 1862; McClure (ed.), *Annals of the War*, 79–80.
[23] McClellan, *Report*, 53, 54; *M.O.S.*, 162–63, 222; 14 *O.R.*, 57–58.

withdrew the Confederate army from Centreville and Manassas to a point behind the Rappahannock, thereby rendering McClellan's Urbanna plan inoperative. But the Union General-in-Chief determined to go ahead with his coastal operation, and disembark his army at Federal-held Fortress Monroe, located at the tip (Old Point Comfort) of the historic peninsula between the York and James rivers—a procedure approved unanimously by McClellan's four corps commanders. These subordinates especially endorsed his proposal to move McDowell's entire First Corps by water up the York River as a "flying column" intended to turn the enemy strongholds of Yorktown and Gloucester, with the assistance of the navy. They believed that 40,000 men should be earmarked by McClellan for the security of Washington.[24]

But on March 11 the fifth of Lincoln's war orders removed McClellan as General-in-Chief, leaving him in command of just the Army of the Potomac. After this humiliating vote of no confidence in the commander about to begin his maiden campaign with that army, no new man was named to the General-in-Chief post for four months, leaving the complex direction of the numerous Union armies in the hands of two military amateurs, Lincoln and Stanton. McClellan showed considerable manliness and cordiality in the way he accepted this sudden demotion.[25]

Despite his insincere protestations of friendship to McClellan, Stanton tried to remove the General in early March from command even of the Army of the Potomac. The Secretary, however, had to go about this scheme in a roundabout way, because Lincoln would not countenance the outright firing of the General from all commands. Stanton brought from St. Louis a sixty-four-year-old hero of the Mexican War, Ethan Allen Hitchcock. A religious mystic,

[24] Morse (ed.), *Welles's Diary*, I, 62–65; 5 *O.R.*, 55–56, 64, 526, 527; *M.O.S.*, 222; 14 *O.R.*, 58; 15 *O.R.*, 223–24; McClellan, *Report*, 59–60; *C.C.W.* (1863), II, 12; Keyes to Stanton, Mar. 14, 1862, Stanton Papers.
[25] Beale (ed.), *Bates's Diary*, 239; Emory Upton, *Military Policy of the United States* (Washington, 1904), 284, 291–92; McClellan to Lincoln, Mar. 12, 1862, Robert Todd Lincoln Collection of the Papers of Abraham Lincoln, Div. of MSS, Library of Congress.

Hitchcock had been retired from the army for fifteen years and was in very poor health. He was offered McClellan's command by Stanton as soon as he reported to the War Department. Hitchcock declined the amazing proffer, and instead accepted a post as special adviser to the Secretary. At another time, Stanton tried to get Senator Orville H. Browning—a friend of Lincoln—to support a Colonel Napoleon Bonaparte Buford, of Illinois, as a replacement for McClellan in command of the Army of the Potomac, but this plan, too, backfired on the Secretary.[26]

The great amphibious invasion by McClellan's army got underway on March 17. This "stride of a giant," as a foreign observer called it, was one of the most colossal in modern military history up to that time. Including the 10,000 men of Wool's garrison at Fortress Monroe, who were to be added to the Army of the Potomac, McClellan's massive host was supposed to aggregate some 155,000 men. Stanton, however, for reasons of his own, began at once to try to reduce this force. On March 30 the Secretary urged that 17,500 men—Blenker's and Hooker's divisions—be taken away from McClellan's invading force and given to the inept John C. Frémont, in command of the superfluous Mountain Department. And the President succumbed to the extent that, on the following day, he did detach Blenker's division of nearly 10,000 men from the Army of the Potomac, and informed McClellan of his decision to do this in an unusually sharp note. McClellan took this blow in stride, replying to Lincoln, "I fully appreciate . . . the circumstances of the case and hasten to assure you that I cheerfully acquiesce in your decision without any mental reservations." The President promised, however, that no further cuts would be made in the Union's main striking force.[27]

When McClellan himself left for the Peninsula on April 1, he

[26] William A. Croffut (ed.), . . . Diary of Ethan Allen Hitchcock (New York, 1909), 437–39.

[27] Swinton, Army of the Potomac, 100; Stanton to Lincoln, Mar. 30, 1862, Stanton Papers; McClellan to Lincoln, Mar. 31, 1862, Lincoln Papers; M.O.S., 164–65.

left behind for the Secretary a table which showed that 73,456 men had been stationed in the rear for the defense of Washington, although only about 18,000 were to be left in the actual fortifications of the capital. While these figures were not quite accurate, McClellan had left Washington amply protected when he departed for the Peninsula, despite Lincoln's and Stanton's contrary opinion. Later events showed, however, that the General would have done better to have explained in person to his superiors exactly what the defense strategy was for the capital, for the President and the Secretary did not understand it.[28]

Meanwhile, on April 2, with heavy rain falling, McClellan himself arrived at Fortress Monroe to take personal command of the Army of the Potomac. The amphibian movement down the bay was proceeding without a hitch. John Tucker, Stanton's assistant secretary of war, wired from the Peninsula that, "for economy and celerity of movement, this expedition is without a parallel on record." Then, with the advance guard of his army slogging up through the heaviest rainy season in twenty years toward Yorktown, McClellan received another blow from his superiors, and this one was crippling.[29]

James S. Wadsworth, the elderly political general in command of the fortifications at Washington, reported in alarm to Stanton on April 2 that there were but 20,477 men in the forts there. Considering the other forces left by McClellan in northern Virginia not to be a part of the defense network for the capital, the frightened President and Secretary panicked and ordered the nearly 40,000 men of McDowell's First Corps to be withheld at Washington instead of proceeding down the bay to join McClellan's army. Also, the promised 10,000 men of Wool's garrison at Fortress Monroe were ordered not to augment the Army of the Potomac. Instead of

[28] McClellan to L. Thomas, Apr. 1, 1862, Lincoln Papers; 14 *O.R.*, 59–60; Colin R. Ballard, *The Military Genius of Abraham Lincoln* . . . (London, 1926), 74–75.

[29] Heintzelman's Journal, Apr. 2, 1862; Swinton, *Army of the Potomac*, 100.

155,000 men, McClellan now had but 95,000 or 100,000. Operating on the offensive in enemy country, McClellan had ample need for a sizeable numerical superiority over his foe, acting on the defensive. Finally, to add to McClellan's discomfiture, he was informed on April 3 that Stanton had halted recruiting in the North, and that the Union navy could not assist in the reduction of Yorktown or Gloucester.[30]

Without McDowell's flying column to sweep up the York River to West Point and turn the two Confederate strongholds, McClellan was obliged to do the job himself with his land-moving divisions. Shortly after landing on the Peninsula, McClellan had 42,000 men confronting the enemy's Yorktown-Warwick River defensive line. This river did not run parallel to the York and James, as McClellan's inaccurate maps showed, but actually ran across the Peninsula perpendicular to his line of advance. Much of the area had been purposely flooded by the Confederates; and while the local commander there had at first but 13,000 to 15,000 men to face the Federals, Johnston's gray army on the Peninsula was soon built up to 53,000 effectives.[31]

It is likely, as we see it now, that had McClellan attacked at once in heavy force, the Warwick-Yorktown lines could have been carried. But, at that time, no Union officer, including McClellan, believed such a course feasible. So, after testing the defenses with several sorties in force, the National commander settled down in the seas of mud to regular siege operations, which lasted one month. While these were proceeding, McClellan bombarded the administration to send him all or a part of McDowell's idle First Corps. Finally, Franklin's division was released to McClellan on April 10, and began to arrive on the Peninsula twelve days later. At this time, however, Lincoln told Senator Browning that "he was becoming impatient and dissatisfied with McClellan's sluggishness of action." Actually, McClellan and his men were working to

[30] See Hassler, *General George B. McClellan,* 83–86.
[31] *B. & L.,* II, 170; Swinton, *Army of the Potomac,* 101; Johnston, *Narrative,* 117.

the limit of human ability to conclude the siege of Yorktown successfully. "The difficulties of transportation," telegraphed Tucker from the Peninsula to Stanton, "have been so great that some of the cavalry horses had to be sent back to keep them from starving. . . . I see an earnest determination to lose no time in attacking the enemy." This statement was echoed by Hitchcock, who had also been sent down to the Peninsula by Stanton to keep an eye on Little Mac. Finally, just as McClellan was about to open a devastating fire on the Confederates at Yorktown, Johnston suddenly evacuated his works and retreated toward Williamsburg. This ended the one-month siege. But Johnston had been obliged to leave behind seventy-seven badly needed heavy siege guns, which the Federals captured.[32]

McClellan determined to move the bulk of his army by land toward Williamsburg, while he, with Franklin's division, would go by water up the York to West Point in a movement designed to entrap or else speed up Johnston's forces in retreat. The Federal divisions moving by land became engaged with the enemy early on the morning of May 5 just outside of Williamsburg. However, the Union forces were somewhat clumsily handled by Sumner. McClellan was called to the field at Williamsburg from Yorktown, where he had been engaged in solving several engineering problems connected with the embarkation of Franklin's division. He arrived at the scene of combat before 5:00 P.M., just as Brigadier General Winfield S. Hancock's brigade had brilliantly turned the Confederate left in a flanking attack. McClellan personally reorganized the Union lines, but the enemy withdrew from the field toward Barhamsville. The total Federal casualties in the stiff little engagement at Williamsburg totaled 2,239 killed, wounded, and missing; the Confederates, fighting on the defensive behind fixed positions, lost a total of 1,703 men.[33]

[32] See Hassler, *General George B. McClellan*, 89–96.
[33] 12 *O.R.*, 275, 450–51, 454–59, 465, 467, 512; *B. & L.*, II, 94–99, 194; Alexander S. Webb, *The Peninsula* . . . (New York, 1881), 70–71, 80–81; *M.O.S.*, 301, 327–30; Livermore, *Numbers and Losses*, 80–81.

McClellan tried to pursue Johnston at once; but the fearful condition of the muddy tracts, cut to shreds by the Confederate wagons going ahead, made it impossible for him to supply men or horses. Meanwhile, Franklin's division, having landed at Brick House Point, across from West Point, near Eltham's Landing, was attacked on May 7 by the enemy. After an initial Union setback, the Confederates were repulsed. This turning movement, moreover, ensured that Johnston's retreat would continue to be rapid, and that it would carry the gray legions back almost to the environs of Richmond. No one can say what would have happened had the administration in Washington permitted McClellan to have moved McDowell's entire First Corps—uselessly tied down south of the Federal capital—by water up the York River *at the beginning* of the campaign. It might be noted here that, as early as May 10, McClellan was seriously contemplating the shifting of his base and line of operations to the James River.[34]

By May 17 McClellan's advance had reached Bottom's Bridge and New Bridge over the Chickahominy River. This important stream rises to the north of Richmond and flows in a general northwest to southeast direction, finally emptying into the James River. The Chickahominy was a serious military obstacle for the Federals because its low banks, in such an abnormally heavy rainy season, had been overflowed by the water for a distance of nearly a mile on each side, making the entire river basin one vast bog. McClellan was obliged to cross his army to the southwest bank of the stream in order to move against the Confederate capital. But first a halt was required to build some eleven bridges over the Chickahominy so as to maintain safe communications if part of the National army was to be on one side of the river and part on the other. These bridges required elaborate corduroy approaches, and even then could be swept away by a rise in the surging tide below.[35]

Meantime, the administration ordered McDowell's First Corps of

[34] McClellan, *Report*, 91–93; 12 *O.R.*, 24, 276, 614–17, 627–30, 631–32.
[35] 12 *O.R.*, 110–11.

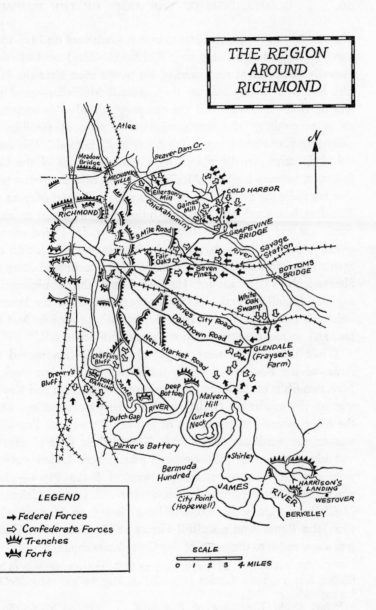

THE REGION
AROUND
RICHMOND

N

Atlee

Meadow
Bridge

Beaver Dam Cr.

MECHANICS
VILLE

Ellerson's
Mill

COLD HARBOR

Gaines
Mill

Chickahominy

RICHMOND

GRAPEVINE
BRIDGE

9 Mile Road

River

Savage
Station

Fair
Oaks

Seven
Pines

BOTTOMS
BRIDGE

White
Oak
Swamp

Charles City Road

Darbytown Road

GLENDALE
(Frayser's
Farm)

Chaffin's
Bluff

New Market Road

Drewry's
Bluff

FORT
DARLING

JAMES

Deep
Bottom

Malvern
Hill

Curles
Neck

Dutch Gap

RIVER

Parker's Battery

S.A.L. R.R.

Bermuda
Hundred

Shirley

JAMES

RIVER

HARRISON'S
LANDING

City Point
(Hopewell)

WESTOVER

BERKELEY

LEGEND

→ Federal Forces
⇨ Confederate Forces
♛ Trenches
♛ Forts

SCALE

0 1 2 3 4 MILES

38,000, then at Fredericksburg, to march southward on May 17 to join McClellan's right wing near Richmond—McDowell to retain virtually independent command of his troops even after the juncture had been made. Stanton then ordered McClellan—and this was of vital importance for the campaign ahead—"to cooperate, so as to establish this communication as soon as possible, by extending your right wing to the north of Richmond." This unrevoked directive actually played right into the hands of the Confederates, because it placed McClellan's army in a dangerous position astraddle the swollen Chickahominy River. But on May 24 the President instructed McClellan as follows: "I wish you to move cautiously and safely." Unfortunately, however, for Union strategy —being directed from the offices in Washington by Lincoln and Stanton—when the wily Jackson made a feint northward down the Shenandoah Valley toward Harper's Ferry, the administration, against McClellan's and McDowell's protests, ordered the latter to defer his march southward from Fredericksburg to join McClellan, and to move westward to try to capture Stonewall.[36]

While these events were taking place, McClellan moved the Army of the Potomac closer to Richmond. By the last week in May, two-fifths of the army (the corps of Heintzelman and Keyes) was on the southwest (right) bank of the Chickahominy, while the other three-fifths (the corps of Sumner, Porter, and Franklin) was on the northeast (left) bank. The furthest Federal advance was along the main Williamsburg pike, where Union outposts were one and three-quarter miles west of Seven Pines—which placed them some four and three-quarter miles from Richmond. McClellan's right wing, too, had been cleared on May 27 when Fitz John Porter won a skillful victory at Hanover Court House, just a few miles to the north of the Confederate capital.[37]

[36] *C.C.W.* (1863), II, 272, 274, 330; 14 *O.R.,* 176–77; Stanton to McClellan, May 17, 1862, Lincoln to McClellan, May 24, 25, 1862, McClellan Papers.

[37] Joel Cook, *The Siege of Richmond* . . . (Philadelphia, 1862), 122–24; McClellan, *Report,* 92, 93, 107; *B. & L.,* II, 319–23; 12 *O.R.,* 680, 682, 700–706.

Then, on May 31, with McClellan in bed with a bad case of neuralgia and malaria, and with the Union army waiting for the high water—which resulted from a great storm on the thirtieth—to go down, Joe Johnston attacked. He had 74,000 men as against nearly 100,000 Federals. The Confederate general threw twenty-three of his twenty-seven brigades against McClellan's left wing on the southwest bank of the Chickahominy. In the initial gray attacks, begun at approximately 1:00 P.M., the Union left was pushed back and seriously threatened with destruction. Learning of the critical situation, McClellan got up from his sick bed and promptly ordered Sumner's Second Corps across the crumbling bridges to the aid of the hard-pressed left. In a most efficacious performance, old Sumner threw his troops across the now-floating Grapevine Bridge, and, at the last moment, fell upon the victorious, advancing enemy. Sumner checked the Confederates, and then hurled them back with heavy loss. The fighting was renewed at 7:00 A.M. on June 1, with McClellan's forces successfully driving the enemy back into the environs of Richmond. Johnston was severely wounded, and Lee succeeded him on June 1 in command of the defeated Army of Northern Virginia. In this battle of Fair Oaks, or Seven Pines, McClellan lost a total of 5,031 men, while the Confederates suffered 6,134 casualties. In his first large-scale battle, McClellan, although ill, had handled his forces creditably, had checked and thrown back the foe, and had retained the initiative in his invasion.[38]

In the early days of June, while rebuilding his washed-away bridges, McClellan inched closer to Richmond. By the last week of June all his army was on the southwest bank of the Chickahominy except Porter's Fifth Corps, which remained on the left bank near Mechanicsville, awaiting the expected arrival of McDowell. However, delays in the Valley prevented the First Corps from ever reaching McClellan. A raid by Jeb Stuart's Confederate cavalry warned McClellan of the exposed condition of his great base of supplies at White House on the Pamunkey River, and the Union

[38] See Hassler, *General George B. McClellan,* 119–28.

commander began sending off supplies by water to the James River in the anticipation that perhaps he might have to change his base to the latter stream.[39]

Meanwhile, the officials in Washington were losing confidence in McClellan. They sent Major General Ambrose E. Burnside to relieve McClellan if he saw fit. But, the two generals being old friends, "Burn" did not exercise this discretionary power. Also, the announcement came from Washington that Major General John Pope had been named commander of the newly created Army of Virginia—a collection of the previously scattered Federal forces in northern Virginia. Pope had been brought from the West, and, upon his arrival in Washington, had snuggled up to the Radicals, trumpeted loudly about his own prowess, and warned Lincoln to recall McClellan's army at once from the vicinity of Richmond. While all this was transpiring on the Union side, Lee was moving Jackson's force from the Valley to Richmond, and otherwise beefing up his army until it totaled at least 85,000 men—almost as many as McClellan had.[40]

The great Seven Days battle began on June 25 with a minor success for McClellan at Oak Grove, on the Williamsburg pike near Seven Pines. On the following day the Federals won another and larger victory at Mechanicsville (or Beaver Dam), the attacking Southerners losing 1,484 killed and wounded to McClellan's total loss of but 361 men. Now, however, the initiative had shifted to Lee. McClellan drew back Porter's embattled Fifth Corps to a new position behind Boatswain Creek, near Gaines's Mill. This was necessary because Jackson's forces, moving onto the field from the Valley, were threatening to turn the Union right flank. In the battle of Gaines's Mill, fought on June 27, Porter's 25,000 effectives were opposed by some 57,000 Confederates. McClellan,

[39] 12 O.R., 44, 64, 119, 153, 159, 169; McClellan, Report, 113, 116; B. & L., 113, 116; 13 O.R., 19, 193, 228; M.O.S., 411; C.C.W. (1863), II, 633.

[40] Montgomery C. Meigs, "The Relations of President Lincoln and Secretary Stanton to the Military Commanders in the Civil War," American Historical Review (XXVI), 291; C.C.W. (1863), II, 279; Livermore, Numbers and Losses, 86.

accepting Pinkerton's estimate of "over 180,000" troops in Lee's army, felt himself unable to reinforce Porter with more than two brigades—although in reality he could have sent more—or to attack the Confederates elsewhere. In the heavy day-long battle, the Federals repulsed with severe losses most of the enemy's desperate attacks, until sheer weight of numbers broke Porter's lines and impelled McClellan to withdraw him to the south side of the Chickahominy. The Nationals had lost the only tactical decision they were to lose during the Seven Days battle, plus casualties amounting to 6,837. Confederate losses were about 8,751 killed and wounded.[41]

The Southerners now believed that McClellan was cut off from his supposed base of supplies at White House, and that he would be forced to retreat back down the Peninsula, to surrender his army, or to see it cut to pieces. What the Confederates did not know was that McClellan had already made the fateful decision to change his base to the James. He would attempt to move his army of some 82,000 men, 25,000 tons of supplies, 25,000 horses and mules, and 2,500 beeves across the narrow bottleneck at White Oak Bridge. This was the only practicable way across the gloomy and extensive White Oak Swamp which lay athwart his sole route of escape to the James. This tremendous mass of men, animals, and equipment was jammed into the cramped space between the Chickahominy and the swamp, and all had to be gotten to safety across the vital White Oak Bridge. Lee, however, was baffled for some time as to McClellan's position and daring plan. Nonetheless, the Union movement, undertaken involuntarily and under great pressure from the soon-to-be-pursuing Confederates, assumed somewhat the aspect of a retreat after Gaines's Mill.[42]

Early on the morning of June 28, McClellan sent to Stanton the famous "Savage's Station Dispatch," certainly one of the most unusual and disrespectful ever sent to a civilian superior by a soldier in the field, regardless of whether the charges were accurate or not.

[41] See Hassler, *General George B. McClellan*, 139–49.
[42] Ropes, *Story of the Civil War*, II, 180, 211; 12 *O.R.*, 60; *B. & L.*, II, 325.

In it, the General intoned, "I have lost this battle [of Gaines's Mill] because my force was too small. I again repeat that I am not responsible for this, and I say it with the earnestness of a general who feels in his heart the loss of every brave man who has been needlessly sacrificed. . . . I have seen too many dead and wounded comrades to feel otherwise than that the government has not sustained this army. If you do not do so now the game is lost. If I save this army now, I tell you plainly I owe no thanks to you or to any other persons in Washington. You have done your best to sacrifice this army." Three weeks later, McClellan admitted to his wife that the dispatch "was pretty frank and quite true. Of course they will never forgive me for that. I knew it when I wrote it; but as I thought it possible that it might be the last I ever wrote, it seemed better to have it exactly true." For reasons of his own, the Secretary never replied to these serious charges, although it is well known that he wanted McClellan removed from command.[43]

On the Peninsula, June 28 was a day of marching by the Federals, with only one small combat fought—that near Golding's, in which the Northerners were victorious. McClellan himself had gone ahead of his marching army, down the Quaker Road from White Oak Swamp through Glendale to Malvern Hill, locating routes of advance and selecting and preparing defensive positions from which portions of his army could fight while the rest of the troops, animals, and wagons were making their way safely to the new haven on the James. After the masterful feat of getting his huge forces across the forbidding White Oak Swamp barrier, McClellan successfully fought off and defeated the pursuing foe in two sharp battles on June 29—at Allen's Farm and at Savage's Station—in which the Confederates suffered much heavier losses than did the Federals.[44]

The hot sunny day of June 30, 1862, was the crucial day for McClellan's delicate operation. He had to keep the enemy at bay to the north of White Oak Swamp in his rear, while at the same

[43] McClellan to Stanton, June 28, 1862, McClellan Papers; *M.O.S.*, 452.
[44] *B. & L.*, II, 369–75; 13 *O.R.*, 50–51, 661, 706; McClellan, *Report*, 131–34.

time keeping the Confederate units on his right flank at arm's length to the west of the vital crossroads at Glendale. And McClellan's forces succeeded in accomplishing these necessary tasks. At the swamp, Franklin, with about 18,000 men, encountered 30,000 Confederates under Jackson. The Unionists repulsed the redoubtable Stonewall's feeble sorties, and kept him north of the morass. At the same time, just west of the Glendale intersection, Federal units—although some were forced back a few hundred yards—essentially repelled with severe loss a whole series of heavy enemy assaults, thus maintaining the integrity of McClellan's long-strung-out army, moving necessarily at a snail's pace southward along the Quaker Road.[45]

Finally, at Malvern Hill, near the James River, the Union army sent Lee's forces reeling back on July 1 in one of the great Confederate commander's worst defeats. McClellan himself had ably posted the units and selected the defensive positions on this wide, open, plateau-like hill. Beginning in the afternoon, and continuing until after dark, the Southerners made persistent and gallant efforts to drive McClellan's army from this key position, but all the assaults melted away with fearful casualties to the attackers. "Few steps could be taken," writes Porter of the battlefield after the combat, "without trampling upon the body of a dead or wounded soldier. . . . In some places the bodies were in continuous lines and heaps." Confederate General D. H. Hill acknowledges that "the Battle of Malvern Hill was a disaster to the Confederates," ending all hope of destroying McClellan's army. Southern losses were somewhere between 5,000 and 7,000 men, while the Federals suffered barely a third of that number. But McClellan did not retain the field of battle. By July 2 the Army of the Potomac, badly in need of food and ammunition, had reached its water-borne supplies, and was safely ensconced in strong defensive lines laid out by McClellan around the new base at Harrison's Landing on the James River.[46]

The mighty Seven Days battle—the greatest ever fought on the

[45] See Hassler, *General George B. McClellan,* 160–65.
[46] *Ibid.,* 166–70.

shores of the New World up to that time, and one of the epic battles of the entire Civil War—was over. The Federals, with some 90,000 effectives, had only slightly outnumbered their foes. McClellan's forces suffered the following casualties: 1,734 killed; 8,062 wounded; 6,053 missing—a total loss of 15,849. Lee had lost 3,479 killed; 16,261 wounded; 875 missing—total losses of 20,614. It was one of the few times during the war that Lee suffered heavier casualties than he inflicted, and it was the only time in the war that he had almost equal numbers with the Federals. "Under ordinary circumstances," Lee admitted in his official report, "the Federal army should have been destroyed." D. H. Hill owns that "throughout this campaign we attacked just when and where the enemy wished us to attack." Nonetheless, Lee had saved Richmond, and had seized and maintained the initiative. But McClellan's performance during the Seven Days was a most competent one. Not long after the Army of the Potomac reached Harrison's Bar, however, the General unburdened himself to his wife in an amazingly frank letter: "I have tried to do my best, honestly and faithfully, for my country. That I have to a certain extent failed I do not believe to be my fault, though my self-conceit probably blinds me to many errors that others see." [47]

The sequel to the Seven Days, on the Union side, was an extremely melancholy one. Lincoln arrived on the night of July 7 at Harrison's Bar. At the President's request, McClellan presented to him a paper concerning the general military situation throughout the country. But this famous "Harrison's Bar Letter" touched also on political matters, McClellan urging the President to adhere to a conservative policy regarding slavery. He recommended also that someone be named quickly to the vacant General-in-Chief position. He closed the paper to Lincoln by remarking, "I may be on the brink of eternity; and as I hope forgiveness from my Maker, I have written this letter with sincerity towards you and from love of my country." While Lincoln was not the least upset by this

[47] B. & L., II, 315, 317, 395; Livermore, Numbers and Losses, 86; 13 O.R., 497.

missive, the communication was anti-Radical in tenor and, according to Welles, helped "Stanton get rid of McClellan at headquarters." In reply to the President's implied view that perhaps the best course of action would be to bring the Army of the Potomac back to the front of Washington to be joined to Pope's Army of Virginia for a new overland thrust toward Richmond, McClellan and the other top Union generals at Harrison's Landing were almost unanimous in their conviction that the best policy was for the Army of the Potomac to stay and fight it out where they were.[48]

Meanwhile, back in Washington, Pope's friend, Major General Henry Wager Halleck, who had received credit for several of his subordinates' victories in the West, was ordered to the capital on July 11 as General-in-Chief of all the Union armies. The impetus for bringing "Old Brains," as he was known (or, among his enemies, "Woodenhead"), to Washington was the plot of Stanton, Chase, and Pope to get rid of McClellan. Being informed of Stanton's machinations, McClellan exploded in a letter home on July 13: "I think that [Stanton] is the most unmitigated scoundrel I ever knew, heard, or read of; I think that (I do not wish to be irreverent) had he lived in the time of the Savior, Judas Iscariot would have remained a respected member of the fraternity of the Apostles, and that the magnificent treachery and rascality of E. M. Stanton would have caused Judas to have raised his arms in holy terror and unaffected wonder." [49]

Halleck was forty-seven years old in 1862, although he looked older. He had a large, melon-shaped head, ever tilted forward or to one side, which topped a small, stoop-shouldered body. He had

[48] Heintzelman's Journal, July 8, 9, 1862; McClellan, *Report*, 144; Mc-Clellan to Lincoln, "Confidential," July 7, 1862, Lincoln Papers; *M.O.S.*, 487; Welles, *Lincoln and Seward*, 191; *C.C.W.* (1863), II, 612–13; Lincoln's talks with generals, July 8, 9, 1862, Lincoln Papers.

[49] 14 *O.R.*, 314, 371; Morse (ed.), *Welles's Diary*, I, 83, 105, 108, 109; Chase, *Diary and Correspondence of Salmon P. Chase* (Washington, 1903), 46–48; *C.C.W.* (1863), II, 279; McClellan to his wife, July 13, 1862, McClellan Papers.

chin whiskers, flabby cheeks, a double chin, and bulging, fish-like eyes that always watered. His paunch was as ample as his complexion was sallow. Halleck spoke in a halting way, chewed and smoked cigars, scratched his elbows incessantly, and was harsh and rude in manner. He had seen little action in the Mexican War after graduating third in the class of 1839 at West Point. But he had taught at Harvard, had been head of a mining company and a railroad, had drawn up the California constitution, and had written books on bitumen, international law, and military art and science.[50]

The chief talent—and it was an important one—which Halleck brought to his trying position as General-in-Chief was his ability to interpret military language into conventional terms for his civilian superiors, and to translate their thoughts into proper military jargon for the field commanders. But Halleck unfortunately was a moral coward who evaded responsibility like the plague. Lincoln felt that he was "little more . . . than a first-rate clerk." Stanton termed him "probably the greatest scoundrel and most bare-faced villain in America"—much too harsh a view. McClellan wrote after the war that, "of all men whom I have encountered in high position, Halleck was the most hopelessly stupid." The Secretary of the Navy, Gideon Welles, who understood Halleck's character better than most people, described him as follows: "He has a scholarly intellect and . . . some military acquirements, but his mind is heavy and irresolute. It appears to me that he does not possess originality and that he has little real talent. What he has is educational." Welles went on to say that "Halleck originates nothing, anticipates nothing, to assist others; takes no responsiblity, plans nothing, suggests nothing, is good for nothing." Yet it was a most onerous and difficult position which Halleck held, and Lincoln kept him on as General-in-Chief for over a year and a half.[51]

[50] New York *Tribune*, May 31, 1862; Beale (ed.), *Bates's Diary*, 293; Wilson, *Under the Old Flag*, I, 98–99; Cullum, *Biographical Register*, I, 573–74.

[51] Morse (ed.), *Welles's Diary*, I, 107, 119, 121, 180, 216, 320, 329, 364, 373, 383, 384, 444; Pease and Randall (eds.), *Browning's Diary*, I, 605; *M.O.S.*, 137.

On the afternoon of July 25, Halleck arrived at Harrison's Landing to see the army and to talk with McClellan. He rejected McClellan's proposal to cross the army to the south side of the James and operate against Petersburg, the railroad key to Richmond. After agreeing to advance against Richmond with the 20,-000 reinforcements which Halleck said were available, McClellan and the Federal generals, who were eager to press on toward the Confederate capital from Harrison's, were astonished when, on August 3, an order, sent over Halleck's signature, directed McClellan to bring the army back to the vicinity of Washington immediately. Despite McClellan's very strong and convincingly argued message against this dubious step—including the prophetic words, "Here, directly in front of this army, is the heart of the rebellion. . . . Here is the true defense of Washington; it is here, on the banks of the James, that the fate of the Union should be decided"—the order was not rescinded, and the Army of the Potomac was withdrawn by water to the front of Washington as rapidly as possible.[52]

McClellan himself arrived at Alexandria on August 27. With his troops being sent down toward Manassas to join Pope's army in the field, he was left at Alexandria to cool his heels—a general without an army to command. On the evening of August 30, while many of his soldiers under Pope were in battle at Manassas, McClellan, with the distant rumbling of the guns reaching his ears, wrote to his wife, "I feel too blue and disgusted to write any more now, so I will smoke a cigar and try to get into a better humor. They have taken all my troops from me! I have even sent off my personal escort and camp-guard, and am here with a few orderlies and the aides. I have been listening to the sound of a great battle in the distance. My men engaged in it and I away. I never felt worse in my life." [53]

[52] See Hassler, *General George B. McClellan*, 188–204.
[53] *Ibid.*, 215.

CHAPTER THREE

John Pope

> [Pope] was utterly outgeneralled; he
> never knew where his enemy was; he
> fought to no purpose. But when he did
> fight, it was with a will beyond his dis-
> cretion.
>
> —*Theodore A. Dodge*

THE THIRD UNION COMMANDER TO CROSS SWORDS WITH THE
Confederates on the road to Richmond was, like his two predecessors, of imposing appearance. Major General John Pope was
sturdily built, and, while not so tall as McDowell, was nonetheless soldierly in bearing and carriage. He had rather long, straight,
dark hair, an upturned nose, a penetrating eye, and a large beard
which reached his chest. His visage was, however, marred somewhat by an often vain and surly expression. All in all, if one were
judging only by physical appearances, the forty-year-old Pope
seemed to measure up well to his task.[1]

The new Federal commander's pre-Civil War career had been
ordinary. Louisville, Kentucky, was the place of his birth on March
16, 1822. He graduated seventeenth in the class of 1842 at West
Point. At the Academy, according to James Longstreet, Pope "stood
at the head for riding," but "he did not apply himself to his books
very closely." Pope served in routine assignments until the war
with Mexico, where he won two brevets. Then followed more conventional service until the Civil War. He had been married in
1859 to Clara Pomeroy Horton, who bore him four children. In

[1] John Richards Boyle, *Soldiers True* . . . (New York, 1903), 41;
Leech, *Reveille in Washington*, 178; *B. & L.*, II, 524.

February, 1861, Pope was a captain, engaged in building light-houses on the Great Lakes.[2]

From the start of the secession crisis, Pope had stood foursquare for the Union. In late February, 1861, he had accompanied President-elect Lincoln and his party on the adventurous trip from Springfield to Washington, D. C. Afterward, while serving as a mustering officer in Chicago, Pope had bombarded the administration with letters, written by himself and by influential politicians, and had even visited Washington briefly—all in an attempt to secure a high appointment. Finally, on May 17, 1861, he was commissioned a brigadier general of volunteers. Among old army men, however, this news did not sit well, if one is to go by the comment made by that grizzled old veteran, Heintzelman, who snorted, "What an additional outrage on the Army."[3]

Pope's subsequent activities before being called East brought laurels to him as well as to the Union cause. From July 17, 1861, to February 18, 1862, he was a district commander in Missouri, where some minor successes were won against Confederate forces under Sterling Price. Pope was then named to command the Army of the Mississippi, which captured New Madrid, Missouri, and Island No. 10, in the Mississippi, in March and April, 1862. He had been promoted to major general of volunteers on March 21, 1862. Under Halleck's overall direction, Pope's army participated in the snail-like crawl to Corinth in April and May, 1862, and was engaged in the pursuit of the enemy to Baldwyn up through June 10, 1862.[4]

Before he left on the morning of June 21 for Washington, Pope had been guilty of currying favor by deliberately overstating,

[2] B. & L., II, 524; Cullum, Biographical Register, II, 49–50; D.A.B., XV, 76–77.
[3] Beale (ed.), Bates's Diary, 242 n; Nicolay and Hay, Abraham Lincoln, III, 314; Cullum, Biographical Register, II, 50; Pope to W. H. Lamon, April 20, 1861, Pope to Lincoln, April 20, 1861, L. Trumbull to Lincoln, May 9, 1861, Lincoln Papers; Heintzelman's Journal, June 14, 1861.
[4] Cullum, Biographical Register, II, 50.

tenfold, the number of Confederate troops and arms he had captured. Upon his arrival in the capital, he was told that the administration intended that he should lead a new army, composed of the scattered forces in northern Virginia, and that he was to operate just east of the Blue Ridge Mountains. It was hoped that such action would menace the enemy forces in western Virginia and thereby draw troops away from Lee's main army, which was facing McClellan near Richmond. Pope and his family were long-time friends of Lincoln, and the General had been suggested by Stanton and Chase as a successor to McClellan in command of the Army of the Potomac. Welles relates that "Pope himself had great influence in bringing Halleck [to Washington], and the two, with Stanton and Chase, got possession of McC[lellan]'s army and withdrew it from before Richmond." Welles observed also that "the introduction of Pope here, followed by Halleck, is an intrigue of Stanton's and Chase's to get rid of McClellan." [5]

Pope served at first as military adviser to Lincoln, and, as John C. Ropes avers, "It is probable that until the arrival of General Halleck, his advice was largely relied on by the President and Cabinet." Hitchcock had held this preferred position for some time, but, while his military reputation was high, he labored under the disadvantage of having never commanded large forces in combat. During the Seven Days battle, Pope's advice to the President was far from brilliant. He urged Lincoln to impel McClellan to keep his army on the York or Pamunkey and not to allow him to move over to the James River. While Pope's idea of trying to get the two main Union armies in the East together was sound, his lack of knowledge and appreciation of the situation confronting McClellan at that crucial time on the Peninsula was unfortunate for Federal strategy.[6]

[5] Villard, Memoirs, I, 279–81; 25 O.R., 17, 18; B. & L., II, 449–51; Morse (ed.), Welles's Diary, I, 105, 108, 120; Nicolay and Hay, Abraham Lincoln, VI, 2.
[6] 18 O.R., 487, 488; John C. Ropes, The Army Under Pope (New York, 1881), 7.

On June 26, 1862, Lincoln issued the order naming Pope to the command of the Army of Virginia, composed of the forces—now called corps—of Banks, McDowell, and Frémont (soon to be replaced by Franz Sigel). One sentence of the President's order bears notice: "When the Army of the Potomac and the Army of Virginia shall be in position to communicate and directly cooperate at or before Richmond the chief command, while so operating together, shall be governed, as in like cases, by the Rules and Articles of War"—in other words, McClellan, who was senior to Pope, would command the combined armies, if and when they got together. Pope issued a general order on June 27, formally assuming command of the Army of Virginia, with headquarters for the time being in Washington. When he appeared on the floor of Congress at this time to meet the solons, to denounce McClellan, and to tell the administration how to run the war, his confidence and unrestrained enthusiasm in himself won over most of the newspaper reporters present, as well as the lawmakers.[7]

With Pope now officially in command of what was soon to be the main Union army in the East, his personal traits and characteristics assumed vital proportions, as they did with all commanders. The new Federal leader was known, by those who were well acquainted with him, as a "humbug" and a "bag of wind." "Personally," writes Lieutenant Colonel Charles P. Horton, "Gen. Pope was of quick temper, impatient of contradiction, rude in manner, and gifted with a vivid imagination." Speaking of Pope's "impetuous nature," General Jacob D. Cox adds that "his reputation in 1861 was that of an able and energetic man, vehement and positive in character, apt to be choleric and even violent toward those who displeased him." "An impulsive and sanguine man," the General was, according to Ropes, "a vigorous, active, resolute man. He had many of the peculiarly military virtues, courage, persistency, confidence in himself"; yet he was also a person "sub-

[7] 18 *O.R.*, 435–37, 444; Theodore F. Dwight (ed.), *The Virginia Campaign of General Pope in 1862* (Boston, 1886), II, 35; New York *Tribune*, June 26, 27, 1862.

ject to sudden and violent changes of opinion." "He had," reports Henry Villard, "two very marked failings—first, he talked too much of himself, of what he could do and of what ought to be done; and, secondly, he indulged, contrary to good discipline and all propriety, in very free comments upon his superiors and fellow-commanders." [8]

Secretary of the Navy Welles quotes Postmaster General Montgomery Blair, "who had known [Pope] intimately," as saying that the General was "a braggart and a liar, with some courage, perhaps, but not much capacity." The President, affirms Welles, "said Pope had great cunning." The Secretary states that "Blair . . . said he was a blower and a liar." Flag Officer Andrew Foote, who knew Pope during the earlier campaigns on the Mississippi, declares Welles, "used to laugh at the gasconade and bluster of Pope." The navy diary keeper added his own observation: "Pope . . . has the reputation among those who know him of being untruthful and wholly unreliable." More important, the new Union commander appeared to Colonel Theodore Lyman as being "so bombastic and so destitute of *savoir faire* as to alienate his subordinates." If these views of Pope's makeup by his associates seem hard and unfair, the General proved all of them to be accurate during his relatively brief tenure as main army commander in the East.[9]

On July 8 Pope gave a dramatic and fantastic testimony before the Committee on the Conduct of the War, the Radical majority of which was friendly to the General. He declared that he was for attack, and not delay; that he favored fighting, and not employing strategy; that all of the Radicals' war aims and policies were fine with him; that McClellan's proposed crossing of the James and

[8] Bigelow, *Retrospections*, I, 542; Leech, *Reveille in Washington*, 178; Dwight (ed.), *The Virginia Campaign*, II, 35, 61; Jacob D. Cox, *Military Reminiscences* . . . (New York, 1900), I, 247–48; Ropes, *Story of the Civil War*, II, 252; Villard, *Memoirs*, I, 272.

[9] Morse (ed.), *Welles's Diary*, I, 104, 120, 126, 221; Dwight (ed.), *The Virginia Campaign*, II, 305.

investing Petersburg was "the most hazardous operation of all"; that the Peninsula scheme was a dreadful blunder and should be given up at once, and the Army of the Potomac recalled by water to the front of Washington and incorporated with his own. Pope asserted that he could march not only to Richmond, but could go all the way through the Confederacy to New Orleans! He was not fearful for the safety of Washington, even if his army was not directly between the capital and the enemy. "I think the best way to defend Washington is to attack Richmond," he said. Then the General showed his lack of grasp of the military probabilities by stating, "I myself doubt very much whether [the Confederates] will move any of their troops in this direction at all, even if they succeed in removing General McClellan's army from where it now is." [10]

In the order constituting the new Army of Virginia, the President had given Pope a threefold task: (1) to cover Washington; (2) to safeguard the Shenandoah Valley; (3) to operate against the enemy's communication lines in the direction of Gordonsville and Charlottesville, so that a part of Lee's army facing McClellan might be drawn away from Richmond toward the west. Pope commenced his campaign in early July by concentrating his army—numbering then almost 50,000—first around Warrenton, and then at Culpeper Court House and along the Rapidan River. Pope himself stayed in the rear at his headquarters in Washington, awaiting the repairing of the Orange & Alexandria Railroad as far as Culpeper. The advance to Culpeper and the Rapidan was quite dangerous, since, with McClellan being withdrawn from near Richmond, Lee was free to move strong forces against the Army of Virginia. Pope was absolutely convinced that bold action on his part would keep the Confederates on the defensive, and that they would seek safety in retreat. "To the very last of his campaign," remarks Colonel Gustave J. Fiebeger, "he therefore placed great reliance in any rumors or reports to the effect that the enemy was trying to get away from him." This was a fatal flaw in Pope's

[10] *C.C.W.* (1863), I, 276–82.

makeup, and would cost him dearly in the unfolding operations.[11]

In an effort to establish a good rapport with his troops, Pope committed an almost unbelievable error in mid-July. He issued, over his signature, a proclamation to his soldiers which was both belittling and highly insulting, and which got him off on the wrong foot with his men at the start of the campaign. This remarkable manifesto deserves to be quoted rather fully. In it, Pope said:

I have come to you from the West, where we have always seen the backs of our enemies; from an army whose business it has been to seek the adversary and to beat him when he was found; whose policy has been attack, and not defense. . . . I presume that I have been called here to pursue the same system and to lead you against the enemy. It is my purpose to do so, and that speedily. . . . I desire you to dismiss from your minds certain phrases which I am sorry to find so much in vogue amongst you. I hear constantly of "taking strong positions, and holding them"; of "lines of retreat," and of "bases of supplies." Let us discard such ideas. The strongest position a soldier should desire to occupy is one from which he can most easily advance against the enemy. Let us study the probable lines of retreat of our opponents, and leave our own to take care of themselves. Let us look before us, and not behind. Success and glory are in the advance, disaster and shame lurk in the rear.

This proclamation is filled with grim irony when reread in the light of Pope's disastrous campaign. The reaction of Fitz John Porter to this manifesto was indicated in a letter to a friend: "I regret . . . that Gen Pope has not improved since his youth and has now written himself down what the military world has long known, an ass. His address to his troops will make him ridiculous in the eyes of military men." Pope later acknowledged that this proclamation, and a whole series of extremely harsh "Radical" orders aimed at the Confederate civilian population in Virginia which were issued with it, were dictated to him by Stanton.[12]

[11] 16 O.R., 21; 18 O.R., 439 ff.; Gustave J. Fiebeger, Campaigns of the American Civil War (West Point, 1910), 54–55, 63.

[12] 18 O.R., 473–74; 16 O.R., 50–52; F. J. Porter to J. C. G. Kennedy, July 17, 1862, McClellan Papers; Chase, Diary, 46–47; Cox, Military Reminiscences, I, 222–23.

Near the end of July, Pope left Washington and assumed command of his army in person at the front. The Army of Virginia, at this time, numbered approximately 50,000 effectives. Strictly speaking, of course, Pope's forces around Culpeper were not yet really an army; they were merely a collection of divisions which had not as yet fought together. In contrast, Lee and his subordinates, as well as his army units, had been together on the Peninsula.[13]

Then, Jackson began moving northward from Gordonsville toward Culpeper on August 7. Pope threw part of his force southward from the latter point to check Stonewall, but the orders he gave to Banks and Sigel were so vague and imprecise as to lead Ropes to remark, "We shall see again and again . . . the same ill-digested plans, the same sanguine view of the future, followed as suddenly by the same unexpected change for the worse in the military situation." The result was that, on August 9, in the battle of Cedar Mountain, Banks, after an initial success, was thrown back in rout, losing 2,381 of about 8,000 men engaged. Jackson lost approximately 1,300 of some 20,000 involved. Pope—who had failed to examine the ground himself or to reinforce Banks properly—nonetheless claimed on the sixteenth that his defeat was really a victory, and congratulated his troops. The commander had a way of twisting things around 180 degrees.[14]

On August 14–15, Pope was reinforced by the two divisions—Major General Jesse L. Reno's and Major General Isaac I. Stevens'—of Burnside's Ninth Corps. Burnside himself remained at Falmouth, across the Rappahannock from Fredericksburg, probably because he ranked Pope. Pope then assumed a line some nine miles in length along the Rapidan River and astride the Orange & Alexandria Railroad. But the Federal position was weak because of the proximity of Clark's Mountain on the Union left flank,

[13] *B. & L.*, II, 460; Dwight (ed.), *The Virginia Campaign*, II, 40; *16 O.R.*, 53–54; *18 O.R.*, 523.
[14] Walter Geer, *Campaigns of the Civil War* (New York, 1926), 129–30; Ropes, *Story of the Civil War*, II, 247–50; Ropes, *Army Under Pope*, 20–30; George H. Gordon, *History of the Campaign of the Army of Virginia* . . . (Boston, 1880), 461.

behind which the enemy could mass his whole army, and because of the fact that the railroad, upon which Pope depended for his supplies and communications, took a sharp bend to the east at Culpeper which made it vulnerable to an enemy thrust around Pope's left flank. Lee, determining to overwhelm Pope before the Army of the Potomac could join him, had moved Longstreet's corps into position on Jackson's right, behind Clark Mountain, and, on August 15, had assumed command in person of his army of 55,000 men. Luckily for Pope, Lee's plan to turn the Union left and seize the railroad was delayed for two days because the Confederate cavalry was not ready to move.[15]

Although warned by Halleck on August 18 about the exposed nature of his flanks, Pope was completely unaware of his danger and thought his position was "strong." But then the Confederate plans to turn his left flank were captured by Pope's cavalry, and he fell back quickly behind the Rappahannock, aided by fog, where Halleck urged him to "stand firm." Of course, Pope's army should have been brought back to Bull Run, or even closer to Alexandria, in order to be reinforced for certain by the bulk of the Army of the Potomac before fighting a major battle with Lee. But Pope was being augmented by the splendid division of Brigadier General John F. Reynolds and by Porter's staunch Fifth Corps. However, Pope had neglected to give Porter any orders as to where he should station his troops or to inform him where the other Federal units were located. So Porter was left to wander aimlessly westward along the northern bank of the Rappahannock River.[16]

Then, on the night of August 22, two Confederate cavalry brigades under Fitzhugh Lee crossed the Rappahannock on the Sperryville road, rode around Warrenton, and charged in upon Pope's headquarters at Catlett's Station, just northeast of Warren-

[15] Geer, *Campaigns*, 130–31; Alexander, *Military Memoirs*, 186.
[16] 18 *O.R.*, 589–91; W. Birkbeck Wood and J. E. Edmonds, *A History of the Civil War* . . . (New York, 1905), 100; Ropes, *Army Under Pope*, 33, 38–40; *B. & L.*, II, 461 n, 515; Burnside to Halleck, Aug. 24, 1862, F. J. Porter Papers.

ton Junction. The brilliant enemy dash just missed capturing Pope himself, who had only a few minutes before walked away from his tent through the woods to another general's headquarters. But the gray riders did capture Pope's dispatch book, telling of the reinforcements he was receiving, as well as giving other useful information. They found also a warm supper on the table, and seized Pope's dress uniform, including his fine plumed hat. Not the least of the booty found in the General's tent was a chest containing $350,000 in Federal greenbacks. The enemy appropriated the meal, the money, and the dress uniform, much to Pope's humiliation. The Union commander, after this raid, was now convinced that Lee had abandoned his plans to turn the Federal right. He telegraphed Halleck on August 24 that he felt the enemy "is not yet ready to force the passage of [the Rappahannock] river for any forward movement." [17]

But at this very moment Lee was planning to strike the railroad in the rear of the Union army by sending Jackson on a wide-sweeping turning movement around and behind Pope's right flank. The Federal commander was, at the same time, preparing to smite Lee's right and rear. But he was handicapped when he and McDowell carelessly lost some of the best maps of the region, and was stymied further by heavy rain on August 24. Pope then began concentrating his army around Warrenton and along the roads leading from that point to the Rappahannock crossings of Waterloo, Sulphur Springs, and Kelly's Ford. Actually, he should have fallen back at once to a line running from Thoroughfare Gap through Gainesville to Manassas. On the very day that Jackson began his great turning movement—August 25—Pope wired Halleck his repeated opinion that the enemy was not as yet prepared to cross the Rappahannock. [18]

While Lee with Longstreet's command of some 30,000 men re-

[17] B. & L., II, 528; Wood and Edmonds, The Civil War, 100–101; **18** O.R., 640.

[18] Ropes, Army Under Pope, 39, 45–46; Roebling's Journal, Aug. 24, 1862, Porter Papers; B. & L., II, 457, 463; 16 O.R., 65–66.

mained in position along the south bank of the Rappahannock, Jackson, with about 25,000 men, moved at daybreak on the twenty-fifth around Pope's right, crossed the Bull Run Mountains at Thoroughfare Gap, and, moving along the Manassas Gap Railroad through Gainesville, reached Bristoe Station on the afternoon of August 26. After tearing up track and telegraph lines there, Stonewall seized Pope's great supply base at Manassas on the morning of the twenty-seventh, capturing enormous quantities of valuable stores and destroying the rest.[19]

Pope was promptly apprised by his lookouts on August 25 that Jackson was on the march. He felt, however, along with Halleck, that the movement was merely another enemy raid down the Shenandoah Valley, and he did not bother to have Jackson shadowed by his own vedettes. Actually, it should have been obvious to Pope that Lee would not allow Jackson to move down the Valley and thereby leave Longstreet's 30,000 men to face the combined armies of Virginia and the Potomac. Characteristically, Pope was not perturbed, due perhaps in part to the fact that he was about to be reinforced by the two excellent corps of Heintzelman and Porter. Even if he believed that Jackson was headed for the Valley, Pope should have abandoned the Warrenton area and concentrated the bulk of his army at Thoroughfare Gap and Gainesville. Such a disposition by the Federal commander, declares James Ford Rhodes, "would have frustrated Lee's plan at the outset." But Pope made no major movement on August 26. Consequently, Lee moved Longstreet's wing after Jackson, Longstreet halting that night at Orleans.[20]

On the night of the twenty-sixth, Pope finally realized that Jackson was coming through Thoroughfare Gap. At first acting judiciously, the Union general ordered most of his units from Warrenton toward Gainesville, to occupy that important point

[19] Geer, *Campaigns*, 132; *B. & L.*, II, 511.
[20] Heintzelman's Journal, Aug. 26, 28, 1862; James Ford Rhodes, *History of the United States* . . . (New York, 1899), IV, 122–23.

which was directly between Jackson and Longstreet. But then, on the evening of the twenty-seventh, he undid his earlier good work by directing practically his entire army to march on Manassas. The developing crisis found Pope far from calm. An officer present at his headquarters found that place in a turmoil. "Everything and everybody bore the semblance of the greatest excitement—especially Gen. Pope," he reported. As to the movements and positions of his units, "Pope . . . was . . . in a great stew about them." He would, Pope crowed, march "at the earliest blush of dawn" on the twenty-eighth, and "bag the whole crowd" of Confederates. This concentration on Manassas, when Pope really did not know where Jackson was situated, was most unwise; it lost the Federals one full day and helped to lead to greater disaster.[21]

After having demolished Pope's base at Manassas, Jackson moved his units to the vicinity of Sudley Church on August 28. Longstreet's command, accompanied by Lee, was marching in Jackson's tracks and was, on the night of the twenty-seventh, still west of Thoroughfare Gap, where Federal cavalry discovered them and reported their position to Pope on the night of the twenty-seventh. The Union commander, however, continued on the twenty-eighth to neglect the possible movements of Longstreet's force.[22]

While obeying Pope's orders to move from Gainesville toward Manassas with his wing of the Union army, McDowell had the good sense on the twenty-eighth to order, on his own responsibility, Ricketts' division to Thoroughfare Gap, where Longstreet was detained long enough to give Pope the whole of the twenty-eighth to fight Jackson alone. But Pope disapproved of this wise decision by McDowell because he was convinced that Longstreet could not reach the field before the evening of August 30. In the early afternoon of the twenty-eighth, Reynolds' division had a

[21] Ropes, *Army Under Pope,* 52 ff.; 16 *O.R.,* 72; Roebling's Journal, Aug. 27, 1862, Porter Papers.
[22] Fiebeger, *Campaigns,* 59; Wood and Edmonds, *The Civil War,* 105–106.

brush with Bradley T. Johnson's brigade just east of Gainesville. Unfortunately, McDowell failed to examine more closely the source and positions of these enemy forces.[23]

Pope himself reached Manassas at noon on the twenth-eighth to find his depot destroyed and the elusive Jackson gone. After jumping to a false conclusion and issuing useless orders, Pope changed his mind, and, at 4:15 that afternoon, directed practically his entire army to march toward Centreville. The Union commander was convinced that Stonewall was east of Bull Run and moving on Alexandria. Consequently, on the night of August 28–29, the Federal right wing, composed of the corps of Heintzelman and Reno, bivouacked between Bull Run and Centreville. The twenty-eighth had been a wasted day for the Nationals, with the bewildered Pope having some 60,000 of his troops aimlessly marching and countermarching. Only when he received word of Rufus King's vicious clash—along the Warrenton pike between Groveton and Gainesville—with a part of Jackson's command at dusk on the twenty-eighth, did Pope finally learn Stonewall's true position north of Groveton.[24]

And how did the Federal commander react to this information? Typically, Pope assumed that Jackson was in a bad way and was retreating. "I see no possibility of his escape," trumpeted Pope. Once again—inexplicably—Pope ignored Longstreet's corps and continued, fatuously, to do so during the whole of the twenty-ninth. Actually, during the afternoon of the twenty-eighth, Ricketts had been driven back from Thoroughfare Gap by Longstreet, and forced to retreat first to Gainesville, from which point he was ordered to Bristoe Station. King, after having fought well on the evening of the twenty-eighth at the so-called battle of Gainesville, had fallen back to Gainesville, and had then taken up the march toward Manassas. These rather unwise final movements by Ricketts and King were due chiefly to McDowell's absence

[23] Ropes, *Army Under Pope,* 67–69, 71; 16 *O.R.,* 533.
[24] Wood and Edmonds, *The Civil War,* 106–108; Ropes, *Army Under Pope,* 72–74.

from his command, for which he was later censured by a court of inquiry.[25]

August 29 was another day of intense heat. With practically all of the fatigued, badly scattered Union forces on or east of the Manassas-Sudley road on the morning of the twenty-ninth, Jackson had taken up a position facing southeastward along the embankment of an unfinished railroad, mostly in the woods, and somewhat elevated, stretching southwestward from near Sudley Church to the pike near Groveton; while Longstreet's wing was marching rapidly through Thoroughfare Gap toward Gainesville and Jackson's right flank. Pope himself arrived "in good spirits" in Centreville about 6:00 A.M. on the twenty-ninth, thinking he had Jackson trapped. His best course would have been to withdraw his army to the high ground about Centreville, rest and feed his soldiers, and receive succor in a day or two from the powerful corps of Franklin and Sumner, then at Alexandria. Still, Pope had some 70,000 men as against Lee's 49,000. Ropes thinks that "it was probably possible to inflict a severe blow on the corps of Jackson before it could be joined by that of Longstreet," but it would require a general of clearer head and better grasp of the situation than Pope.[26]

Meanwhile, north of Groveton, the main action of the twenty-ninth was beginning. During the morning Sigel launched two badly directed attacks against Jackson's strong railroad position, and both were rather easily repelled. Pope himself arrived on the battlefield shortly after noon to assume personal command. He failed to see that the sensitive and vulnerable point in Jackson's position was his left flank, near Sudley Spring. Throughout the remainder of the battle, under Pope's immediate command, the Federal assaults were made in a piecemeal fashion. The third Union attack of the day was ordered by Pope at 1:00 P.M., and, after fierce fighting, was again thrown back. Then, about 3:00 P.M., came the memorable and truly magnificent charge of

---

[25] 16 O.R., 75; B. & L., II, 517; 15 O.R., 330–31.
[26] Davis, Three Years, 108; C.C.W. (1863), I, 384; Dwight (ed.), The Virginia Campaign, II, 197–219; Geer, Campaigns, 137.

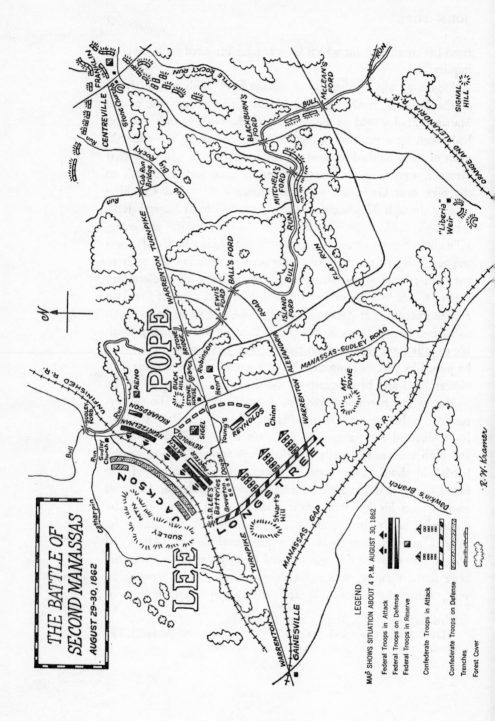

THE BATTLE OF
SECOND MANASSAS

AUGUST 29-30, 1862

LEGEND

MAP SHOWS SITUATION ABOUT 4 P.M. AUGUST 30, 1862

Federal Troops in Attack
Federal Troops on Defense
Federal Troops in Reserve

Confederate Troops in Attack

Confederate Troops on Defense
Trenches
Forest Cover

- R. W. Kramer

Brigadier General Cuvier Grover's brigade—one of the finest of the war—which pierced the first two enemy lines near the Deep Cut and scattered the defenders, but which was finally checked and thrown back by Jackson's third line and reserves when Pope failed to support Grover. Now, after some nine hours of fighting, and four desperate assaults, over 4,000 Federal soldiers had fallen and Jackson's line remained intact. Too few men had been used to enable any of the attacks to have succeeded, and when gains were made, the assaulting force had not been properly supported.[27]

On the Union left, in the meantime, near Manassas on the Orange & Alexandria Railroad, important events were shaping themselves. Porter, whose head of column had passed just beyond Manassas on its march toward Centreville, received an order from Pope at 9:30 on the morning of the twenty-ninth to reverse his march and to move with his own two divisions and with King's toward Gainesville in order to gain Jackson's rear. Porter immediately began to do this. Then, at approximately 10:00 A.M., Pope, laboring under the impression that Jackson was retreating and that Longstreet was still distant, drew up the famous "Joint Order" to McDowell and Porter. It directed these two generals to move their commands on the road from Manassas to Gainesville, near which latter point they would link up with the left flank of Pope's right wing, then contending with Jackson just north of the Warrenton pike near Groveton. The directive contained this important sentence: "If any considerable advantages are to be gained by departing from this order, it will not be strictly carried out." It warned also that they would probably be pulled back east of Bull Run that night in order to be resupplied. Porter and McDowell received the order at approximately 11:30 A.M.; but Porter's advance, at just that time, was encountering at Dawkin's Branch the advance of Longstreet's corps coming onto the field on Jackson's right. The result was that McDowell, who then commanded the Fifth Corps as well as his own, directed Porter to contain Long-

[27] Wood and Edmonds, *The Civil War*, 110; *B. & L.*, II, 474; Dwight (ed.), *The Virginia Campaign*, II, 89–90.

street along Dawkin's Branch while he (McDowell) moved with King's division from Manassas along the Sudley road to join Pope's right wing.[28]

Despite the fact that he had been informed of Confederate troops in large numbers south of the pike, Pope, who was in a blue funk as to what was going on, issued the following order to Porter at 4:30 P.M.: "I desire you to push forward into action at once on the enemy's flank and if possible on his rear." Receiving this directive at 6:30 P.M., Porter instantly began making preparations with his 9,000 men to attack Longstreet's 30,000, but darkness came on before he could undertake the operation. After the campaign, however, Pope and the Radicals, in order to make Porter the scapegoat for Pope's own failure and defeat, had him court-martialed for not obeying this impossible order, which was based on the false belief that Longstreet was not up. After being convicted and cashiered from the army, Porter was finally vindicated and cleared by a court of inquiry in 1879, which stated that his holding action on the twenty-ninth had saved Pope's army from overwhelming defeat then and there.[29]

Before the day was over, Pope hurled two more attacks—the fifth and sixth—against Jackson. That made by Kearny and Stevens against Stonewall's left wing at 5:00 P.M. gained some 300 yards before being thrown back, while King's attack along the Warrenton pike at dusk was easily repelled. This latter assault was made by Pope after ample warnings from Porter, Reynolds, and John Buford that Longstreet was on the field, continuing Jackson's right in a southeastwardly direction south of the pike. But instead of desisting and pulling his weary army back to Centreville for badly needed supplies, Pope was determined to renew the attack on the thirtieth. He decided to concentrate practi-

---

[28] 16 *O.R.*, 40, 76, 518–21; Ropes, *Army Under Pope*, 89–100; *B. & L.*, II, 518–28.

[29] Ropes, *Story of the Civil War*, II, 277–82, 285; 16 *O.R.*, 18, 523, 525–26, 533; *Senate Documents*, No. 37, 1st Sess., 46th Cong., pt. i, 251, pt. 3, 1707, 1709.

cally his entire force on and north of the pike to crush Jackson. So at 8:50 P.M. on the twenty-ninth, Pope sent Porter a curt, distrustful order, directing him to move his corps through Manassas and along the Sudley road to the pike and thence westward to Groveton, and to have it at this latter point by daylight of the thirtieth. While Porter was able to do this, it was a serious blunder on Pope's part, for it exposed the left and rear of the Union army to a devastating attack by Longstreet's powerful corps on the thirtieth. It is also not known why Pope failed to employ Banks's corps, at Bristoe Station, in the action on the twenty-ninth, or, especially, on the thirtieth. He possibly forgot about the existence of this force.[30]

The heavy combat on August 30 was something of an anticlimax, for, in reality, Pope had lost the battle on the several previous days. On the morning of the scorching hot thirtieth, the top Federal generals met with Pope at his headquarters, and found him "bragging and over-confident." He "was very sanguine that [the enemy] had retreated." In a boisterous dispatch to Halleck at 5:00 A.M., Pope blatantly proclaimed a great victory on the twenty-ninth over "the combined forces of the enemy." He now determined to assail the Confederates with Porter's corps on the pike, supported in the second and third lines by King's and Reynolds' divisions, and on the right by Ricketts. But Pope delayed until noon in issuing these orders, and failed to mount his great attack until 3:30 in the afternoon. He continued to ignore the existence of Longstreet south of the pike, and had denuded his front of all blueclad troops south of that highway. The result was that, despite much gallantry and three efforts in all, the Federal attacks were smashed with heavy loss, Longstreet crushing the Union left flank with a massive attack which endangered Pope's whole army. Only heroic stands, first at Bald Hill and then at Henry Hill, enabled Pope to extricate his forces north of the pike. At 8:00 P.M., he ordered his retreating forces back to Centreville,

[30] Geer, *Campaigns,* 141; 16 *O.R.,* 529–30; Dwight (ed.), *The Virginia Campaign,* II, 93.

where he believed a stand could be made. It was First Bull Run all over again.[31]

The casualties at the Battle of Second Manassas were heavy. Out of a total effective force of over 70,000, Pope lost, according to Livermore, 16,054 men killed, wounded, and missing. Confederate losses amounted to 9,197 of a total force available to Lee of some 55,000 men.[32]

To add to the gloom, it began raining at daylight on the thirty-first of August. Later that morning Pope sent a telegram to Halleck from Centreville which must have chilled the marrow of the administration: "I should like to know whether you feel secure about Washington should this army be destroyed." Minutes later the General-in-Chief tried to cheer Pope by wiring him, "My dear General: You have done nobly. Don't yield another inch if you can avoid it. . . . I am doing all I can for you and your noble army. God bless you and it." [33]

The thirty-first was spent by Pope in resupplying his army at Centreville and in trying to reorganize it. Later that day he wired Halleck, urging him to direct the army to withdraw into the works of Washington. He claimed, untruthfully, that the officers of the Army of the Potomac units with him had failed to co-operate with him and were responsible for his defeat and disorganization. On September 1 Pope's right flank was saved in a combat in a driving rain at Chantilly (Ox Hill), where Philip Kearny and Stevens checked Jackson's movement, although it cost them their lives. But Pope could not prevent the army from resuming its retrograde movement toward Washington. Early on the morning of September 2 he sent to Halleck the following almost unprecedented confession of failure by an army commander: "Unless something can be done to restore tone to this army it will melt away before

[31] John D. Vautier, *History of the 88th Pennsylvania Volunteers* . . . (Philadelphia, 1894), 53, 54; Roebling's Journal, Aug. 30, 1862, Porter Papers; *B. & L.,* II, 489, 520–21.

[32] Livermore, *Numbers and Losses,* 88; Dwight (ed.), *The Virginia Campaign,* II, 197; 16 *O.R.,* 249–62.

[33] 16 *O.R.,* 80; *B. & L.,* II, 491.

you know it. . . . These forces under my command are not able to [stop the Confederates] in the open field, and if again checked I fear the force will be useless afterwards." On the following day Lincoln and Halleck placed McClellan in command of the defenses of the capital, and of all the troops falling back thereto— in effect relieving Pope of his command and terminating his campaign.[34]

At the time of his removal from command, Pope came to Washington and visited Lincoln and the Secretary of War. Noted John Hay in his diary: "Stanton seemed to believe very strongly in Pope. So did the President for that matter." In fact, according to Chase, "the President . . . assured [Pope] of his entire satisfaction with his conduct; assured him that McClellan's command was only temporary; and gave him some reason to expect that another army of active operations would be organized at once, which he (Pope) would lead." Pope, in his conversation, and later in his blistering official report, charged McClellan, Porter, and other Army of the Potomac officers with everything up to treason. The President forbade him to publish his report, but Pope released it to the newspapers anyway. After being relieved Pope continued to blame these officers and others for his defeat. He later went so far as to flay the administration, Halleck, and Lincoln for not sustaining him, and he could not even be assuaged by a manly letter written to him by Halleck.[35]

On September 7, 1862, Pope was named to a department command in the northwest, with headquarters at St. Paul, Minnesota, and left Washington, D. C., on that date. While riding herd on the recalcitrant Indians of the plains, Pope vented his spleen against

[34] *B. & L.,* II, 490, 492; 16 *O.R.,* 80, 82–83; 18 *O.R.,* 796–97; Dwight (ed.), *The Virginia Campaign,* II, 166–67.

[35] Dennett (ed.), *Diaries and Letters of Hay,* 46; Chase, *Diary,* 65–68; Morse (ed.), *Welles's Diary,* I, 109–10; Pope to Stanton, Sept. 5, 1862, Dec. 25, 1864, Stanton Papers; *C.C.W.* (1866), Suppl., II, 189–90; Pope to Lincoln, Sept. 5, 1862, Lincoln Papers; 18 *O.R.,* 812–23; Pope to E. B. Washburne, Feb. 1, 1863, Elihu B. Washburne Papers, Div. of MSS, Library of Congress.

the redmen. Wrote Welles in his diary on October 14, 1862: "Stanton read a dispatch from General Pope, stating that the Indians in the Northwest had surrendered and he was anxious to execute a number of them. . . . He has . . . destroyed the crops of the Indians." "The tone and opinions of the dispatch," concluded Welles, "are discreditable. It was not the production of a good man or a great one." [36]

In 1867 Pope was given command of the Third Military District in the South, comprising the "reconstructing" states of Georgia, Alabama, and Florida. He was one of the most detested of the Federal generals in the occupation of the former Confederate states. Then, from 1868 until his retirement (on account of age, in 1886), Pope commanded, at different times, the departments of the Lakes, Missouri, California, and the Pacific. In 1882 he had been made a major general in the regular army. He died of nervous prostration on September 23, 1892, in Sandusky, Ohio, at the age of seventy.[37]

[36] 16 O.R., 46; Cullum, *Biographical Register*, II, 50; Morse (ed.), *Welles's Diary*, I, 171.
[37] Cullum, *Biographical Register*, II, 50; *D.A.B.*, XV, 76, 77.

CHAPTER FOUR

McClellan Again

> As regards General McClellan, I have
> always entertained a high opinion of his
> capacity, and have no reason to think
> that he omitted to do anything that
> was in his power.
> —*Robert E. Lee*

HALLECK WAS COWED. WITH POPE'S DEFEATED ARMY RESTING
for the moment at Centreville on August 31, 1862, the General-
in-Chief in Washington began to show signs of disintegration.
Late on that evening he telegraphed in an unusually courteous
manner to McClellan at Alexandria, "I beg of you to assist me in
this crisis with your ability and experience. I am utterly tired out."
On the following morning McClellan rode into Washington, unaware that Burnside had just turned down a second offer by the
administration to command the united Federal armies on the
grounds that McClellan was the best man for the job.[1]

Arriving in the capital on the morning of September 1, Mc-
Clellan went to army headquarters and urged Halleck himself to
assume command in the field of the Union forces. But the General-
in-Chief shied away from this task. The administration had just
received a frantic message from Pope, who charged, untruthfully,
that Porter and other officers of the Army of the Potomac with
him "are mere tools and parasites," and that they were responsible
for not fighting or co-operating with him.[2]

The General-in-Chief and McClellan conferred that afternoon

[1] 12 *O.R.*, 103; *C.C.W.* (1863), II, 650; Cox, *Military Reminiscences*,
I, 254.
[2] McClellan, *Report*, 182–83; *B. & L.*, II, 549.

with the President at Halleck's home. In the interview, Lincoln said that he had "always been a friend" of McClellan, and requested that Little Mac, as a personal favor to him, wire Porter and ask him and the other Army of the Potomac generals to cooperate wholeheartedly with Pope. While staunchly denying that any of his officers had done less than their full duty, McClellan agreed to this request, and sent the following dispatch to Porter: "I ask of you, for my sake, that of the country, and the old Army of the Potomac, that you and all my friends will lend the fullest and most cordial cooperation to General Pope in all of the operations now going on. The destinies of our country, the honor of our arms, are at stake, and all depends now upon the cheerful cooperation of all in the field. This week is the crisis of our fate. Say the same thing to my friends in the Army of the Potomac, and that the last request I have to make of them is, that for their country's sake they will extend to General Pope the same support they ever have to me." Porter's reply reassured McClellan in the manner he expected, the message concluding with the words, "Our killed, wounded, and enfeebled troops attest our devoted duty." [3]

McClellan was eating breakfast at his home in Washington on September 2 when, at 7:30, he was interrupted by a personal visit from Lincoln and Halleck. The President stated that Pope had been terribly beaten, that there were 30,000 stragglers choking the roads south of Washington, and that he considered the capital lost. A steam warship was at anchor in the Potomac to carry the Chief Executive and other high government officials to safety. Lincoln then asked McClellan, verbally, "as a favor to him," to "take steps at once to stop and collect the stragglers, to place the works in a proper state of defense, and to go out to meet and take command of the army when it approached the vicinity of the works—committing everything," McClellan said, "to my hands." He assured the distraught President that he could save the capital, but Lincoln remained unconvinced. [4]

[3] 12 O.R., 104. See also Heintzelman's Journal, Aug. 31, 1862.
[4] 12 O.R., 105; M.O.S., 535, 566; B. & L., II, 549–50; McClellan Papers, Vol. 109.

The Chief Executive was then obliged to defend before the cabinet his decision to restore McClellan to command, and the opposition to this appointment from Chase and Stanton was virulent. They "actually declared that they would prefer the loss of the capital to the restoration of McClellan to command." Only Blair defended the General. It was one of the great Union President's wisest and most courageous decisions in a lifetime of wisdom and courage.[5]

McClellan determined to ride out to meet the retreating troops— still nominally under Pope's control until the vicinity of the capital was reached—on the late afternoon of September 2, and to get them posted to meet any threatened onslaught upon Washington. Riding along the road from Alexandria to Fairfax Court House, McClellan began to encounter the debris of Pope's routed army, many units being intermingled and disorganized. He soon came upon Pope and McDowell, and instructed the former where to station the various divisions in the fortifications of Washington. The word of McClellan's reappointment to command and of his presence with the troops swiftly reached the ears of the men. Clamorous cheers for the General broke upon the clear evening air. "The scene that followed," noted an eyewitness, "can be more easily imagined than described. From the extreme sadness we passed in a twinkling to a delirium of delight. A Deliverer had come." Another officer present remarked that "many of the soldiers . . . wept with joy at having again for their commander one upon whom they could place implicit reliance."[6]

While these events were transpiring in North America, an ominous situation for the Lincoln government was developing on the foreign scene in Europe. British Prime Minister Lord Palmerston and Foreign Minister John Russell were seriously considering steps toward recognizing the independence of the Confederacy.

[5] Morse (ed.), *Welles's Diary*, I, 104–106; Chase, *Diary*, 64–65; *M.O.S.*, 545; M. Blair to F. J. Porter, April 22, 1870, and April 3, 1879, McClellan Papers.

[6] Cox, *Military Reminiscences*, I, 243–45; Swinton, *Army of the Potomac*, 195; Comte de Paris, *History of the Civil War* . . . (Philadelphia, 1875), II, 300, 306.

This, if realized, would mean at the very least that the Union blockade of Southern ports would be broken. Palmerston declared that, with a battle in the offing to the northwest of Washington, he would await its outcome before acting. Russell asserted to W. E. Gladstone, "The views which Palmerston and I entertain . . . had the offer of mediation to both parties in the first place, and in the case of refusal by the North, to recognition of the South." If McClellan suffered a severe defeat it would be ruinous to the Union cause. It is the opinion of Thomas A. Bailey that the Confederates were closer to final victory at the start of the Maryland campaign than at any other time during the war.[7]

With Lee at Frederick, Maryland, McClellan pushed cautiously but steadily westward from Washington to confront him. The National army, however, after the rough handling it had received under Pope in the Manassas campaign, was in a poor state of organization, and lacked such supplies as shoes, clothing, and ammunition. The cavalry was in wretched condition. McClellan had hoped that Lee would give him a respite so that he could reorganize and resupply the Federal army near Washington; but the gray chieftain was unco-operative, and McClellan had to press on westward after him, and organize his force as well as he could on the march.[8]

Now, the Union garrison of approximately 13,000 at Harper's Ferry, under the command of old Colonel Dixon S. Miles, presented a serious problem. Halleck unwisely ordered Miles to hold that place in the face of Lee's threatening posture at Fredrick. McClellan, however, perceiving that Miles was in a death-trap in the pocket at the ferry, telegraphed the General-in-Chief on September 11, "Colonel Miles . . . can do nothing where he is, but could be of great service if ordered to join me. I suggest that he be ordered at once to join me by the most practicable route." But Halleck refused this request.[9]

[7] Ephraim D. Adams, *Great Britain and the American Civil War* (London, 1925), II, 31–43; Thomas A. Bailey, *A Diplomatic History of the American People* (New York, 1946), 363, 364.

[8] Meade, *Life and Letters of Meade,* I, 309; *M.O.S.,* 551–52.

[9] *B. & L.,* II, 612; 28 *O.R.,* 254.

Lee's reaction was, as usual, prompt and positive. On September 9, seeing with almost unbelieving eyes that Halleck had offered up Miles's garrison to the slaughter, Lee at Frederick split his army in two, half of it under Jackson going back to Harper's Ferry to capture the Federals there, and the other half under Longstreet, accompanied by Lee, proceeding on along the National Turnpike toward Boonsboro and Hagerstown. It was at this time that the Confederate commander voiced an opinion of McClellan. "He is an able general," declared Lee, "but a very cautious one. His enemies among his own people think him too much so. His army is in a very demoralized and chaotic condition and will not be prepared for offensive operations—or he will not think it so—for three or four weeks. Before that time I hope to be on the Susquehanna." [10]

In his march to Frederick, McClellan was dogged by contradictory orders from Washington. Lincoln directed him to pursue Lee more swiftly; Halleck instructed him to slow down his pursuit and stay closer to the Federal capital. On September 13, Army of the Potomac units entered Frederick, where they and McClellan received a tumultuous ovation from the happy townsfolk. On the same day McClellan captured a copy of Lee's marching orders which gave the enemy dispositions—as of four days previous—and told of the Confederate plan to capture Harper's Ferry. But on the day before, McClellan had already divined the enemy's intentions. "I feel perfectly confident," he wired Halleck on the twelfth, "that the enemy has abandoned Frederick, moving in two directions, viz: On the Hagerstown and Harper's Ferry roads." [11]

McClellan reacted energetically to the situation. Too late, Halleck had placed Miles's garrison at the ferry under his orders. Miles sent a message to McClellan on the fourteenth stating that he could assuredly hold out until the sixteenth. On the fourteenth McClellan sent the following directive to him: "You may count on our making every effort to relieve you. Hold out to the last extremity." Franklin

[10] 28 *O.R.*, 603–604; 27 *O.R.*, 42, 145; *B. & L.*, II, 605–606.
[11] *C.C.W.* (1863), I, 439, 482–84; *M.O.S.*, 571–72; *B. & L.*, II, 603.

was then instructed, on the evening of the thirteenth, to push the left wing of the army through Crampton's Gap the following morning to the relief of Miles. McClellan made an urgent appeal to Franklin: "I ask of you, at this important moment, all your intellect and the utmost activity that a general can exercise." The rest of the army would march at daylight on the fourteenth along the National Pike toward Turner's Gap, where the road breaks through the South Mountain barrier at a high pass. McClellan would have done better, however, to have pressed on that night with his forces. With half of his army under Jackson at Harper's Ferry, and with the other half under Longstreet between Boonsboro and Hagerstown, Lee was in a dangerous position. However, a Confederate sympathizer came into possession of McClellan's plans and immediately turned this vital information over to the Southerners. Lee was thus enabled to bring back troops to Turner's Gap to contest McClellan's passage of this key crossing of the South Mountain range.[12]

On September 14 McClellan pushed forward to South Mountain. Seeing that the main pass at Turner's Gap could not be carried by frontal assault, he outflanked the Confederate left, north of the gap, and also threw units against Fox's Gap, one mile south, on the enemy's right flank. At the same time, Franklin was pressing forward against Crampton's Gap, six miles south of Turner's. The blueclad soldiers were forced to climb the steep sides of the mountain wall with the Confederates firing down their throats. Severe fighting raged all day at the three gaps, the troops at Turner's and Fox's being under McClellan's personal command. By nightfall the Federals had forced the passage of all three gaps. So rapid had been McClellan's penetration of the passes that Jackson had this to say of his former West Point classmate: "I thought I knew McClellan, but this movement of his puzzles me." Lee, realizing his defeat, admitted, "The day has gone against us," and Ropes avers

[12] McClellan, *Report*, 191; Francis W. Palfrey, *The Antietam and Fredericksburg* (New York, 1882), 25, 28–30; Alexander, *Military Memoirs*, 230.

that the Confederates indeed "had been badly beaten." The total
Union casualties at the battle of South Mountain amounted to
2,346, while the Southerners lost at least 3,434 men.[13]

During the afternoon of the battle, McClellan had set up his
command post along the National Turnpike at the eastern foot
of the mountain range, where he directed the Union fighting.
Around the army commander swirled an extraordinary scene
which demonstrated the hold he had over the Federal soldiers. It is
described in this way by one of the men in the ranks who witnessed
it:

Here, upon our arrival, we found General McClellan sitting upon his
horse in the road. . . . As each organization passed the general, the
men became apparently forgetful of everything but their love for him.
They cheered and cheered again, until they became so hoarse they
could cheer no longer. It seemed as if an intermission had been declared in order that a reception might be tendered to the general.
. . . A great crowd continually surrounded him, and the most extrava-
gant demonstrations were indulged in. Hundreds even hugged the
horse's legs and caressed his head and mane. While the troops were
thus surging by, the general continually pointed with his finger to the
gap in the mountain through which our path lay. It was like a great
scene in a play, with the roar of the guns for an accompaniment.[14]

The chief significance of the battle of South Mountain was that
McClellan had wrested the all-important initiative from Lee, just
as the Confederate had done to him at the start of the Seven Days
battle on the Peninsula. "This victory," writes James Ford Rhodes
of South Mountain, "restored the morale of the Union army, and
gave heart to the President and the people of the North." In reply
to McClellan's telegram reporting his victory, the anxious Lincoln
wired back, "God bless you, and all with you. Destroy the rebel
army if possible." In reality, the Confederate invasion of the
North had failed with their defeat at South Mountain; Antietam
was to prove something of an anticlimax. All that McClellan had

[13] See Warren W. Hassler, Jr., "The Battle of South Mountain," *Maryland Historical Magazine*, LII (March, 1957), 39–64.

[14] *B. & L.*, II, 551 n.

to do in the concluding great battle of the campaign was to hold Lee on even terms, and the enemy incursion into the North, and their hopes of British recognition and intervention, would go up in smoke.[15]

While Lee was falling back with Longstreet's corps to Sharpsburg, Jackson was completing the investment of Harper's Ferry. Despite McClellan's order to "hold out to the last," Miles, after suffering only a relatively few casualties from an artillery bombardment on the morning of September 15, shamefully hoisted the white flag at 9:00 A.M. He himself was killed just as the firing died down. Some 12,000 Federal soldiers were surrendered to Jackson—the greatest capitulation of United States soldiers in war up to that time. The Confederates captured also seventy-three artillery pieces, 13,000 muskets, and great quantities of other valuable military stores. Jackson then marched with most of his command to the rendezvous with Lee and Longstreet at Sharpsburg, arriving there early on the sixteenth. A. P. Hill's division remained at the ferry, paroling prisoners and gathering in the booty seized. The only bright episode for the Federals at Harper's Ferry was the brilliant escape from the besieged town of Colonel B. F. "Grimes" Davis and his cavalry brigade.[16]

McClellan, meanwhile, rode on from Boonsboro ahead of his troops, and reached the hills bordering the east bank of the Antietam Creek in the late afternoon of September 15. Through his field glasses he saw Longstreet's men and guns in position across the stream on the elevated ground just to the east of Sharpsburg. The Confederate gunners spotted McClellan's party and opened fire. Getting the range quickly, the enemy sent shells bursting quite close to the General and his staff. McClellan sent his aides behind the cover of the ridge and, ignoring the projectiles whining

[15] Rhodes, *History of the United States*, IV, 146; *C.C.W.* (1863), I, 489.
[16] *B. & L.*, II, 609–18; Douglas S. Freeman, *Lee's Lieutenants* . . . (New York, 1943), II, 193–200; Alexander, *Military Memoirs*, 232–37; Palfrey, *The Antietam*, 27.

past his head, continued to peer through the glasses at the enemy position. "I noted with satisfaction," writes Jacob Cox, "the cool and business-like air with which he made his examination under fire." [17]

McClellan deployed his troops on the ridge along the eastern bank of the Antietam as soon as they arrived on the field, while Lee did the same along the high ground which runs north and south and passes just to the east of the town of Sharpsburg. All of the Federal units except the Sixth Corps reached the field before dark on the fifteenth. However, McClellan had been informed that Lee had 120,000 troops, and, being a circumspect man, he was not going to be hasty in assailing this veteran force. Actually, during the forthcoming Battle of Antietam, McClellan's 69,732 effectives were to be pitted against Lee's force of 52,000 to 58,000 men.[18]

The sixteenth of September dawned cool and foggy. The heavy mists delayed McClellan's reconnaissances until almost noon. Most of the day was spent in reconnoitering the enemy position, posting the Federal troops, bringing up ammunition and supplies, and feeding the hungry men. In deferring his attack until the seventeenth, however, the Union commander lost valuable time. McClellan himself placed many of his units in position, again disregarding a wrathful enemy fire. The General paid a visit to his left and told Burnside, in command at that end of the field "that he would probably be required to attack the enemy's right on the following morning"—a warning that was repeated at sunset on the sixteenth.[19]

In the early afternoon of September 16, McClellan evolved his plan of battle. He would first attack heavily the Confederate left

[17] M.O.S., 586–87; McClellan, Report, 200; Cox, Military Reminiscences, I, 300.
[18] Cox, Military Reminiscences, I, 302; C.C.W. (1863), I, 441; Palfrey, The Antietam, 69–72; Hassler, General George B. McClellan, 271–72, 273 n.
[19] Palfrey, The Antietam, 56–61; 28 O.R., 307–308; 27 O.R., 1026; Cox, Military Reminiscences, I, 384.

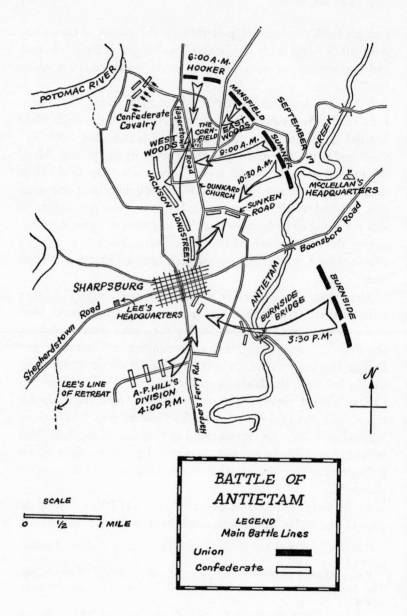

BATTLE OF
ANTIETAM

LEGEND
Main Battle Lines

Union ▬▬▬

Confederate ▭

in the vicinity of the East Woods. Then, when that offensive was well underway, Burnside was to assail the enemy right near the so-called Burnside Bridge over the Antietam. If these attacks were successful, McClellan would strike the Confederate center with whatever troops were available. As was his custom, the Union leader would leave the actual fighting of the battle to his corps commanders, although, due to the failure of several of these generals, McClellan would have done better to have exercised a greater degree of personal control of the action—as he had done at South Mountain. Nonetheless, his plan of battle was a good one, and should have fared somewhat better than it did. By late afternoon of the sixteenth, Hooker's First Corps had crossed the Antietam by the upper bridge, and, after a sharp joust in the evening with the Confederate left, had succeeded in placing itself in position, facing southward, just to the north of the East Woods and the Cornfield.[20]

The fateful day of September 17, 1862, broke misty and gray, but a warm sun was to appear soon and bring on a perfect Indian summer day. McClellan's battle opened at 5:30 A.M. with Hooker strenuously attacking Jackson's left. The Confederates were driven, in furious fighting, through the East Woods and the Cornfield, across the Hagerstown road, and into the West Woods near the higher ground around the Dunker Church. Lee had to rush reinforcements from his right, near the Burnside Bridge, to check Hooker. The First Corps had inflicted heavy losses and had sustained similar ones. Hooker himself was one of the casualties, having been wounded in the heel. Only a few of his men, however, could hold the ground they had temporarily won about the church; the rest had to fall back to a point near their starting place. Hooker, in command of Joseph K. F. Mansfield's Twelfth Corps, had failed to have that force in close support of his own corps at the start of the action. Consequently, Mansfield, at 7:30 A.M., attacked alone in a southwestward direction and drove Jackson

[20] McClellan, *Report,* 201–202, 208; Palfrey, *The Antietam,* 59–60, 61, 73; *M.O.S.,* 588 ff.; Swinton, *Army of the Potomac,* 209–10.

back again into the West Woods near the church. But Mansfield was mortally wounded, and at about 9:00 o'clock only a small part of his corps was able barely to hold on to the ground near the church.[21]

Fortunately, reinforcements were at hand for the Federals. Sumner's Second Corps came into position somewhat tardily about 9:00 A.M. to attack in a westerly direction to the left of Mansfield. Sumner, however, with his fighting blood up, neglected to make any reconnaissances. He attacked piecemeal with his three divisions. John Sedgwick's division ran into a terrible ambush in the West Woods just north of the church, and was decimated and forced to retreat. McClellan himself then made a brief but dramatic appearance on the front lines, helping to rally the broken division. But Sumner's other two divisions drove the Confederates, after a ferocious conflict, from the Sunken Road back to a point just northeast of the town. The situation was now critical for Lee's center. The wounding of several of his division commanders, however, and the fact that he himself had been shaken by Sedgwick's bad defeat, kept the usually combative Sumner from making a final push through the weakened Confederate center, despite the urging of his junior in rank, Franklin. McClellan again came up to the front lines, but Confederate reinforcements from right and left had now strengthened the enemy center, and the Union commander reluctantly allowed Sumner to have his way. A splendid opportunity to pierce Lee's center and knock his army to pieces had been lost by the hesitation of the top National generals.[22]

But the chief reason for McClellan's inability to crush Lee at Antietam was Burnside's almost criminal dilatoriness and failure to obey orders. Beginning at 8:00 A.M., and through the morning until noon, McClellan issued four urgent directives to Burnside to

[21] J. L. Smith, *History of the 118th Pennsylvania Volunteers* . . . (Philadelphia, 1905), 140–41; 27 *O.R.*, 119, 217, 218, 475–76; Stine, *Army of the Potomac*, 191 ff.

[22] Francis A. Walker, *History of the Second Army Corps* . . . (New York, 1886), 101–19; Ropes, *Story of the Civil War*, II, 364–69; Wilson, *Under the Old Flag*, I, 113–14.

attack in force and drive away the tiny Confederate force holding
the Burnside Bridge. Finally, at 1:00 P.M., the bridge was carried
by but two Union regiments. Then Burnside sat down and did
nothing *until 3:00 o'clock!* A final order from McClellan, threatening to remove him from his command if he did not press forward,
impelled Burnside to advance at 4:00 P.M. toward the town of
Sharpsburg. McClellan should have taken such drastic action
earlier, and should have visited his left during the morning hours.
The inexcusable delays by Burnside since early morning had permitted Lee to draw large numbers of troops from opposite the
Union left to contend with the powerful attacks of McClellan's
right and center, and, though losing considerable ground, essentially to contain them. Just as Burnside's troops reached the outskirts of the town, and seemed to have won the battle, A. P. Hill's
last units arrived in the nick of time from Harper's Ferry, fell upon
Burnside's left flank, and threw him back to a point just west of the
bridge which he had carried. Both armies, completely exhausted,
remained in position on September 18, although McClellan was receiving reinforcements; and that evening Lee abandoned the field
of battle—including a great many of his dead and wounded—and
retreated across the Potomac at Shepherdstown.[23]

Thus ended the battle of Antietam. It was the bloodiest single
day's battle of the war, and was a combat which claimed more
casualties in fourteen hours than have ever been suffered before or
since by the American people in arms. According to Livermore,
McClellan's army lost 2,108 killed; 9,549 wounded; and 753 missing—a total loss of 12,410. Lee suffered the following casualties:
2,700 killed; 9,024 wounded; 2,000 missing—an aggregate loss of
13,724 men. On the morning of the eighteenth McClellan wrote
his wife his frank impressions of the great combat. "We fought
yesterday," he said, "a terrible battle against the entire rebel army.
The battle continued for fourteen hours; the fighting on both sides
was superb. The general result was in our favor; that is to say, we
gained a great deal of ground and held it. It was a success, but

[23] Hassler, *General George B. McClellan*, 285–89.

whether a decided victory depends on what occurs today." This
was all fine and accurate; but then McClellan added the following
exaggerated statement: "Those in whose judgment I rely tell me
that I fought the battle splendidly and that it was a masterpiece of
art." It was far from that.[24]

Antietam, while little more than a drawn battle tactically for Mc-
Clellan, was, more importantly, a strategic victory of inestimable
value to the Union. "To one who is biassed," writes James Ford
Rhodes, "by the feeling that Lee had by this time shown himself
almost invincible, it will be natural to speak well of the general who
overcame him in any way on any terms. . . . Let us note the
change of feeling at the North from depression before South Mountain to buoyancy after Antietam; let us reflect that a signal Confederate victory in Maryland might have caused the Northern voters
at the approaching fall elections to declare for the peace that Jefferson Davis would offer from the head of Lee's victorious army,
and that without McClellan's victory the Emancipation Proclamation would have been postponed and might never have been issued!" Then, too, the triumph helped lessen the threat of British
recognition and intervention on behalf of the Confederacy. General Longstreet acknowledges in this way the Confederate failure in
Maryland against McClellan and his Army of the Potomac: "The
razing of the walls of Jericho by encircling marches of priests and
soldiers, at the signal of long-drawn blasts of sacred horns and
shouts of the multitude, was scarcely a greater miracle than the
transformation of the conquering army of the South into a horde
of disordered fugitives before an army that two weeks earlier was
flying to cover under its homeward ramparts." [25]

After Antietam there ensued a period of five weeks of debate and
contention between McClellan and the authorities in Washington

[24] Livermore, *Numbers and Losses,* 92–94; Joseph K. Barnes (ed.), *The
Medical and Surgical History of the War of the Rebellion* . . . (Washington, 1875–88), Part I, lviii; McClellan, *Report,* 213; *M.O.S.,* 612–13.
[25] Rhodes, *History of the United States,* IV, 154, 156; Longstreet, *From
Manassas to Appomattox,* 239, 283.

as to when, and by what route, the Union army would advance across the Potomac into Virginia against Lee. McClellan had not had time to organize his army properly after he had been named commander in early September. Now, after Sharpsburg, there was found to be a great lack of shoes, clothing, camp equipment, cavalry, artillery, wagon horses, and other supplies. The army had lost ten general officers in casualties in the Maryland campaign, and several corps had been severely shattered. All this required time to rectify, and the sometimes overcautious McClellan determined to take the time before embarking on a sustained fall and winter campaign deep into Virginia.[26]

The Radicals in Congress now resumed their old smear tactics against McClellan. They termed him a procrastinator, a coward, and even a traitor. They circulated false stories that "McNapoleon" —as they called him—had sneaked into Lee's tent on the eve of the battle of Antietam to receive his "orders" from the gray leader as to how Lee wanted him to fight the battle the next day. McClellan was also charged by the Radicals with having received and obeyed instructions from Lee not to pursue the retreating Confederate army until it could cross the Potomac to safety.[27]

On September 22, 1862, Lincoln issued his celebrated Emancipation Proclamation. This was followed on October 1 by a visit of the President to McClellan and the army near Harper's Ferry. Lincoln was impatient at the delay in crossing the Potomac into Virginia. The General escorted the Chief Executive over the battlefields of Antietam and South Mountain. According to McClellan, Lincoln complimented him on his handling of the army in these successes, seemed to comprehend the reasons why an immediate invasion of Virginia had to be delayed a bit, and pledged to stand by McClellan as army commander until the enemy was beaten and the war ended. "That will be impossible," the General said frankly

[26] McClellan, *Report*, 216; Paris, *The Civil War*, II, 538–39.
[27] E. Conckling to J. Holt, Nov. 8, 1864, Joseph Holt Papers, Div. of MSS, Library of Congress; Rhodes, *History of the United States*, IV, 184–85.

to Lincoln. "We need time. The influences at Washington will be too strong for you, Mr. President." But Lincoln insisted that he would stand firmly behind McClellan. And so they parted, for the last time.[28]

Then, just two days after Lincoln's departure to Washington, McClellan was astounded to receive the following message from Halleck on October 6: "The President directs that you cross the Potomac and give battle to the enemy, or drive him south." The administration wanted McClellan to advance, "as soon as possible," east of the Blue Ridge Mountains, whereas the General wanted to move up the Shenandoah Valley. If he could not reach the Confederate rear, McClellan hoped to defeat the enemy in detail or else force him back to Gordonsville, whereupon the Federals would move against Richmond. Not until October 26 did McClellan begin crossing the Potomac. In order to receive additional reinforcements, he adopted the administration's preferred route east of the Blue Ridge. With Warrenton as the marching objective, McClellan's army made such rapid progress as to threaten seriously to interpose between Jackson's corps, then near Winchester in the Valley, and Longstreet's corps, which was further south and east of the mountains. So swift was McClellan's advance that it elicited this compliment from the President on October 29: "I am much pleased with the movement of the army." And the tempo of the Union advance was even speeded up after the General had received Lincoln's encomium. Lee was also aware of McClellan's rapid progress, and his messages to Richmond took on something of a tone of apprehension.[29]

By November 7 McClellan had his army well concentrated near Warrenton. The Confederate army, on the other hand, was widely split: Longstreet's corps was at Culpeper Court House and Jackson's

[28] See Hassler, *General George B. McClellan,* 298–301.
[29] *C.C.W.* (1863), I, 507–508, 514–15, 516–17, 517–18, 556; McClellan, *Report,* 235–36; 27 *O.R.,* 11; 28 *O.R.,* 82 ff., 464, 501, 504, 626, 697; Alexander, *Military Memoirs,* 279, 281.

was still in the Valley near Winchester, the two Confederate wings
being some fifty miles apart—a good two days' march. McClellan
proposed by a short march to the southwest to interpose between
the separated segments of the gray army, and his chances of doing
this appeared good. Only a precipitate retreat by Jackson toward
Gordonsville could save Lee from serious trouble. The Union commander had approximately 142,000 men as opposed to some 85,-
000 Southerners.[30]

McClellan was alone in his tent on November 7 examining some
maps and papers when out of the snowstorm that was raging appeared two men, Burnside and Brigadier General C. P. Buckingham—the latter a special messenger from Washington. Receiving the visitors in his usual courteous way, McClellan engaged them
in conversation for some time. Then, Buckingham handed him an
order which relieved him from command of the Army of the
Potomac and instructed him to turn over the army to Burnside. In
full control of himself, McClellan said to Burnside with a smile,
"I turn the command over to you." [31]

After the two generals had left his tent, McClellan picked up his
pen and wrote his wife, "Another interruption—this time more important. It was in the shape of Burnside, accompanied by Gen.
Buckingham. . . . They brought with them the order relieving
me from command of the Army of the Potomac. . . . No cause is
given." Then, knowing well the glaring limitations of his friend
and successor, Burnside, McClellan declared in his letter, "They
[the administration] have made a great mistake. Alas for my
poor country! I know in my inmost heart she never had a truer
servant. . . . Do not be at all worried—I am not. I have done
the best I could for my country; to the last I have done my duty as
I understand it. That I must have made many mistakes I cannot

---

[30] 28 O.R., 695–98, 701–705, 710; Swinton, Army of the Potomac,
226–27; B. & L., III, 103 n.
[31] B. & L., III, 103; Stine, Army of the Potomac, 241–42; M.O.S.,
651–52.

deny. I do not see any great blunders; but no one can judge of himself. Our consolation must be that we have tried to do what was right." [32]

No specific, official reason was ever given for McClellan's removal. The Radicals in Congress, however, and in the cabinet, had from the first been hostile to McClellan, chiefly on political grounds, and they had placed such great pressure on the President that even Lincoln could not withstand it. During the crisis immediately after Pope's crushing defeat, Lincoln had said to his private secretary that this feeling against McClellan "will make it expedient to take important command from him. . . . But he is too useful just now to sacrifice." Lincoln himself had felt that the General had been much too slow to invade Virginia after Antietam, and that when once he had done this, he had allowed Lee to get away from him. Therefore, on November 5, the day after the fall elections—which had gone against the administration—Lincoln had drawn up his order deposing McClellan.[33]

So great was the outcry in the Army of the Potomac against McClellan's removal that the General was obliged to stay on for several days in order to quiet the men and suppress the mutinous talk which was being freely bandied about. In fact, when his special train was about to pull out from Warrenton Junction to take him away from the army, the men, drawn up in formation, broke ranks, uncoupled his car from the rest of the train, and insisted that they would not let him go. They beseeched him to allow them to march on Washington and deal summarily with those who had relieved him of command. But, at this crisis, according to an eyewitness, "McClellan stepped upon the front platform of the car, and there was instant silence. His address was short. It ended with the memorable words, 'Stand by General Burnside as you have stood by me, and all will be well.'" The car was then recoupled and the train rolled away. Wrote an officer in blue then with the army: "What do you think of such a man? He had it in his power

[32] M.O.S., 660.
[33] See Hassler, *General George B. McClellan*, 317–23.

to be dictator—anything he chose to name—if he would but say the word, but he preferred retirement rather than ambition. He was not a Caesar." [34]

McClellan's feelings at his departure were given in the usual letter to his wife, written on November 10: "I am very well and taking leave of the men. I did not know before how much they loved me nor how dear they were to me. Gray-haired men came to me with tears streaming down their cheeks. I never had to exercise so much self-control. The scenes of today repay me for all that I have endured." [35]

Although he had, earlier in his career, issued a number of flamboyant, Napoleonic manifestoes to his troops, the final address of McClellan upon his departure from the army was an earnest and eloquent one. It read:

OFFICERS AND SOLDIERS OF THE ARMY OF THE POTOMAC:
An order from the President devolves upon Major-General Burnside the command of this army.

In parting from you, I cannot express the love and gratitude I bear to you. As an army, you have grown up under my care. In you, I have never found doubt or coldness. The battles you fought under my command will proudly live in our nation's history. The glory you have achieved, our mutual peril and fatigues, the graves of our comrades, fallen in battle and by disease, the broken forms of those whom wounds and sickness have disabled—the strongest associations which can exist among men—unite us still by an indissoluble tie. We shall ever be comrades in supporting the Constitution of our country and the nationality of its people.

GEO. B. McCLELLAN
Major-General, U. S. Army. [36]

In his final official report, McClellan read his superiors a pithy lecture on the conduct of general military policy: "In the arrangement and conduct of campaigns the direction should be left to professional soldiers. A statesman may, perhaps, be more compe-

[34] *Ibid.*, 316–17, 327–29.
[35] *M.O.S.*, 661.
[36] 28 *O.R.*, 551; *M.O.S.*, 653.

tent than a soldier to determine the political objects and direction of a campaign; but those once decided upon, everything should be left to the responsible military head, without interference from civilians. In no other manner is success probable. The meddling of individual members of committees of Congress with subjects which, from lack of experience, they are of course incapable of comprehending, and which they are apt to view through the distorted medium of partisan or personal prejudice, can do no good, and is certain to produce incalculable mischief." [37]

After his removal from the command of the Army of the Potomac, McClellan reported for orders to Trenton, New Jersey. When no orders ever came, the General established his home in Orange, New Jersey. In November, 1864, he resigned from the army on election day when he ran for President on the Democratic ticket. Although heavily defeated in the electoral college, he ran much closer to Lincoln in popular votes. McClellan then spent time abroad in Europe from 1864 to 1867, where he could indulge his historical and literary tastes, and engage in mountain climbing. Returning to the United States in 1867, he was placed in charge of construction of a new type of steam warship until 1869. In 1868 he had been asked to accept the presidency of the University of California, but had declined. The following year he turned down a similar bid from Union College. From 1870 to 1872 McClellan was Chief Engineer of the Department of Docks of New York. He declined the comptrollership of New York in 1871. McClellan then served as governor of New Jersey from 1878 to 1881, and earned a reputation as being one of the ablest and most popular chief executives that state ever had. He died of heart trouble at his home in Orange on October 29, 1885. Among his pallbearers was Joseph E. Johnston. [38]

[37] McClellan, *Report,* 238–39, 242.
[38] *D.A.B.,* XI, 583–84.

CHAPTER FIVE

Ambrose E. Burnside

> There was no . . . intention to sacrifice but, if stupidity be culpability, few generals of ancient or modern times rank with Burnside in the guilt of manslaughter.
>
> —*Carl Russell Fish*

"BURNSIDE IS A BRICK." THIS QUAINT EXPRESSION OF AFFECtion was almost universally applied to McClellan's successor in 1862, nor was it inappropriate to Ambrose E. Burnside before or after the Civil War. And the thirty-eight-year-old soldier looked the part of an army commander. "He was," declared Charles A. Dana, "rather a large man physically, about six feet tall, with a large face and a small head." General Cox, who knew him well, states that "Burnside's flashing eyes, his beard trimmed to the 'Burnside cut' with the mustache running into the side whiskers whilst the square, clean-shaven chin and jaws gave a tone of decision and force to his features, made up a picture that at once arrested the eye." He had "large, fine eyes [and a] winning smile." Cox went on to say that Burnside "had a hearty and jovial manner, a good-humored cordiality toward everybody." Burnside's dress caused comment also. "His seeming carelessness about his uniform," asserts Cox, "was really a calculated affair, but it made him more picturesque. His hat was the stiff broad-rimmed, high-crowned regulation hat, worn rather rakishly, with gold corn, acorn-tipped; his pistol-belt was a loose one, allowing the holster to hang on his hip instead of being buckled tight about the waist; his boots were the high cavalry boots reaching to the knee; his large buckskin gauntlets covered his forearm." He could easily fall asleep while signing papers, and even when standing. In short, he had something of a "brigandish air" about him that appealed to people.[1]

Burnside's career prior to his being named to command the Army of the Potomac had been a series of ups and downs. He had been born in a log cabin in Liberty, Indiana, on May 23, 1824, of Scottish ancestry. Educated in a seminary there, Ambrose was apprenticed to a tailor at the age of eighteen, largely because his family was large and at that time poor. A change in his father's fortunes, however, helped gain for Burnside an appointment to West Point in 1843. He graduated eighteenth in a class of thirty-eight in 1847. The war south of the border ended just as he arrived in Mexico City. Following routine assignments, Burnside resigned from the army in 1853, hoping to manufacture a breech-loading carbine which he had developed. This project fell through, however, and he was obliged to turn to his friend, McClellan, to bail him out. McClellan, then vice-president of the Illinois Central Railroad, got "Burn" a job, first in the land department of the railway and then as treasurer, and the latter's fortunes began an upswing.[2]

Burnside had been a major general in the Rhode Island militia, and when civil strife erupted, he brought to Washington, as its colonel, the First Rhode Island regiment. He participated in the First Bull Run campaign as a brigade commander and, although his performance left something to be desired, he was promoted to brigadier general of volunteers on August 6, 1861. In the early months of 1862, Burnside led an amphibious force to the North Carolina littoral which, against practically no opposition, captured Roanoke Island and New Bern. For this he was made major gen-

---

[1] Nevins and Thomas (eds.), *Strong's Diary*, III, 179; Charles A. Dana, *Recollections of the Civil War* . . . (New York, 1902), 138; Cox, *Military Reminiscences*, I, 389–90; D. R. Larned to H. Larned, Dec. 21, 1861, Daniel Reed Larned Papers, Div. of MSS, Library of Congress.

[2] Cullum, *Biographical Register*, II, 191; *D.A.B.*, III, 309.

eral of volunteers on March 18, 1862. He held an anomalous and ineffective position at Fredericksburg during Pope's ill-starred Manassas campaign, and was a corps and wing commander under McClellan at South Mountain and at Antietam. Burnside's action—or rather lack of action—at Antietam probably cost McClellan a more decisive victory. But he was highly regarded by the authorities in Washington—chiefly because of his easy and minor successes on the North Carolina coast—and had turned down two previous offers to command the Army of the Potomac before being given the positive order to take over from McClellan in November, 1862.[3]

Burnside's characteristics and personal traits added up to both strengths and weaknesses. "Few men, probably," writes General F. W. Palfrey, "have risen so high upon so slight a foundation as he. . . . Nobody could encounter his smile and receive the grasp of his hand without being for some time under a potent influence. It is probably true that that man's manners made his fortune. . . ." "His bearing under fire was good," declares Cox, "and his personal courage beyond question. He shrank from responsibility with sincere modesty, because he questioned his own capacity to deal with affairs of great magnitude." Charles A. Dana reports that "when [Burnside] first talked with you, you would think he had a great deal more intelligence than he really possessed. You had to know him some time before you really took his measure." "He was," states Ben: Perley Poore, "alike earnest in the performance of his duty, spotless in reputation, loyally patriotic, and faithful in his friendships. . . . He made loving kindness the guide of his life," and a more lovable man could not be found. But he was often too lenient, and was, as General Regis DeTrobriand observed, "too much inclined to be obstinate" in his views of a proper course of action to be taken. And, as will be seen, Burnside could, on occasion, play the political game, and shift his principles as well as his friendships. This momentary and uncharacteristic deviousness was evinced principally in the weeks after his defeat at Fredericksburg

[3] Cullum, *Biographical Register*, II, 191–92.

and his removal from command. "In a great army," asserts Cox, "[Burnside] was at a disadvantage from lack of true system in handling great and complicated affairs when he was in chief command." [4]

When General Buckingham arrived in the snowstorm on the evening of November 7, 1862, at Burnside's headquarters, fifteen miles south of Salem, Virginia, he found the Ninth Corps commander alone in a small room. According to Buckingham, as soon as Burnside read the order naming him to McClellan's post, "he at once declined the command." "Among other objections, he urged his want of confidence in himself, and his particularly friendly relations to McClellan, to whom he felt under the strongest obligations." Only after a two-hour discussion with several of his staff officers and Buckingham did Burnside reluctantly agree that, since the order was a positive one, allowing him no discretion, it had to be complied with—a view that the outgoing McClellan also voiced. The statement by Buckingham that, if Burnside refused to comply with the directive, Hooker would be given the command, probably helped convince Burnside to accept the inevitable. [5]

Although perhaps a natural move at that time, it was, of course, most unfortunate for the Union cause to supplant the able McClellan with an officer such as Burnside. He was probably the most incompetent of all the general officers then serving with the Army of the Potomac, although Washington was apparently largely ignorant of the low opinion held of him by his brother officers. "Those of us," declares Major General Darius N. Couch, "who were well acquainted with Burnside knew that he was a brave,

[4] Palfrey, *The Antietam and Fredericksburg,* 54–55; Cox, *Military Reminiscences,* I, 264, 389–90, II, 40; Dana, *Recollections,* 138; Ben: Perley Poore, *The Life and Public Services of Ambrose E. Burnside . . .* (Providence, 1882), 17–18; Regis DeTrobriand, *Four Years with the Army of the Potomac* (Boston, 1889), 351; Williams, *Lincoln and the Radicals,* 197; *B. & L.,* III, 119 n.

[5] Stine, *Army of the Potomac,* 241–42; *B. & L.,* III, 106; *C.C.W.* (1863), II, 650.

loyal man, but we did not think that he had the military ability to command the Army of the Potomac." Actually, the selection of Franklin to succeed McClellan would probably have been received with the widest approval in the Army of the Potomac at that time. And Major General Henry W. Slocum insists that Franklin was really Lincoln's choice, except that there was strong political opposition to him. Even Halleck himself—who could play politics when necessary—exclaimed to a friend at the time of Burnside's appointment, "Oh, the curse of political expediency! It has almost ruined the army, and if carried out will soon ruin the country." [6]

Burnside at once "felt the weight of the responsibility which had now come upon him. . . . It was a large command—in a letter . . . at the time, he called it 'enormous.' " When McClellan and Burnside rode up to Couch's headquarters at dusk on November 8, Couch offered the new commander his congratulations; but Burnside "turned away his head, and made a broad gesture as he exclaimed, 'Couch, don't say a word about it.' His manner indicated that he did not wish to talk about the change." That same day, Meade wrote as follows: "Burnside, it is said, wept like a child, and is the most distressed man in the army, openly says he is not fit for the position, and that McClellan is the only man we have who can handle the large army collected together, one hundred and twenty thousand men." Burnside knew that he was incompetent to head such a massive host—a belief shared by the Confederates— and in the days immediately after his elevation to its command he fretted, worked long hours, drove himself hard, got very little sleep, and actually became physically ill as a result.[7]

When he took over the reins of the army on November 9, 1862,

[6] Wood and Edmonds, *The Civil War*, 142–43; *B. & L.*, III, 106; S. R. Franklin, *Memoirs of a Rear-Admiral* (New York, 1898), 9, 10; 13 *O.R.*, 654.
[7] *Personal Narratives of Events in the War of the Rebellion . . .* (Providence, 1882), 36; *B. & L.*, III, 106; Meade, *Life and Letters of Meade*, I, 325; Gen. John Cochrane to Lincoln, Nov. 14, 1862, Lincoln Papers; Howard, *Autobiography*, I, 314; D. R. Larned to H. L. Larned, Nov. 22, 1862, Larned Papers.

Burnside knew well that he had been given his post with the understanding that he would strike an offensive blow before the army
went into winter quarters; this was expected of him by the public,
the press, and the politicians. With the two wings of the Confederate
army nearly fifty miles apart—as noted before—Burnside had an
opportunity, had he followed McClellan's plan, to interpose between these wings and defeat them in detail, or else to force the
enemy to concentrate precipitately far back at Gordonsville. Longstreet thinks that Burnside should have done this, and says that it
"was the move about which we felt serious apprehension." Or, as
Ropes believes would have been best, Burnside could have moved
toward Culpeper, crossed the Rappahannock and Rapidan at the
upper fords, and moved on Spotsylvania Court House—as Grant
did in 1864—which would have obviated going through Fredericksburg. Hooker actually proposed this scheme to Burnside on November 19, 1862.[8]

Instead, Burnside, after conferring with his chief subordinates
and his makeshift staff, chose another alternative, which he dispatched to Halleck as his plan of operations. He had just been told
by Herman Haupt (who was in charge of transportation and construction on the United States military railroads) of the brittle nature of the Orange and Alexandria Railroad, and decided to abandon McClellan's promising design. First, he hoped to surprise Lee
by a rapid movement. Therefore, although it would mean giving
up much logistical material, Burnside would shift his line of operations and communications from the Orange & Alexandria eastward to the line of the Richmond, Fredericksburg, and Potomac
Railroad. A swift march of his army from Warrenton to Fredericksburg would be preceded by a feint toward Culpeper and Gordonsville. From Fredericksburg, Burnside said he would move rapidly
southward along the R. F. & P. to Richmond, hoping to arrive there
before Lee could intervene with his divided forces. Two chroniclers

---

[8] Palfrey, *The Antietam*, 136; 28 *O.R.*, 546; *B. & L.*, III, 85; Ropes,
Story of the Civil War, II, 447–49; 31 *O.R.*, 355; *C.C.W.* (1863), I, 654,
666.

of the Army of the Potomac, however, contend that Burnside really wanted to evade a battle until spring, and then move the army to the Peninsula, and that Fredericksburg would be a convenient winter base in the meantime.[9]

Actually, while Burnside might well have fared better had he adhered to McClellan's project, his own plan had much to recommend it. The ten-mile-long segment of the R. F. & P. between Aquia Creek Landing and Fredericksburg was far safer and less vulnerable than the long, circuitous Orange & Alexandria. Then, too, operating on the Fredericksburg line would place the Federal army directly between the enemy and Washington—a favorite defensive move for the safety of the capital which was supported by the administration. A disadvantage of Burnside's plan was that, when once at Fredericksburg, a number of rivers intervened between the Federal army and Richmond. Also, to be successful, Union intensions would have to be masked from Lee up to the last moment. Once Burnside began his movement it had to continue without interruption, and was undertaken with the understanding that bridging material would be sent to Fredericksburg in time to enable the army to cross at that point as soon as it arrived.[10]

While his plan was being considered on November 11 by his superiors, Burnside called a meeting of his corps commanders, where he announced the details of his scheme, as well as telling of his intention to divide his army into grand divisions of two corps each. Sumner, Hooker, and Franklin were to command these grand divisions, and each was to have in addition a cavalry brigade, except Sumner, who would be given a cavalry division. Some writers contend that this was a mistake on Burnside's part, and claim that the grand divisions proved too clumsy and unwieldy, and placed one more general between the army commander and his basic maneuver unit, the division. However, Grant used this arrangement at Chattanooga and Sherman did likewise in his Georgia campaign. Apparently forgotten by Burnside during the forthcoming battle

[9] 28 *O.R.,* 552–54; 31 *O.R.,* 99.
[10] See Palfrey, *The Antietam,* 138.

were Sigel's Eleventh Corps and Slocum's Twelfth Corps, available as reinforcements, but kept in the rear at Warrenton and Harper's Ferry, respectively.[11]

When Lincoln and Halleck received Burnside's plan of campaign, the General-in-Chief was not impressed with it. So, accompanied by Montgomery Meigs and Haupt, Halleck journeyed to Warrenton, where he spent November 12 and 13 conferring with Burnside. Halleck favored McClellan's plan, but Burnside held out for his own Fredericksburg move. The General-in-Chief would not approve the new army commander's plan, and said, characteristically, that he would leave the decision up to the President. A grave misunderstanding occurred at this conclave between Halleck and Burnside which went far toward encouraging failure in the near future. Somehow or other Halleck thought, erroneously, that Burnside was going to march the bulk of his army down the right (south) bank of the Rappahannock and seize the heights back (west) of Fredericksburg; whereas, actually, Burnside's plan called for his moving the army down the north bank of the river to Falmouth, at which point the troops would be crossed over into Fredericksburg by means of pontoon bridges which would be provided by the Washington officials. Returning to Washington, Halleck telegraphed Burnside on November 14 Lincoln's decision: "The President has just assented to your plan. He thinks it will succeed, if you move very rapidly; otherwise not." [12]

But almost at the start of his operation, Burnside was frustrated by looseness on the part of the Union high command, and he himself must bear a certain degree of the blame. Although in his written campaign plan Burnside had not dwelt too much on rushing pontoon bridging material to Fredericksburg, he claims that in his meeting with Halleck at Warrenton he emphasized the need for speed in this matter, and that the General-in-Chief had pledged that he would have the pontoons on time where Burnside wanted them. Halleck, however, contends that he told Burnside that the latter's

---

[11] 28 *O.R.*, 570, 583–84; *B. & L.*, III, 107; 31 *O.R.*, 815.
[12] 31 *O.R.*, 47–48, 83, 84; *C.C.W.* (1863), I, 650; 28 *O.R.*, 579.

officers would have to look after this matter. Actually, through a series of unfortunate delays, in part avoidable, the bridging material did not arrive at Falmouth, across the Rappahannock from Fredericksburg, until November 25. Halleck apparently believed the bulk of the Army of the Potomac to be moving down the south bank of the river, and failed to follow through on his orders for the forwarding of the pontoons. Burnside, on his part, washed his hands of the whole matter, assuming that Halleck was taking care of everything.[13]

On the morning of November 15 Burnside began moving his forces out of the Warrenton area by multiple columns for Falmouth. The march was made with celerity. By the nineteenth, his entire army had arrived in the vicinity of Falmouth, except for the Federal cavalry, which was "covering the fords of the Rappahannock further up the stream." The blue horsemen, however, should have been ordered by Burnside to make a strong feint toward Culpeper to distract Lee, if possible, from the real Union objective. Divining Burnside's intentions, the Confederate commander ordered Longstreet on November 18 to march to Fredericksburg. On the twenty-second Jackson was instructed to move to the same place, to take position on Longstreet's right, and to cover the river against a possible Union crossing below Fredericksburg. Directed by Jefferson Davis to fight at Fredericksburg instead of along the North Anna, as he had wished to do, Lee himself arrived in Fredericksburg on November 23.[14]

The Rappahannock at Fredericksburg is over 400 feet wide. The left (or northeast) bank is bordered by Stafford Heights, which dominate Fredericksburg across the river. The town is situated on a plain which is almost one mile wide, from east to west, and which is bounded on the west by Spotsylvania Heights, a range of hills

---

[13] Geer, *Campaigns of the Civil War*, 180–81; 31 *O.R.*, 84–86, 148–49, 793–800; *C.C.W.* (1863), I, 665–75; *B. & L.*, III, 122; 28 *O.R.*, 714–17, 1014.

[14] Palfrey, *The Antietam*, 138; Henderson, *Stonewall Jackson*, II, 370, 375.

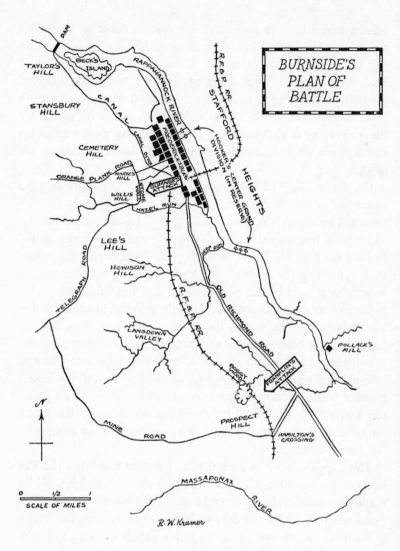

BURNSIDE'S
PLAN OF
BATTLE

TAYLOR'S HILL

DAM

BECK'S ISLAND

RAPPAHANNOCK RIVER

CANAL

STANSBURY HILL

CEMETERY HILL

CANAL DITCH

FREDERICKSBURG

R.F.&P. RR.

STAFFORD

HEIGHTS

HOOKER'S CENTER GRAND DIVISION (IN RESERVE)

ORANGE PLANK ROAD

MARYE'S HILL

WILLIS HILL

STONE WALL

SUMNER'S ATTACK

HAZEL RUN

LEE'S HILL

DEEP RUN

HOWISON HILL

TELEGRAPH ROAD

R.F.&P. RR

LANSDOWN VALLEY

OLD RICHMOND ROAD

POLLACK'S MILL

BOGGY WOODS

FRANKLIN'S ATTACK

N

MINE ROAD

PROSPECT HILL

HAMILTON'S CROSSING

0   1/2   1
SCALE OF MILES

MASSAPONAX RIVER

R. W. Kramer

which runs in a general north-and-south direction. The northern part of this range is known as Marye's Heights, and is some 100 to 150 feet in elevation. The plain between this high ground and the western edge of the town was open ground in 1862, and was bisected by a southward-running millrace and its low bluff just beyond the town. The Orange Plank Road ran westward from Fredericksburg, while south of this highway the Telegraph Road pursued the same course until it reached the foot of Marye's Heights, where it turned abruptly ninety degrees and ran southward along the foot of the ridge as a sunken road, bounded by stone retaining walls.[15]

When Sumner arrived at Falmouth and found the enemy to be in light force on the western bank, he asked Burnside to allow him to cross and seize Fredericksburg. Hooker requested permission also to cross at a ford four miles from Hartwood and take in flank and rear any Confederate force on Marye's Heights. But Burnside refused both entreaties, stating that he did not wish to have his army split by a wide river which was capable of rising at any time. While this would normally have been a safe and sound thing to do, Burnside, in this case, given the positions and numbers of the hostile forces, would have done better to have followed Sumner's and Hooker's suggestions. Throughout this campaign, however, Burnside failed to send out proper reconnaissances, his inflexible mind rigidly adhering to his preconceptions and earlier plans. He felt that it was "necessary to make arrangements to cross in the face of a vigilant and formidable foe." His lack of practical imagination during his entire tenure as a commander of the Army of the Potomac is all too apparent.[16]

Shortly after arriving at Falmouth, Burnside called a conference of his grand division and corps commanders, and told them that he had decided to cross the river at Skinker's Neck, some thirteen miles below Fredericksburg, and offer battle to Lee there. Only

[15] 31 O.R., 171, 1021; Geer, Campaigns of the Civil War, 182-83.
[16] William H. Powell, The Fifth Army Corps . . . (London, 1896), 354-56, 360-63; Palfrey, The Antietam, 138-40.

Hooker opposed such a move. When the attempt was made, in the first days of December, Burnside found that Lee had anticipated him and had moved sufficient artillery and infantry forces to Skinker's Neck to contain the threat; while at another possible crossing point, Port Royal, twenty-six miles below Fredericksburg, Federal gunboats, trying to succor the army, were shelled on December 4 and forced to drop downstream. Part of Jackson's Confederate command was kept down the river near these points for some time. Burnside then abandoned this plan of campaign, and sought another more promising one.[17]

The Confederates were assisted by the fact that, for nearly three weeks after the Union pontoon trains did arrive on November 25, Burnside made no effort to cross the Rappahannock near Fredericksburg. Since Jackson did not appear on the scene until later, had Burnside been ready to cross when the bridging material did arrive, he would have found Lee with only Longstreet available to meet him. A golden opportunity had thus been missed. The National commander had wired Halleck on November 22, when the pontoons were delayed in arriving, "I cannot feel that the move indicated in my plan of operations will be successful after two very important parts of the plan have not been carried out, no matter for what reason." Burnside was still working long hours, and was still ill from overexertion.[18]

Irked with Burnside's slowness, Lincoln conferred with him on November 26 and 27. The General told the President that he thought he could force a passage of the river at Fredericksburg, but that the effort would be "somewhat risky." Unable to agree on a specific plan, Lincoln and Halleck probably told Burnside to proceed on his own judgment. The latter declared after the battle that he himself had devised all his movements, and that they were not influenced by Lincoln, Stanton, or Halleck. On December 4 Burnside announced that he had given up trying to cross below Fredericks-

---

[17] B. & L., III, 128–29; 31 O.R., 87, 811; Wood and Edmonds, The Civil War, 145.

[18] Wood and Edmonds, The Civil War, 145; C.C.W. (1863), I, 645–46.

burg at Skinker's Neck, and that he now intended to span the river at Fredericksburg and at a point just below the town. When William F. Smith asked him about the enemy-held heights just west of Fredericksburg, Burnside replied, "Oh! I know where Lee's forces are, and I expect to surprise him. I expect to cross and occupy the hills before Lee can bring anything serious to meet me." Apparently, the Federal commander ignored the fine opportunity to cross by the fords above Fredericksburg, as Hooker was to do so successfully in May of the following year. In order to cover the intended crossings at and near Fredericksburg, Burnside directed Henry J. Hunt to mass sufficient batteries on Stafford Heights.[19]

The weather turned quite cold at the end of the first week of December. There was ice in the river and four inches of snow on the ground. And it was not only the weather that was chilly. Burnside had learned of freely expressed criticisms of himself, his plan, and the probable results therefrom, by Hooker and other officers. So, on December 8, the army commander called a meeting of all his top line and staff officers, and addressed them, according to Howard, as follows: "I have heard your criticisms, gentlemen, and your complaints. You know how reluctantly I assumed the responsibilities of command. I was conscious of what I lacked; but still I have been placed here where I am and will do my best. I rely on God for wisdom and strength. Your duty is not to throw cold water, but to aid me loyally with your advice and hearty service." This sad state of affairs in the high command of the Army of the Potomac existed just as Burnside had decided to attack Lee in force. He had 120,281 men to Lee's 78,513.[20]

Burnside convened his grand division commanders at noon on December 9, and issued orders for his offensive movement, which

[19] B. & L., III, 129–30; G. F. R. Henderson, *The Campaign of Fredericksburg* (London, 1891), 37; 31 *O.R.,* 180–81, 797–98; Roy P. Basler (ed.), *The Collected Works of Abraham Lincoln,* (New Brunswick, N. J., 1953–55), V, 509, 511, 514; Pease and Randall (eds.), *Browning's Diary,* I, 590; Williams, *Lincoln and His Generals,* 198, 199.

[20] 31 *O.R.,* 61, 105; Howard, *Autobiography,* I, 321; Livermore, *Numbers and Losses,* 96.

was to commence at daybreak on the eleventh. The orders were rather vague and general. Sumner was to cross at Fredericksburg, advance through the town, and seize Marye's Heights near the Telegraph and Plank roads. Hooker was to follow Sumner across the same bridges and closely support the latter's attack, as well as to hold himself in readiness to support Franklin's movement on the Federal left. Franklin was directed to cross just below the town and move southward down the Old Richmond Stage Road. He was told to expect additional orders during the movement, and his future actions were to be determined by circumstances. That night Burnside telegraphed Halleck his belief that the enemy "will be more surprised by a crossing immediately in our front than in any other part of the river." He said he was "convinced that a large force of the enemy is now concentrated in the vicinity of Port Royal, its left resting near Fredericksburg, which we hope to turn." While no dissent was voiced to Burnside by his subordinates at the council of war, Couch notes that after the army commander left, "marked disapprobation" in Burnside's plan was voiced by many.[21]

In commenting on the Union commander's scheme, Palfrey says that "it seems to be true that Burnside formed no definite plan of battle at all. . . . How ill-defined and shadowy his plans were, may be gathered from his own language in his official report: 'I hoped to be able to seize some point on the enemy's line near the Massaponax, and thereby separate his forces on the river below from those occupying the crest or ridge in rear of the town.'" Actually, Burnside was doing exactly what the Confederates wanted him to do. "He had abandoned strategy" by not attempting any flanking movements, "and tied himself down to narrow tactical possibilities," writes Palfrey.[22]

Early on the morning of December 11, while the fog was still on the river, the Federal engineers began work on three pontoon bridges opposite Fredericksburg and two below the town near the

[21] 31 *O.R.*, 63, 64, 106, 107; *B. & L.*, III, 107, 126; *C.C.W.* (1863), I, 660.

[22] Palfrey, *The Antietam*, 141, 143–44; 31 *O.R.*, 88.

mouth of Deep Run. However, Confederate sharpshooters in Fredericksburg time and again broke up work on the spans. Burnside tried to drive them out near midday by a heavy two-hour artillery bombardment of the town by 183 guns. But the cannonade, which did much damage to buildings, failed to budge the enemy snipers. Continued delay was ruining whatever chances Burnside had left of striking Lee while some of Jackson's units were downstream toward Skinker's Neck. Only when Hunt suggested to Burnside that troops cross the river in the pontoon boats themselves did the Federals succeed in the late afternoon in clearing the Southerners out of Fredericksburg. By night, all the bridges were completed. But instead of moving his forces across after dark on December 11, as his generals expected, Burnside waited until daylight on the twelfth to do this, and much of the day was spent in completing this operation. This put the Federal commander's plan twenty-four hours behind schedule, and gave Lee time to concentrate his army in position from Marye's Heights to Hamilton's Crossing. Nor did Burnside make any real effort to prevent the looting in town which some of his men engaged in during the night of December 11–12.[23]

On the afternoon of the twelfth Burnside himself crossed the river to the west bank. Incredibly, with the majority of his troops now directly confronting the enemy, he still had not centered upon any specific and distinct battle plan. When word was brought to the General from Couch concerning the serious obstacle of the canal millrace ditch, Burnside, obstinate in his nervous state, tartly replied that "he himself had occupied Fredericksburg with the Ninth Corps the August before" and knew the terrain well, and that Couch was wrong. Then he rode along his lines and discussed possible plans of action with his top generals.[24]

At approximately 5:00 P.M. on the twelfth, Burnside rode up to

[23] Alexander, *Military Memoirs,* 289–92; 31 *O.R.,* 184, 190, 283, 344, 485; *B. & L.,* III, 86–88, 108, 121; Swinton, *Army of the Potomac,* 241; Palfrey, *The Antietam,* 146–47.

[24] Palfrey, *The Antietam,* 151; Walker, *Second Corps,* 137, 155; 31 *O.R.,* 89.

Franklin's position on the Union left. Prior to his arrival, Franklin, Reynolds, and Smith had conferred together and had agreed that the only feasible plan was for Burnside to throw at least 40,000 men of the Left Grand Division against Lee's right flank. When the army commander arrived, the three generals presented this project to him. The matter was discussed for an hour before Burnside departed. All three generals were of the firm belief that Burnside had agreed to their plan. At any rate, he pledged to issue to Franklin within two or three hours the necessary orders for it. When midnight came without any word, Franklin sent an orderly to army headquarters. This aide was told that the orders would soon be forthcoming. However, they did not reach Franklin until 7:45 A.M. on December 13, and then they were entirely different from what Franklin, Reynolds, and Smith expected them to be.[25]

Burnside apparently returned to his headquarters at the Phillips house, high on Stafford Heights, soon after midnight on the morning of the thirteenth, and went to sleep. He probably arose about 5:15 A.M. and drew up his battle order, which bore the time of 5:55 A.M.; but it did not reach Franklin for one hour and fifty minutes. "It is a pitiful picture," says Palfrey sadly, "but is probably a true one, that Burnside passed the evening of the 12th riding about, not quite at his wits' end, but very near it." Then, he concludes sardonically, "As far as can be made out, he finally came to the conclusion that he would attempt to do something, he did not quite know what, with his left, and if he succeeded, to do something with his right." [26]

Saturday, December 13, 1862, dawned foggy and cold, with a light snow on the ground. Lacking adequate information of the enemy, due to his feeble reconnaissances, Burnside's intentions apparently kept changing, and his orders, which Franklin and the other grand division commanders received about 7:45 A.M., were

[25] B. & L., III, 132–34; C.C.W. (1863), I, 707; William B. Franklin, Reply of Major-General W. B. Franklin . . . (New York, 1867), 1, 2.
[26] Powell, Fifth Corps, 375; B. & L., III, 134–35; Palfrey, The Antietam, 151.

vague and indefinite. They "showed," as William Allan avers, "but a very inadequate grasp of the situation." Franklin was ordered to *seize* Prospect Hill, just north of Hamilton's Crossing, with one division, well supported, while, somewhat contradictorily, he was told at the same time to hold his command in a position to move swiftly south on the Old Richmond Stage Road. When Franklin's attack was seen to be successful, Sumner—when Burnside gave the word—was to *seize* Marye's Heights to the west of the town with one division, well supported. Hooker was to be ready to support either Franklin or Sumner.[27]

The use of the word "seize," instead of "carry," indicates that Burnside expected Franklin and Sumner to meet comparatively weak opposition which would crumble away if tapped lightly in front with a division or two. Swinton declares that "the dispositions were such that it would be difficult to imagine any worse suited to the circumstances"; while Ropes asserts that "one rises from the perusal of this famous order with a feeling of hopeless amazement that such a wild and absurd plan of battle should ever have been entertained by anyone."[28]

When Franklin received this vague and inconsistent order at 7:45 A.M., he consulted with Reynolds and "Baldy" Smith, and all three generals agreed that Burnside meant the main movement to be one down the Richmond road, with but a reconnaissance in force to be made against Prospect Hill. To prevent any erroneous interpretation of his directive, and to telegraph back to him the events transpiring at Franklin's end of the field, Burnside had sent along with his order his adjutant general, and the latter at no time during the day showed by word or tone any indication but that Franklin was carrying out Burnside's order properly. At approximately 8:30 A.M. Franklin made the attack against Prospect Hill

---

[27] *B. & L.*, III, 97, 109, 139, 308; Theodore F. Dwight (ed.), *Campaigns in Virginia, Maryland, and Pennsylvania, 1862–1863* (Boston, 1903), 133–34.

[28] Swinton, *Army of the Potomac*, 244–45; Ropes, *Story of the Civil War*, II, 461.

with two divisions, supported by another. After heavy fighting, and after a temporary breakthrough by Meade, the assaults were thrown back by 1:00 P.M. Franklin had suffered over 4,000 casualties, and had to be bolstered by two of Hooker's divisions and one of Sumner's.[29]

During the peak of Franklin's attack, at 12:30 P.M., a messenger who brought Burnside word of the fighting on the Federal left reports that the army commander "seemed at the time annoyed at the smallness of the force engaged." More than being merely annoyed, Burnside later stated that "his first impulse was to ride off as fast as possible, confront [Franklin], and *shoot him;* but that considering the demoralization it would have produced, and the critical position of the army with a river in its rear, he decided that it would not do." However, when asked a few days after the battle by the Committee on the Conduct of the War his opinion as to why Franklin had failed to carry Prospect Hill, Burnside said that it was due "to the great strength of the position, and the accumulation of the enemy's forces there." [30]

Waiting impatiently at his headquarters on the east bank of the river for word of the progress of Franklin's attack from the Union left, Burnside sent an aide at 10:30 A.M. to determine the exact situation there. Then, Burnside committed an act of extreme folly. Without waiting for the aide to return (he came back at 12:30 P.M.), Burnside, at noon, in his own words, "feeling the importance of haste . . . now directed General Sumner to commence his attack." Thus, Burnside abandoned his plan of battle, as issued early that morning, whereby Sumner was to attack only when definite word was received from the Federal left that Franklin had so shattered the enemy's lines in his front that a power drive by Sumner from the Union right would have a good chance of taking Marye's Heights.[31]

[29] Ropes, *Story of the Civil War*, II, 463; *C.C.W.* (1863), I, 707–14; *B. & L.*, III, 135, 141 n; Henderson, *Stonewall Jackson*, II, 386–93; 31 *O.R.*, 133–42.

[30] 31 *O.R.*, 93–94; Nevins and Thomas (eds.), *Strong's Diary*, III, 297; *C.C.W.* (1863), I, 655.

[31] See 31 *O.R.*, 94.

Promptly at 12:10 P.M., Sumner's first assault on the stone wall along the sunken road began. With the fog now lifted, the blue-clad forces, in full battle array, came magnificently into view on the open plain, in full sight of the breathless men in gray. It was one of the most splendid of martial displays, and no more gallant or hopeless attacks were made by either side during the war. One brigade after another of Sumner's command were thrown forward —necessarily piecemeal, because of the nature of the terrain and obstacles, especially the canal ditch—into a storm of artillery and musketry fire. No brigade could get closer than fifty yards to the stone wall, although a few intrepid individuals fell some twenty-five paces from the wall. In about an hour and a half, the bulk of Sumner's grand division had attacked and had been heavily repulsed. Meanwhile, the desperate Burnside, pacing up and down on the eastern bank of the river, was heard to be muttering vehemently, "That height must be carried this evening." Then, at 1:30 P.M., he ordered Hooker to support Sumner by attacking with the two divisions still under his immediate command.[32]

Hooker received the attack order at 2:00 P.M., made a personal reconnaissance, and sent an aide to Burnside requesting the order be countermanded because further assaults on Marye's Heights were hopeless. Fighting Joe then went himself to remonstrate vociferously with Burnside. Despite the fact that Hooker even cursed Burnside for the mismanagement of the battle, the latter was unmoved, and insisted that the attacks continue. Hooker's men made valiant efforts to do what Sumner had been unable to do, but the task was beyond the capabilities of human flesh. The Federal attacks came to an end at sundown—about 5:30 P.M. As Hooker baldly stated in his testimony after the battle, "Finding that I had lost as many men as my orders required me to lose, I suspended the attack."[33]

In all, in front of the stone wall at Marye's Heights, Burnside

[32] 31 O.R., 222, 287; Palfrey, *The Antietam*, 161–73; Swinton, *Army of the Potomac*, 251, 254.

[33] C.C.W. (1863), I, 668; 31 O.R., 120, 356; Stine, *Army of the Potomac*, 289–90.

had hurled no less than sixteen separate, piecemeal attacks against the impregnable Confederate lines. Almost 8,000 Federal soldiers had fallen on that fearful plain, and not one of them had gotten closer than twenty-five yards to the sunken road. A Confederate officer, speaking of the field of battle, writes, "I saw it the day after the fight, and from the heights it looked as blue as if it had been covered with a blue cloth. At no one spot during our war were there as many bodies on the same space as here." Southern losses on this part of the field came to only some 1,500 men.[34]

At the peak of the attacks from the Union right, Burnside unrealistically sought further assistance again from Franklin on the left. "Tell General Franklin," said Burnside to the officer bearing the verbal message, "with my compliments, that I wish him to make a vigorous attack with his whole force; our right is hard pressed." This wish was received by Franklin at about 2:30 P.M., just as Meade's remnants were streaming back in retreat from the woods near Prospect Hill. However, it was then too late in the afternoon for Franklin to rearrange his forces—strung out along a front two miles in length—and deliver an assault that could come close to driving Jackson from his easily defended position. He informed Burnside of the inability to execute this attack.[35]

With the falling of darkness and the cessation of his futile attacks on the stone wall, Burnside rode across the river into Fredericksburg to talk with officers and men, and to try to arrive at some measures to retrieve the situation. The night was quite cold and the troops suffered terribly, no fires being permitted. Burnside could hear the eerie, almost unreal chorus of the moaning of thousands of Federal wounded who still lay on the plain between the two lines. Couch, whom Burnside visited, noted that "it was plain that he felt he had led us to a great disaster, and one knowing him so

[34] Ropes, *Story of the Civil War*, II, 467; Dwight (ed.), *Campaigns in Virginia, Maryland, and Pennsylvania*, 137; William W. Blackford, *War Years with Jeb Stuart* (New York, 1945), 196.

[35] 31 *O.R.*, 118, 128; *C.C.W.* (1863), I, 711; Henderson, *Stonewall Jackson*, II, 393.

long and well as myself could see that he wished his body was also lying in front of Marye's Heights. I never felt so badly for a man in my life." [36]

All this, and the trying, frustrating events of the day, had unnerved Burnside to the extent that he was little better than a raving madman. Smith found him back at his headquarters before daylight, convulsed in agony, pacing the floor, and crying, "Oh! Oh those men! oh, those men!" Pointing across the river in the direction of the stone wall, he exclaimed again, "Those men over there! I am thinking of them all the time." Then he abruptly interrupted his lamentation to inquire of Smith, "Do you know what I do when you fellows all get away from here at night?" When Smith answered in the negative, Burnside declared, "I call Robert in here and have a long talk with him, certain that I shall get honest opinions." Robert was a former Negro slave from New Mexico whom Burnside had brought with him to Bristol, Rhode Island, to operate some machinery in his gun factory, and who was now the General's cook and servant.[37]

The battle of Fredericksburg was the most one-sided major combat in the Eastern theatre of operations during the war so far as the spread in casualties between the two armies was concerned. Of Burnside's 120,281 men, the following losses were suffered: 1,284 killed; 9,600 wounded; 1,769 missing—a total loss of 12,653. Lee, out of 78,513 men, suffered total casualties of 4,756.[38]

Before daylight on December 14, Burnside met with his chief officers at the Phillips house. As he entered the room where they were gathered, he shouted, "Well, its all arranged; we attack at early dawn, the Ninth Corps in the center, which I shall lead in person . . . we'll make up for the bad work of today." To Burnside's astonishment and pain, his remarks were greeted with

[36] C.C.W. (1863), I, 653; B. & L., III, 116–17; see Henry Steele Commager (ed.), The Blue and the Gray (Indianapolis, 1950), I, 247.

[37] B. & L., III, 138; see Clarence E. Macartney, Grant and His Generals (New York, 1953), 221–22.

[38] Livermore, Numbers and Losses, 96; B. & L., III, 146–47.

silence. Then, led by Sumner and Hooker, the high-ranking officers present voiced their strongest opposition to a resumption of the battle in that manner. Maps were examined. By this time, Burnside was raving wildly about his top officers disobeying his orders and being strenuously opposed to him. He asserted that if he only had reliable generals under him he could trounce the foe; but, not possessing any such officers, he would be obliged reluctantly to give up the contest, countermand the orders to have the Ninth Corps charge the sunken road, and retreat across the river. When he actually issued the withdrawal order, Burnside wept.[39]

The Union commander skillfully withdrew his army to the northeastern bank of the river. As soon as it was safely on the left bank of the Rappahannock, Burnside said, according to Smith, "that he had it in his mind to relieve Sumner from command, place Hooker in arrest, and Franklin in command of the army." Halleck telegraphed Burnside on the fifteenth that he still had confidence in him, and that, "in regard to movements we cannot judge here; you are the best judge." Burnside replied that "for the failure in the attack I am responsible, as the extreme gallantry, courage, and endurance shown by [the troops] was never excelled, and would have carried the points, had it been possible." Then Burnside made the following grave admission to Halleck: "The fact that I decided to move from Warrenton onto this line against the opinion of the President, Secretary, and yourself, and that you have left the whole management in my hands, without giving me orders, makes me the more responsible." [40]

The Radicals, as in the case of Pope at Second Manassas, now needed another scapegoat; so, having selected upon Franklin as their victim, four members of the notorious Committee on the Con-

[39] Franklin to McClellan, Dec. 23, 1862, McClellan Papers; D. R. Larned to H. Larned, Dec. 16, 1862, Larned Papers; *B. & L.*, III, 127; *C. C. W.* (1863), I, 653.

[40] *B. & L.*, III, 138; Meade, *Life and Letters of Meade*, I, 362; *C.C.W.* (1863), I, 711; 31 *O.R.*, 65–67, 122; Boston *Courier*, Dec. 23, 1862; New York *Herald*, Jan. 10, 1863; *Congressional Globe*, Appendix, Jan. 30, 1863, 76.

duct of the War went down to Falmouth on December 19 to catch
the "fool and traitor generals." Testifying under oath, Burnside still
supported Franklin's conduct in the battle. The intriguing Hooker,
however, severely castigated Franklin's generalship. Although at
this time disappointing the Radicals in his testimony on Franklin,
Burnside nonetheless did perform a sudden about-face as to his
political views, and now freely mouthed Radical tenets. Returning
to Washington on the night of December 20, the committee did
not condemn Burnside. While the members felt that his assault had
been unwise, they wrote off its failure to the imponderables of
war.[41]

Upon hearing that the administration was being bombarded
with criticism for allegedly forcing him to fight against his will at
Fredericksburg, Burnside went up to Washington late on December 19 and stayed through the twentieth. He told Lincoln that he
was willing to assume all the censure for the Fredericksburg defeat, and that he would issue a statement to that effect. This manly
gesture pleased the relieved President, and he complimented the
General as being the first commander he had discovered who
was ready to relieve him of some of the heavy load of responsibility.[42]

Then, on December 26, Burnside issued orders to prepare the
army for a new offensive movement. Without consulting his generals, he proposed to put his main body across the Rappahannock at
Sedden's house, some six or seven miles below Fredericksburg,
while a feint—which could be converted into a real assault-crossing
if the move below were detected—would be made above the town.

[41] *C.C.W.* (1863), I, 643 ff.; Chandler to his wife, Dec. 18, 1862,
Chandler Papers, Div. of MSS, Library of Congress; Julian, *Political Recollections,* 224–25; Meade, *Life and Letters of Meade,* I, 340; John Cochrane, *The War for the Union* (New York, 1875), 40–48; New York
Tribune, Dec. 19–27, 1862; *Senate Reports,* 37th Cong., 3d Sess., Vol. I,
No. 71.
[42] Burnside to Lincoln, Dec. 19, 20, 1862, Lincoln Papers; 31 *O.R.,*
866–70; *Scribner's Monthly,* XIX (1879), 424; Basler (ed.), *Collected
Works of Lincoln,* VI, 15.

A picked cavalry force was to cross at Kelly's Ford and press southward to the vicinity of Petersburg, where several railroads could be
cut, and then on to Suffolk where the blue riders could be picked
up and brought back by vessel to Aquia. It might be said in advance that just as the operation was actually getting underway on
December 30, it was halted by the order from the President
which directed Burnside to make no general movement without his
(Lincoln's) approval.[43]

This latest of Burnside's projects was squelched by the active opposition of Brigadier Generals John Cochrane and John Newton,
who, along with Franklin and Smith, were convinced that any crossing then by Burnside below Fredericksburg would be repelled.
Cochrane and Newton then went up to Washington on leave on
December 30, and had an audience with the President. They told
Lincoln that no one in the Army of the Potomac had any confidence in Burnside, and that the latter's new plan was doomed to
defeat and should be halted. Cochrane later testified under oath
that "the President . . . was pleased to say that he was glad that
we had visited him, and that good would come of the interview."
Later that very evening, Lincoln wired Burnside not to "make a
general movement of the army without letting me know," and
Burnside canceled his planned operation.[44]

On December 31 Burnside went up to Washington again for a
visit of several days. When he talked with the President alone on
January 1, 1863, he was informed that certain nameless officers of
his army had told Lincoln that none of the top generals had any
confidence in the army commander's plan to cross the river, and
that this design was doomed to failure. Burnside then told the
President of a new scheme, which was simply to cross the river, he
said, at some unspecified point above or below Fredericksburg.
Lincoln expressed his doubt that such a plan—if it can be called
that—would work, and sent out a call for Stanton and Halleck to

[43] *C.C.W.* (1863), I, 716–17, 718.
[44] *Ibid.*, 730–46; 31 *O.R.*, 900–18; Basler (ed.), *Collected Works of Lincoln*, VI, 22.

join the conclave. Prior to the arrival of these two officials, Burnside told the President that he (Burnside) lacked the confidence of
his chief generals and therefore should be relieved of his command,
at which time he would retire to private life. He said further that
the army and the people had no confidence in Stanton and Halleck,
and that they should be fired. Later in the day the General placed
most of these views in a letter and, probably on January 2, handed
it to Lincoln in the presence of Halleck and Stanton, at which time
he boldly told them that he had recommended their ouster. But
Lincoln refused officially to receive this letter, thereby indicating
that he would still retain the Secretary and General-in-Chief. No
decisions were reached at this council of war as to what operation
Burnside should now undertake.[45]

When Burnside returned to the army, he persisted in proposing
another crossing of the river in accordance with his stated plan.
However, he desired direct approval for this operation from some
superior in Washington. He told Lincoln in a communiqué on
January 5 that, although his generals disapproved of his scheme, he
was going to proceed with it anyway, and that if the President would
not approve his plan he would resign. On the same day Burnside
wired Halleck of his intention to cross the Rappahannock again,
saying that he would assume the responsibility for the operation,
but that he would appreciate some general guiding directions from
the General-in-Chief. Halleck, however, in his reply to Burnside on
the seventh, brilliantly evaded assuming any responsibility, and
spoke only in extremely broad and vague terms which were of no
help to the army commander. Lincoln endorsed Halleck's dispatch,
urged Burnside to "be cautious," and said it was not yet advisable to
relieve the General of his command. Burnside then abandoned his
proposed operation, he relates, "intending to make it in some other
form within a few days." [46]

With good weather prevailing since the battle, Burnside planned

[45] C.C.W. (1863), I, 717–18; 31 O.R., 941–42, 945, 1011.
[46] Basler (ed.), Collected Words of Lincoln, VI, 31–32; C.C.W.
(1863), I, 718–19.

still another movement of his army. This time, he would march up the left bank of the Rappahannock to Banks's Ford, some six miles above Fredericksburg, where the main crossing would be made. To divert Lee, feints were to be made just above and just below the town. However, as the movement was about to get underway, the heavens opened and torrents of rain fell. "To start off in the mud as we did," declares Couch, "with the army in its discouraged state was perfect folly. There did not seem to be anything in the move to recommend itself." But Burnside wallowed on through January 20 and 21 in his famous but futile "Mud March," until he was finally obliged to call it off and bring the weary, disheartened army back to Falmouth.[47]

The morale of the Army of the Potomac now reached a new low, with desertions reaching a peak of some 200 men per day. Reports of this condition even reached the cabinet. At a review of troops, some of the soldiers in blue actually booed Burnside and voiced threatening mutterings about refusing to fight further under his leadership. Word had leaked out also of the visit of Cochrane and Newton to Washington, and the press published the views held of Burnside as given by his subordinates, with Hooker being especially loose-tongued while urging his own elevation to the army command.[48]

Learning of these things, Burnside, on January 23, in a towering rage, drew up General Orders No. 8, in which he would dismiss from the service (actually he could not do this) Hooker, Newton, Cochrane, and Brigadier General W. T. H. Brooks, and relieve from duty in the Army of the Potomac Franklin, Smith, and others. The army commander showed the order to Henry J. Raymond, of the New York *Times,* who was then in camp. When Raymond asked Burnside what he would do if Hooker resisted obeying the

---

[47] Swinton, *Army of the Potomac,* 258; *B. & L.,* III, 118–19.

[48] Swinton, *Army of the Potomac,* 256, 262; *C.C.W.* (1865), I, 3, 73; Villard, *Memoirs,* I, 348, 375–76; New York *Tribune,* Jan. 19, 1863; Cochrane, *War for the Union,* 44–48; John R. Adams, *Memorial and Letters of Reverend John R. Adams* (Cambridge, Mass., 1890), 89–90, 98–99.

order, Burnside replied, with evident relish, that he would hang "Fighting Joe" before the sun set. In a near panic, Raymond rushed up to Washington and informed the President of Burnside's order. The pained Lincoln said he would prevent the issuance of the order, and declared that he would probably have to oust Burnside from command and supplant him with the conniving Hooker, who, more than any other officer, had the country with him.[49]

As for Burnside, one of his aides urged him to let the President examine his order before he issued it, and the General agreed. Arriving in the capital on January 24, Burnside handed two papers to Lincoln: the order, and a letter of resignation, and said that the President would have to accept one or the other because things could not go on as they were now. In reply to this ultimatum the Chief Executive said that he would take the matter up with his chief advisers. On the following day Lincoln informed Burnside that he was relieving him from the command of the Army of the Potomac and replacing him with Hooker. He said, however, that he would not accept Burnside's resignation from the service, and that he would find him another command after the General had had a thirty days' leave of absence. Burnside agreed to this. He made a last trip back to Falmouth to deliver to Hooker the orders changing the command.[50]

Although Stanton and Halleck would have preferred Major General William S. Rosecrans to Hooker as a successor to Burnside, they were overruled by Lincoln. The order of January 25 which announced the change in army commanders stated also that Franklin and Sumner, both of whom outranked Hooker, were relieved from further service with the Army of the Potomac—an unjustified decision on grounds of actual performance during the Fredericksburg campaign and battle. Burnside left the army on the twenty-sixth, after issuing a noble farewell address in which he

[49] 31 O.R., 998–99; Franklin, Reply, 11 n; Scribner's Monthly, XIX (1879), 703–706.

[50] 31 O.R., 998; C.C.W. (1863), I, 719–22; Pease and Randall (eds.), Browning's Diary, I, 619; Basler (ed.), Collected Works of Lincoln, VI, 77 n.

mustered kind and chivalrous words for his unchivalrous nemesis, Hooker, asking "cordial support and cooperation" for the "brave and skillful general" who was taking over the reins from him.[51]

While the Radicals were glad to see Hooker get the command, they did not wish to lose their new convert to Radicalism—Burnside. They decided, therefore, to help Burnside leave the Army of the Potomac with a clean slate so far as Fredericksburg was concerned. The best way to do this was to throw the blame onto a scapegoat, preferably a pro-McClellan general, and Franklin, as noted before, was seized upon as the one to be smeared. In new hearings before the Committee on the Conduct of the War, Burnside, as the first witness, did an about-face in testifying on Franklin's behavior during the battle of Fredericksburg. This time Burnside charged that Franklin had disobeyed his orders by not attacking soon enough or with sufficient force. He asserted that the army would have won the battle had Franklin attacked in the manner in which he had wanted him to attack. Burnside also castigated Hooker for trying twice to dissuade him from attacking after Sumner's repulse, instead of beginning his own assaults at once. In the "findings" of the committee—published in April of 1863—Burnside was acquitted of *any* blame for the Fredericksburg disaster. Instead, the committee stated that Franklin's refusal to attack with his entire force had cost Burnside the battle—a false charge that Franklin answered in a most effective pamphlet.[52]

After his leave of absence, Burnside commanded the Department of the Ohio from March 25, 1863, to December 12, 1863, during which time Morgan's Raiders were captured, Cumberland Gap taken, and eastern Tennessee occupied by the Federals. The high point, perhaps, in Burnside's Civil War career came when he suc-

[51] Statement by John G. Nicolay and John Hay (eds.), *Complete Works of Abraham Lincoln* (New York, 1905), VIII, 206; 31 *O.R.,* 1005.

[52] Chandler to his wife, Jan. 22, Feb. 7, 1863, Chandler Papers; New York *Tribune,* Jan. 24, Feb. 10, Apr. 6, 1863; *C.C.W.* (1863), I, 52–57, 690–92, 716–24; Meade, *Life and Letters of Meade,* I, 358–60, 361–62; Franklin, *Reply, passim.* See also Williams, *Lincoln and the Radicals,* 268–69.

cessfully withstood Longstreet's siege of Knoxville in November, 1863, for which he received the thanks of Congress. During Grant's overland campaign of 1864, Burnside was again in command of the Ninth Corps, but he utterly failed to distinguish himself. In fact, his inept handling of the mine assault at the siege of Petersburg cost him his job, and from August 13, 1864, he was on leave of absence awaiting orders.[53]

The basically honorable and noble nature of the man, however, asserted itself near the end of the war. On March 23, 1865, Burnside wrote Stanton, "If I can be of any service to General Grant or General Sherman as a subordinate commander, or aide-de-camp, or as a bearer of dispatches from you to either of them, I am quite ready." In his final written report, dated November 13, 1865, Burnside made this manly statement concerning his tenure of command of the Army of the Potomac during the Fredericksburg campaign: "I am not disposed to complain of my lack of success in the exercise of the command; and, in view of the glorious results which have since attended the movements of this gallant army, I am quite willing to believe that my removal was for the best."[54]

Burnside's civil career after the war was most successful. He resigned from the army in 1865 to become president of the Cincinnati and Martinsville Railroad. In 1866 he was president of the Rhode Island Locomotive Works, and in the following year became president of the Indianapolis and Vincennes Railroad and director of the Narragansett Steamship Company. Burnside was governor of Rhode Island in 1866, a position to which he was re-elected in 1867 and in 1868. In 1870 he was employed as a medium of communication in efforts to end the Franco-Prussian War. Burnside capped his later career by serving as United States senator from Rhode Island from 1874 until his death in Bristol, Rhode Island, on September 13, 1881.[55]

[53] Cullum, *Biographical Register*, II, 192.
[54] See Macartney, *Grant and His Generals*, 265; 31 *O.R.*, 96.
[55] *D.A.B.*, III, 313.

CHAPTER SIX

Joseph Hooker

> My God! it is horrible—horrible;
> and to think of it, 130,000 magnificent
> soldiers so cut to pieces by less than
> 60,000 half-starved ragamuffins.
> —*Horace Greeley*

HE WAS A MOST COLORFUL-LOOKING INDIVIDUAL, WITH RED, white, and blue predominating. Most descriptions of Major General Joseph Hooker emphasize his florid complexion, his great shock of light hair, and his blue eyes. He "was fully six feet high," according to Villard, "finely proportioned, with a soldierly, erect carriage, handsome and noble features . . . a rosy complexion, abundant blond hair, a fine and expressive mouth, and—most striking of all—great, speaking gray-blue eyes." This *"beau-ideal* of a soldier in all physical qualities"—and only W. S. Hancock, perhaps, excelled him in appearance—had only one flaw in his physiognomy, and that was "a fatally weak chin." What attracted attention most, however, was the General's skin. "His roseate hue is natural to him," writes a contemporary. "His complexion is red and white most beautifully blended, and he looks as rosy as the most healthy woman alive. His skin never tans nor bleaches, but peels off from exposure, leaving the same rosy complexion always visible." John Hay hints that Hooker's flushed appearance was due perhaps to his use of alcohol.[1]

Except for a peak reached during the Mexican War, Hooker's

[1] Villard, *Memoirs,* I, 347–48; William F. G. Shanks, *Personal Recollections of Distinguished Generals* (New York, 1866), 187–91.

life before the Civil War had been generally a hard and unrewarding one. He was born in Hadley, Massachusetts, on November 13, 1814, and entered West Point in 1833. He graduated twenty-ninth in a class of fifty in 1837, and served as a lieutenant in the Florida War in 1837–1838, and in other routine assignments until the war with Mexico. Here, he won three brevets for gallant and meritorious conduct at Monterey, at the National Bridge, and at Chapultepec. Hooker then served on the Pacific coast for a time, and resigned from the army, as captain, in 1853. For five years he worked as a farmer at Sonoma, California, but was not too successful. From 1858 to 1859 Hooker was superintendent of military roads in Oregon, and from 1859 to 1861 he was a colonel of California militia.[2]

When the Civil War began, Hooker came East from California to Washington, D.C. But because of the unwarranted criticism which he had made of Scott's handling of the American army in the campaign for Mexico City, while testifying in the Worth-Pillow investigation, he was permitted to cool his heels for awhile at the War Department. On May 17, 1861, however, Hooker was made a brigadier general of volunteers. But he continued without a command, and was but a private observer at the First Battle of Bull Run. Shortly after that combat, in desperation, he finally secured an interview with the President. Here, characteristically, Hooker asserted to Lincoln, "I was at Bull Run the other day, Mr. President, and it is no vanity in me to say I am a damned sight better general than you had on that field." His optimism and self-confidence impressed the Chief Executive.[3]

On August 4, 1861, Hooker was named by McClellan to command a brigade in the Army of the Potomac; and on October 15, 1861, he was made a division commander. It was in this latter capacity that Hooker served through the Peninsula campaign and was engaged in most of the battles. On May 5, 1862, he was made a

[2] Cullum, *Biographical Register,* I, 536–37; *D.A.B.,* IX, 198.
[3] *Harper's Magazine,* XXXI, 642.

major general of volunteers. During this campaign he received, through an error which was knowingly permitted to remain in the press, the sobriquet, "Fighting Joe." Hooker did not like this nickname, because, he said, "people will think I am a highwayman or a bandit." During Pope's Second Manassas campaign, Hooker was a division commander, and in McClellan's Maryland campaign he was promoted to the command of the First Corps. He was wounded at Antietam, and was named a brigadier general in the regular army on September 20, 1862. Hooker then served as a grand division commander under Burnside at Fredericksburg. Thus far, he had been an excellent troop leader. "In every engagement," writes Colonel James F. Rusling, "he always seemed to know exactly *what* to do and *when* to do it."[4]

Early in the war, Hooker had been a conservative in politics, and had even opened his camp to men seeking runaway slaves. But, by the late summer of 1862, the easy-principled General had done a flip-flop, and was now trying to get the attention of the Radicals by criticizing McClellan and his friends, Halleck, and even the President. By the fall of 1862 the Radicals were beginning to whoop it up for Fighting Joe for army command. After Fredericksburg, Hooker charged that Burnside was incompetent and that his operations were absurd, that Lincoln and his administration were imbeciles, that nothing would proceed properly until a military dictator was installed, and that this should be done quickly. In early January, 1863, Hooker visited Washington, spoke to newspaper reporters of his prowess in handling an army, and sniffed around as to the possibilities of getting the command. Stanton and Halleck favored Rosecrans, and were definitely opposed to Hooker. Other generals were considered, but the field was finally narrowed down to Reynolds, Meade, and Hooker. Finally, after a somewhat obscure political intrigue involving Chase, Lincoln overruled Stanton and

---

[4] *B. & L.,* II, 112–13, III, 217; John Bigelow, *The Campaign of Chancellorsville* . . . (New Haven, 1910), 6; James F. Rusling, *Men and Things I Saw in the Civil War* (New York, 1899), 53.

Halleck and named Hooker to the command. "It was," as Wood and Edmunds aver, "a dangerous precedent to reward intrigue and insubordination with the chief command." [5]

Few soldiers of history have had the extreme, divergent, sharply etched personal traits and characteristics that Hooker possessed. A voluble talker, frank and outspoken, he was quite nervous, and, as an observer remarks, "goes at everything with a dash." Although he occasionally greeted strangers coldly and stiffly, he was usually courteous and polished in manner, graceful and dignified—"a thorough-bred gentleman." He was courageous under fire, and most popular with the men in the ranks. He believed in destiny and fate, and the exhilarating lure of battle itself intoxicated him. [6]

But other people saw less favorable qualities in Hooker. As Gamaliel Bradford phrases it, "his defects, like evil angels, walked by him always." General Carl Schurz states that Hooker was "a man with no firm moral force but he is a good soldier and in addition has the talent publicly to display his achievements in the most favorable light." Meade, writing in October, 1862, before Hooker was named to command the Army of the Potomac, sized him up perspicaciously: "Hooker is a very good soldier and a capital officer to command an army corps, but I should doubt his qualifications to command a large army." As to Hooker as an army commander, Meade declared, "I should fear his judgment and prudence, as he is apt to think the only thing to be done is to pitch in and

[5] *C.C.W.* (1863), III, 634–41; W. W. Tilghman to Stanton, May 22, 1862, Hooker to Stanton, Nov. 9, 1862, Stanton Papers; Garfield to his wife, Oct. 12, 1862, Theodore C. Smith, *Life and Letters of James A. Garfield* (New York, 1925), I, 251; *C.C.W.* (1865), I, 111–12, 175 *Scribner's Monthly*, XIX (1880), 42, 422; Meade, *Life and Letters of Meade*, I, 346; Nicolay and Hay, *Abraham Lincoln*, VI, 264–72; Walter H. Hebert, *Fighting Joe Hooker* (Indianapolis, 1944), 166; 31 *O.R.*, 1008–1009; Wood and Edmunds, *The Civil War*, 190.

[6] Shanks, *Personal Recollections*, 187–91; Villard, *Memoirs*, I, 347–48; B. & L., III, 155; 27 *O.R.*, 219; Alexander K. McClure, *Colonel Alexander K. McClure's Recollections of Half a Century* . . . (Salem, Mass., 1902), 347.

fight. . . . I fear he is open to temptation and liable to be seduced by flattery." [7]

But there were other harsher opinions of Hooker's reputation and less desirable traits. "In the 'Fifties," writes George Fort Milton, "when out in California at the Gold Rush, he became famous for his 'glad eye' for ladies of easy virtue, whence the Californians invented the name 'Hookers' for the type of ladies the debonaire lieutenant liked so well. Likewise he communed with John Barleycorn and was said to be a three-bottle man." Others testify to Hooker's fondness for drink. He had also a penchant for gossip and criticism. Like Pope, he never wearied of thumping his own chest and expounding on his fancied talents as an army commander. When Burnside had the temerity, in April, 1863, to reprove Hooker's conduct at Fredericksburg, the latter let go a violent broadside at his precursor: "[I] cannot bear to go into battle with the slanders of this wretch uncontradicted. He must swallow his words as soon as I am in a condition to address him, or I will hunt him to the ends of the earth." U. S. Grant, under whom Hooker served at Chattanooga later in the war, spoke of him as follows: "I . . . regarded him as a dangerous man. He was not subordinate to his superiors. He was ambitious to the extent of caring nothing for the rights of others." [8]

On January 26, 1863, Hooker formally took over the helm of the Army of the Potomac. The forty-eight-year-old general was immediately summoned to Washington by the President for a conference. A. K. McClure met him at the War Department, and later recalled, "When I asked him what he thought of his campaign on which he was about to start, he answered in the most enthusiastic

[7] Gamaliel Bradford, *Union Portraits* (Boston, 1916), 59; Frederic Bancroft, *Speeches, Correspondence and Public Papers of Carl Schurz* (New York, 1913), I, 251; Meade, *Life and Letters of Meade*, I, 318, 319.

[8] George Fort Milton, *Conflict: The American Civil War* (New York, 1941), 253; Morse (ed.), *Welles's Diary*, I, 229–30; *Harper's Monthly*, XXXI, 642; *C.C.W.* (1863), I, 575; Villard, *Memoirs*, I, 348; Grant, *Memoirs*, II, 539.

manner, declaring that he had the finest army on the planet; that he could march it to New Orleans; that he would cross the Rapidan without losing a man, and then 'take the rebs where the hair was short.' " In his interview with Lincoln, Hooker stated that the President would have to stand between him and Halleck, who, since their early California days, were enemies. Perhaps as a result of this request, Hooker was given an unusually wide degree of autonomy in handling the army, and was not obliged very often to correspond directly with the General-in-Chief.[9]

The President was privy to several unpleasant sides of Hooker's character, especially his attempts to undermine his predecessors in command of the army. "Hooker talks badly," Lincoln had declared. The President had been informed also that the General was one of those who had called loudest and most frequently about the need for a dictatorship. It was probably at the end of this conference with Hooker on January 26, 1863, that the Chief Executive handed the General his famous letter of advice. In it, Lincoln said, in part:

. . . I think it best for you to know that there are some things in regard to which I am not quite satisfied with you. . . . I . . . believe you do not mix politics with your profession [this was an erroneous belief]. . . . I think that during General Burnside's command of the army, you have taken counsel of your ambition, and thwarted him as much as you could, in which you did a great wrong to the country and to a most meritorious and honorable officer. I have heard, in such a way as to believe it, of your recently saying that both the army and the Government needed a dictator. Of course, it was not for this, but in spite of it, that I have given you the command. Only those generals who gain successes can set up dictators. What I now ask of you is military success, and I will risk the dictatorship. . . . And now beware of rashness. Beware of rashness, but with energy and sleepless vigilance go forward and give us victories.

[9] McClure, *Recollections*, 347–48; Dennett (ed.), *Diaries and Letters of Hay*, 84; *C.C.W.* (1865), I, 111–12, 175–76; Halleck to W. T. Sherman, Sept. 16, 1864, William T. Sherman Papers, Div. of MSS, Library of Congress; 39 *O.R.*, 156; 40 *O.R.*, 12.

Edward Channing says of this missive, "It was an extraordinary letter to write to one whom a great place had just been given, and seems to carry in itself conclusive reasons why the appointment should not have been made." Later, when Fighting Joe read it to other persons, he was moved with emotion, and declared of Lincoln, "He talks to me like a father. I shall not answer this letter until I have won him a great victory." [10]

Hooker's appointment to his new post had far-reaching repercussions. The Radical press hailed him, while the pro-Democratic, conservative papers denounced him as a power-hungry intriguer. The General's elevation was received by the army in the way Couch expresses it: "This appointment, undoubtedly, gave very general satisfaction to the army, except, perhaps to a few, mostly superior officers, who had grown up with it, and had had abundant opportunities to study Hooker's military character; these believed that Mr. Lincoln had committed a grave error in his selection." And, as W. F. G. Shanks states, "He had little of the love or admiration, and consequently little of the genuine support of his subordinate commanders; while he was, by reason of his promotion, further removed from immediate direction of his troops, and the inspiration of his presence was lost on those who had learned to believe in him." On the Confederate side, Lee was not respectful of Hooker's ability to handle the large Army of the Potomac, nor was Beauregard, who declared, "If Hooker had two to one against Lee, then I pity the former." [11]

At the end of January, 1863, extremely cold weather, accompanied by unusually heavy rains and snows set in and lasted for quite some time. Hooker declared that he would not embark on a winter campaign. Therefore, the army stayed in camp around Falmouth and Stafford Heights, across from the battered city of

[10] *Scribner's Monthly,* XIX (1880), 422, 704; 40 *O.R.,* 4; Channing, *History of the United States,* VI, 477; Nicolay and Hay, *Abraham Lincoln,* VII, 87–88.

[11] New York *Tribune,* Feb. 3, 4, 27, 1863; *B. & L.,* III, 154; *Harper's Monthly,* XXI (1865), 641; A. L. Long, *Memoirs of Robert E. Lee* (Richmond, 1886), 248; 109 *O.R.,* 288.

Fredericksburg, and was reorganized and refitted. It numbered then 149,323 men present for duty (not effectives), with 45,019 troops in the defenses of Washington. Lee's Army of Northern Virginia aggregated 73,984 men present for duty, but it was soon to be weakened by the departure from Fredericksburg to Suffolk— some 120 miles—of two divisions under Longstreet's command. In the field of army administration, in which he excelled, Hooker's installation as army head worked wonders. He began by naming Major General Daniel Butterfield as his chief of staff. While not a genius as a troop leader, Butterfield was a good administrator, and was undoubtedly responsible for the success of many of the reforms made in the army at this time. One of these was the elimination of the grand division structure on February 5. The army was now to be composed of seven rather small infantry corps. However, this was too many; four or five would have been better. The cavalry was amalgamated into a cavalry corps, commanded by the well-intentioned but somewhat ineffectual Major General George Stoneman.[12]

Other administrative reforms in the Army of the Potomac ensued. Desertions were curtailed by a new furlough system, and allegedly disloyal officers were dismissed. The shooting of a few deserters in front of the other soldiers had a most salutary effect. A more controversial change was that in which the wagon supply trains were replaced, in large part, by 2,000 pack mules. Rather ill-advised was Hooker's stripping his chief of artillery—the capable Henry J. Hunt—of all executive functions, thus reducing him to a purely administrative status. However, Hooker was wise in expanding the size and competency of the Inspector General's Department, and in setting up a new Bureau of Military Information. Also conducive to raising morale was the General's adoption of Butterfield's suggestion of having distinctive uniform badges to indicate the different divisions and corps. The army commander also tightened up on permitting outsiders to visit the army, especially women; al-

[12] Bigelow, *Chancellorsville,* 11–12, 32–33, 39–40; Francis A. Walker, *General Hancock* (New York, 1894), 73.

though in the latter category, as was perhaps inevitable, little progress was made. The food of the soldiers was improved, as were the uniforms and other clothing. All in all, during the late winter and early spring, Hooker might well have been dubbed "Administrative Joe." [13]

With the campaign season approaching again, Hooker had, on March 31, 136,724 men present for duty, as compared with Lee's 64,799. Shortly before, during a review at Falmouth, Hooker had said to a group of officers, "If the enemy does not run, God help them." On March 29 he asserted to another group, "I have the finest army the sun ever shone on. I can march this army to New Orleans. My plans are perfect, and when I start to carry them out, may God have mercy on General Lee, for I will have none." Hooker said that he "did not mean to drive the enemy, but to bag him"—shades of John Pope! When a party including the President visited the army at Falmouth in early April, Hooker asserted, "I am going straight to Richmond if I live." Bubbling over with enthusiasm, he prefaced many of his remarks with the words, "When I get to Richmond." Said Lincoln to a newspaper friend present, "That is the most distressing thing about Hooker. It seems to me that he is overconfident." To the army commander and his senior corps leader, Couch, Lincoln said, "Gentlemen, in your next battle *put in all your men.*" [14]

Early in April Hooker felt that his army was ready to move, despite the execrable roads. After first considering crossing the river well below Fredericksburg, the General drew up another plan on April 11 whereby Stoneman's cavalry corps would cross up-

---

[13] *C.C.W.* (1865), I, 74, 91–93, 111–12; Bigelow, *Chancellorsville,* 44–50, 126; *B. & L.,* III, 154, 183; 40 *O.R.,* 156–57, 544–63.

[14] Herman Haupt, *Reminiscences* . . . (Milwaukee, 1901), 193; New York *Tribune,* Mar. 21, 1863; Edward L. Pierce, *Memoir and Letters of Charles Sumner* (Boston, 1887–93), IV, 133–34, 138–39; Washington *National Intelligencer,* Apr. 5, 1863; Brooks, *Washington in Lincoln's Time,* 45–57; Basler (ed.), *Collected Works of Lincoln,* VI, 161; Beale (ed.) *Bates's Diary,* 287–88; *Scribner's Monthly,* XV (March, 1878), 673; *B. & L.,* III, 120.

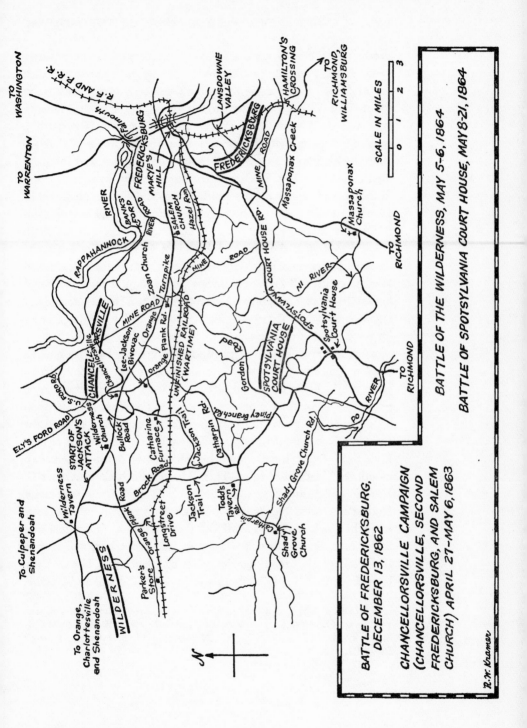

TO WASHINGTON

TO WARRENTON

R. AND P. R. R.

Falmouth

RAPPAHANNOCK RIVER

BANKS' FORD

FREDERICKSBURG

MARYE'S HILL

ELY'S FORD ROAD

C. & S. ROAD

To Culpeper and Shenandoah

WILDERNESS

To Orange, Charlottesville and Shenandoah

Wilderness Tavern

START OF JACKSON'S ATTACK

Wilderness Church

Bullock Road

Brock Road

Parker's Store

Orange Plank Road

Longstreet Drive

MINE ROAD

CHANCELLORSVILLE

Chancellor's

Lee-Jackson Bivouac

Orange Plank Rd.

Zoan Church

Orange Turnpike

MINE ROAD

Catharine Furnace?

Jackson Trail

Catharpin Rd.

Jackson Trail

Todd's Tavern

Catharpin Rd.

Shady Grove Church

Shady Grove Church Rd.

Piney Branch Rd.

Gordon Road

SPOTSYLVANIA COURT HOUSE

SPOTSYLVANIA COURT HOUSE RD.

UNFINISHED RAILROAD (WARTIME)

SALEM CHURCH

Hazel Run

MINE ROAD

Spotsylvania Court House

NI RIVER

Massaponax Church

TO RICHMOND

PO RIVER

TO RICHMOND

FREDERICKSBURG

MINE ROAD

Massaponax Creek

LANSDOWNE VALLEY

HAMILTON'S CROSSING

TO RICHMOND, WILLIAMSBURG

TO RICHMOND

SCALE IN MILES

0 1 2 3

BATTLE OF THE WILDERNESS, MAY 5-6, 1864

BATTLE OF SPOTSYLVANIA COURT HOUSE, MAY 8-21, 1864

BATTLE OF FREDERICKSBURG, DECEMBER 13, 1862

CHANCELLORSVILLE CAMPAIGN (CHANCELLORSVILLE, SECOND FREDERICKSBURG, AND SALEM CHURCH) APRIL 27-MAY 6, 1863

R. K. Kramer

N

stream and move to Lee's rear, doing considerable damage, after which Hooker would cross his main body by the upper fords, turn Lee's left, and hammer the retreating Confederate army back upon the anvil of the Federal cavalry to the south. On the twelfth Lincoln approved the General's plan, and Hooker directed Stoneman to cross the Rapidan with his cavalry west of the Orange and Alexandria, push into Lee's rear, harass the Confederates, and intercept their expected retreat. Stoneman, encumbered with wagons, began a tortoise-paced march up the north bank of the river on the thirteenth. His slowness and the beginning of a heavy two-week rainfall forced him to return with his head tucked back in his shell. Hooker met with the annoyed President at Aquia Creek on the nineteenth, and apparently convinced him that if the rains halted soon he could still employ Stoneman on a similar raid and could himself execute his approved campaign plans. Hooker told Sanitary Commissioner George T. Strong on the following day that he intended "to destroy Lee's army or his own within a week." [15]

Now, however, instead of planning to force Lee back on his line of communications, Hooker determined to attack the Confederate army itself, chiefly by means of turning Lee's left. Stoneman, with practically all of the Union cavalry, was to go off on his raid upon the enemy's communications. Sedgwick's command was to cross the river just below Fredericksburg and make a demonstration against Lee's right. Other forces would be stationed at Banks's Ford, Falmouth, and Stafford Heights. Then, Meade's Fifth Corps, Oliver O. Howard's Eleventh Corps, and Slocum's Twelfth Corps, all under Hooker's personal command, would march upstream and cross the Rappahannock at Kelly's Ford and the Rapidan at Germanna and Ely's Fords, march down the south bank of the river, and reopen Banks's Ford, thus reuniting the wings of the army. If Lee sent any large force from Fredericksburg westward toward Chancellorsville,

[15] C.C.W. (1865), I, 43, 113, 115; Bigelow, *Chancellorsville*, 106–12, 141, 153, 168; 40 O.R., 199–200, 213; 39 O.R., 1066; Basler (ed.), *Collected Works of Lincoln*, VI, 175; Nevins and Thomas (eds.), *Strong's Diary*, III, 312.

Sedgwick was to storm the enemy's works on Marye's Heights at all costs, and get on the rear of the gray force. Lee, however, was undeceived as to Hooker's intentions, and wrote Jackson on April 23, "I think that, if a real attempt is made [by the Federals] to cross the river, it will be above Fredericksburg." [16]

The weakest part of this otherwise admirable design was the need for concerted action between Hooker's main body and Sedgwick's wing. Also, the sending off of almost all of the Federal cavalry force, instead of dispatching some 3,000 troopers on the raid while the remainder of the blue horsemen stayed with Hooker's main body and acted as its antennae, was a mistake. The heavy rains kept Stoneman from crossing anyway until April 28, and then he accomplished little of importance. The impatient Hooker did not even wait a few days to allow Stoneman to sever Lee's communications, but crossed the infantry and artillery over at almost the same time as the cavalry force crossed. The Union commander had been informed quite accurately as to Lee's number of effectives—which was slightly over 60,000. Hooker, in comparison, had a little over 130,000 effectives. [17]

The immense operation began at 5:30 A.M. on April 27. Hooker's movements went smoothly on that day and on the twenty-eighth. Under Slocum's command, the Fifth, Eleventh, and Twelfth corps marched up the Rappahannock to Kelly's Ford. Other Federal units made a demonstration at Falmouth. Except for Hooker's second in command, Couch—who was informed on the twenty-seventh—the Union corps commanders were not told of Hooker's plans until the evening of the twenty-eighth. During the day of the twenty-ninth, Couch's divisions had marched to United States Ford. By midnight of the twenty-ninth, Slocum's three corps were across the Rapidan, and could have pushed on further had Hooker ordered it. As Meade noted at the time, "we are across the river and

[16] 40 O.R., 236 ff., 859; 39 O.R., 256; C.C.W. (1865), I, 74, 116–18.
[17] Abner Doubleday, *Chancellorsville and Gettysburg* (New York, 1882), 3; Hooker to Lincoln, Apr. 27, 1863, Lincoln Papers; 39 O.R., 320, 696.

have outmanoeuvred the enemy, but we are not yet out of the woods." [18]

On April 27 and 28 Sedgwick's force had moved to a point near Franklin's old crossing, three and one-half miles below Fredericksburg. By the twenty-ninth four pontoon bridges were erected there, and by the thirtieth Sedgwick's First and Sixth Corps were across the river on the southwest bank, making feints. As Jackson showed few signs of attacking Sedgwick, Daniel E. Sickles' Third Corps was ordered from Stafford Heights on the night of the thirtieth to join Hooker on the right wing. The army commander on the thirtieth instructed Sedgwick to attack and destroy the force opposite him if the foe exposed a weak point; otherwise, he was merely to make a demonstration, or, if the enemy fell back, to pursue via the Telegraph and Old Richmond Stage roads. Sedgwick was informed that the force under Hooker's own command would "be on the heights west of Fredericksburg" by noon on May 1, or, if opposition was met, by the night of the first.[19]

In a well-conducted movement by Slocum, the Federal Fifth, Eleventh, and Twelfth corps reached Chancellorsville on the afternoon of April 30, while Couch's Second Corps was nearing that place from the north. At a little after 5:00 P.M., Hooker himself arrived at Chancellorsville. He then issued a congratulatory order to his troops, saying, "The enemy must either ingloriously fly or come out from behind his intrenchments and give us battle on our own ground, where certain destruction awaits him." The Federal leader proclaimed that "the rebel army is now the legitimate property of the Army of the Potomac. They may as well pack up their haversacks and make for Richmond. I shall be after them." [20]

Chancellorsville comprised only a brick mansion and a few outhouses which were located at an important road junction situated about one mile in from the eastern edge of an area known as the

---

[18] 40 *O.R.*, 262 ff., 554; 39 *O.R.*, *passim.*; Meade, *Life and Letters of Meade*, I, 370.

[19] 39 *O.R.*, 566; Bigelow, *Chancellorsville*, 230–31.

[20] 39 *O.R.*, 171; *B. & L.*, III, 157; *C.C.W.* (1865), I, 27.

Wilderness. This difficult, tangled region of second-growth black oak and pine extended some ten miles north and south and about fourteen miles east and west. There was a small 300-yard open space to the west of the brick Chancellor house, but such clearings were scarce. Hooker had set up a telegraph line running from United States Ford to Falmouth, from the terminals of which messages were relayed by flag signals or couriers.[21]

The first Federal troops arrived at Chancellorsville at 2:00 P.M. on April 30. Meade and Pleasonton urged Hooker to press on eastward out of the confining Wilderness, especially since a captured Confederate dispatch indicated that Lee knew of the Union concentration at Chancellorsville. But Hooker said that the following morning—May 1—would be "sufficiently early to move on Fredericksburg," a decision that he later admitted was unfortunate. The General was in excellent spirits when he turned in for the night, and well he might have been. His movement and campaign thus far had been magnificently handled, and even though he erred by stopping so soon at Chancellorsville, he was still master of the situation at that moment. He had definitely outgeneralled Lee. "The enemy is in my power," Hooker gloated, "and God Almighty cannot deprive me of them." On the morning of the thirtieth, Lee learned that Hooker had split his huge army and that half of it was already in his rear near Chancellorsville. Undaunted, the Confederate chieftain determined to strike the Federal force of some 72,000 at Chancellorsville with the bulk of the Southern army, while Early with some 10,000 troops would try to contain Sedgwick at Fredericksburg. Nonetheless, the odds were very heavily in favor of the Union commander.[22]

By early morning of May 1, Sickles' Third Corps had arrived in the Chancellorsville area, and was left there as a general reserve. It

[21] Swinton, *Army of the Potomac*, 277, 281; 39 *O.R.*, 217.
[22] 40 *O.R.*, 304–305; Bigelow, *Chancellorsville*, 216, 221–23, 234–35; 39 *O.R., passim.;* B. & L., III, 157, 173–75; Theodore A. Dodge, *The Campaign of Chancellorsville* (Boston, 1881), 53; Walker, *Second Corps,* 218; Morse (ed.), *Welles's Diary,* I, 335–36.

was not until 11:00 A.M. that Hooker pushed his forces eastward from Chancellorsville toward Fredericksburg. However, a Confederate division had arrived on April 30 at a strong position near Tabernacle Church, had entrenched a three-mile line there running perpendicular to the roads upon which the Federals were marching, and was joined on the morning of May 1 by the bulk of Jackson's corps. By a little before 1:00 P.M., Hooker's marching forces were emerging from the forests of the Wilderness when the enemy troops were spotted to the east near the church. The Nationals had reached a good defensive position, with room to maneuver, and with open ground in front for their superior artillery to do execution. The blue troops on the River Road to the left were within a short distance of opening up Banks's Ford on the Confederate right flank—the ford by which the two wings of the Union army could support each other. Light skirmishing ensued.[23]

Hooker was astonished when he heard that Lee was actually confronting him with the intention of fighting. "When I gave the order to General Sedgwick," Hooker testified after the battle, "I expected that Lee would be whipped by manoeuvre." The Union leader, it seems, could not divest his mind of these preconceptions, nor provide for unexpected contingencies. So at 1:00 P.M. he committed a serious blunder: he suddenly ordered his forces, then facing the enemy, to withdraw back into the Wilderness and to fall back to their previous positions around Chancellorsville, and he stuck to this decision in the face of vociferous contrary opinions voiced by many of his best generals. He then sent a dispatch to Butterfield, at Falmouth, saying that he had "hope the enemy will feel emboldened to attack me." Couch, among others, indicates that the army commander had lost his mental and emotional balance, and declares that he "retired from [Hooker's] presence with the belief that my commanding general was a whipped man." Hooker was not drunk at the time, nor at any other time during the campaign or battle,

---

[23] Geer, *Campaigns of the Civil War*, 212–13; *C.C.W.* (1865), I, 44, 124–25; *B. & L.*, III, 217, 218; 39 *O.R.*, 198, 506; 40 *O.R.*, 324, 328; Doubleday, *Chancellorsville*, 11, 13; Walker, *Second Corps*, 220–21.

although perhaps it would have been better had he continued in his habit of consuming considerable quantities of alcohol. As to his sudden loss of nerve at this crisis of the campaign, the Union commander frankly admitted to Abner Doubleday shortly after the battle, "Doubleday . . . for once I lost confidence in Hooker, and that is all there is to it." Meanwhile, throughout May 1, below Fredericksburg, Sedgwick, in light of Hooker's orders, did little more than make a demonstration.[24]

By nightfall on May 1, Hooker had assembled the bulk of the forces with him in a somewhat convex line of about five miles in length around Chancellorsville, facing mostly southward. Lee took up a position generally perpendicular to the Orange Turnpike, facing chiefly westward. Hooker realized that his right flank, comprising Howard's Eleventh Corps, was in the air, but Howard cavalierly refused some reinforcement that Fighting Joe offered him. Deducting losses, there were in the Chancellorsville area, at dusk on May 1, 47,626 Confederate troops, with 144 guns, as opposed to Hooker's 70,267 men and 208 guns. The superior Union artillery, however, could be used in this wooded country only to fire down the roads, or from several of the higher clearings, as at Fairview and Hazel Grove. At 8:45 that evening, Hooker wired Butterfield, "I think the enemy in his desperation will be compelled to attack me on my own ground. . . . I am all right." To Couch, Hooker declared, in reference to his withdrawal back into the Wilderness, "It is all right, Couch, I have got Lee just where I want him; he must fight me on my own ground." Despite his error in pulling back to Chancellorsville, Hooker still dominated the military situation on the night of May 1–2, and victory was still within his reach.[25]

Both armies wielded the axe and spade during the night, strength-

[24] 39 O.R., 198–99, 558; 40 O.R., 322–51; DeTrobriand, *Army of the Potomac*, 436–37; B. & L., III, 159, 161, 170; Doubleday, *Chancellorsville*, 14, 15; C.C.W. (1865), I, xlix, 15, 31, 37, 73, 149; Rhodes, *History of the United States*, IV, 264 n.

[25] Doubleday, *Chancellorsville*, 16–17, 19; 107 O.R., 1034; B. & L., III, 161.

ening their fieldworks. Hooker knew that he had, in the main, a strong position, and Lee saw that a frontal attack on it would be suicidal. But, at their famous last meeting, Lee and Jackson, having learned that Hooker's right flank was in the air, decided to move Stonewall with 32,000 men across the front of the Union army and assail Howard's corps on its right flank on the turnpike, although the whole plan constituted one of the gravest gambles in military history. As Doubleday avers, "nothing short of utter blindness on the part of the Union commanders could make it successful." [26]

Meantime, at 1:55 A.M. on May 2, Hooker drew up an order to Sedgwick to take up all his bridges at Franklin's crossing and to move Reynolds' First Corps at once to Chancellorsville. This directive did not reach Sedgwick until 5:25 A.M. Reynolds was pushed up the left bank of the Rappahannock, crossed the river at United States Ford, and moved to the rear of the Chancellorsville position. At 9:30 A.M., Hooker sent a message to Butterfield to be relayed to Sedgwick in which he instructed Sedgwick to assail the enemy at Fredericksburg if there was a likelihood of success. Hooker added that, as to Sedgwick's attack, "it must be left to his discretion." [27]

Starting early on the morning of May 2, Jackson embarked on his circuitous march across Hooker's front and around to a point just west of Howard's right flank on the Orange Turnpike. For several hours, Jackson's force was plainly seen by Sickles' Federal troops at Hazel Grove, and this information was sent to Hooker—who could see the clouds of dust himself—at his headquarters at the Chancellor house. The Union commander then spread out a map on his cot, and, according to John W. De Peyster, while examining it, mused aloud as follows: "It can't be a retreat; retreat without a fight? That is not Lee. If not retreat, what is it? Lee is trying to flank me." So, at 9:30 A.M., Hooker sent an order—which was repeated—to Howard, urging him to throw out his pickets and to

[26] *C.C.W.* (1865), I, 56–57; 40 *O.R.*, 328–30; Doubleday, *Chancellorsville*, 21.
[27] 39 *O.R.*, 558; Bigelow, *Chancellorsville*, 277.

prepare to receive an attack from the west on his right flank. He urged him to place "heavy reserves" in position to meet such an assault. Howard, however, did little, although he assured the army commander that he was strengthening his right flank. While this probably put Hooker more at ease, he was still responsible for not having reserves within supporting distance of the Eleventh Corps. Still, he justifiably felt that he had given sufficient warning to Howard, and asserted that the Federals "had eighty chances in a hundred to win." [28]

Jackson's forces did not get into position to smite Howard until after 5:30 P.M. And as the hours passed quietly away on May 2, with Sickles nipping at the rear of the southward-moving enemy force at Catherine Furnace, Hooker came to believe that the Confederates were retreating toward Gordonsville. Showing this belief, he directed Howard's reserve brigade to assist Sickles. Of course, Hooker's best move would have been to order a general advance of his entire command. At 4:00 P.M., he ordered Sedgwick to "capture Fredericksburg . . . and vigorously pursue the enemy," adding, "we know the enemy is flying, trying to save his trains." [29]

As the day wore on, Howard, and, to a lesser extent, Hooker, received numerous warnings that Jackson was getting into position to attack in heavy force the right flank of the Eleventh Corps. But Howard foolishly rebuffed all these warnings in a very curt manner. At a little before 6:00 P.M., Jackson's massed forces struck Howard's exposed right flank a crushing, irresistable blow. Howard admitted that he was utterly surprised by the assault, the first indication of which was the rush of game through his lines. Despite heroic but ineffective personal efforts by Howard and others to rally the men, a panic and rout at once ensued, most of the Eleventh Corps soldiers fleeing rapidly eastward down the pike toward Chancellorsville, and suffering in all 2,412 casualties. Despite harsh words which were hurled at Howard's men, no troops on earth, deployed as were

[28] 39 O.R., 231, 386, 651, 652; B. & L., III, 218, 219 n, 220.
[29] Bigelow, *Chancellorsville*, 277, 289; 39 O.R., 386–87, 490; C.C.W. (1865), I, 45; 40 O.R., 363; Dodge, *Chancellorsville*, 75.

these Federals, could have withstood Jackson's thunderbolt. Howard later acknowledged the debacle of his corps to have been his own fault.[30]

Back at army headquarters at Chancellorsville, the sounds of battle were not heard, due to unusual atmospheric conditions. Hooker and several of his staff officers were sitting relaxed on the porch of the mansion at 6:20 P.M., when one of the aides, going down to the pike and peering westward through his field glasses, exclaimed, "My God, here they come!" as the demoralized blueclad fugitives appeared streaming eastward toward the mansion. The General leaped onto his horse and rode forward to try to rally the defeated troops. He ordered his own former division into the breach, shouting to his men, "Receive them on your bayonets, boys! Receive 'em on your bayonets!" and "Don't fire a shot—they can't see you." The situation looked serious for Hooker by 9:00 P.M. But the falling of darkness, the serious wounding of Jackson by his own men, and a stubborn defense by a small number of Union troops checked the brilliantly successful Confederate onslaught. Greatly alarmed at his plight, Hooker in effect abandoned Sickles' corps to its fate; but this force cut its way out to safety.[31]

At 9:00 P.M. on the same evening, Hooker sent an order to Sedgwick to cross the river at Fredericksburg and to press on toward Chancellorsville, arriving there in Lee's rear by dawn. This directive—received at 11:00 P.M. by Sedgwick—stated that "between us we will use him up." Sedgwick began his march northward on the Richmond road at once, but the night was very dark, the road was rough, and some enemy resistance was encountered—all of which slowed down the march. Actually, of course, this order—to reach the vicinity of Chancellorsville by daybreak on the third— was impossible to comply with.[32]

[30] *B. & L.,* III, 163, 183–84, 196–97, 220 n; Doubleday, *Chancellorsville,* 22–32; Augustus C. Hamlin, *Battle of Chancellorsville . . .* (Bangor, Maine, 1896), 55–63, 143–45.

[31] *C.C.W.* (1865), I, 45, 57; *B. & L.,* III, 163–64; Rusling, *Men and Things,* 303.

[32] *B. & L.,* III, 165, 225; 40 *O.R.,* 365.

A valuable reinforcement reached Hooker between 1:00 and 2:00 A.M. on May 3. This was the arrival near the field of Reynolds and his splendid First Corps. However, Hooker's attention was diverted to Hazel Grove, which Sickles correctly insisted was the key to the battlefield. Not until dawn had broken did the Union commander visit this point; and when he did, he promptly ordered Sickles to evacuate it and fall back to Fairview. Confederate guns, soon emplaced at Hazel Grove, would dominate the Federal artillery position at Fairview and lob projectiles onto the Chancellor house and grounds, as well as enfilade other parts of the Union line. Hooker, nonetheless, persisted in this unfortunate order, and, with a few aides, silently and thoughtfully strolled back from Hazel Grove to Chancellorsville. Although the third of May was a beautiful clear day, Hooker was quite downcast, possibly due to his being outgeneralled by Lee. As James Ford Rhodes states, "Hooker, despondent at the rout of the Eleventh Corps, was in mind and nerve unfit for the exercise of his great responsibility. The story of Sunday the third of May is that of an incompetent commander in a state of nervous collapse confronted by an able and alert general." [33]

At daylight on May 3 the entire Confederate line advanced to the attack. Hooker was seen by Couch to be leaning against a pillar on the south veranda of the Chancellor mansion, "looking anxious and much careworn." He issued few orders during the day, and let his corps and division commanders do the fighting without any plan. With the battle increasing in tempo, Hooker rode around his lines. Shortly after 7:30 A.M., he cantered up to a knot of men huddled over the prostrate figure of a dead man, and demanded, "Who have you there, gentlemen?" When told that it was his friend and present commander of his old division, Major General Hiram G. Berry, Hooker leaped to the ground and, with tears in his eyes, kissed his

[33] John C. Ropes and William R. Livermore, *Story of the Civil War* (New York, 1894–1913), I, 172–73; 39 *O.R.*, 390; 40 *O.R.*, 249; Bigelow, *Chancellorsville*, 344–46; Rhodes, *History of the United States*, IV, 462.

forehead, and cried, "My God, Berry, why was this to happen? Why was the man on whom I relied so much to be taken away in this manner?"[34]

Returning to his headquarters about 9:15 A.M., Hooker sent off the following sanguine but inaccurate message to Butterfield at Falmouth: "Communicate with Sedgwick. We are driving the enemy and only need him to complete the job." Then, at approximately 9:30 A.M., the Union commander was the victim of a freak accident. He was standing on the south porch of the Chancellor house, leaning against a column with his right hand, and receiving a paper from a courier below with his left, when a Confederate twelve-pounder solid shot struck the pillar against which he was resting. The concussion waves ran up the column and down his arm to his body, sending him sprawling. Then, as he was reeling under the impact of that blow, part of the severed pillar fell heavily upon his head and the right part of his chest and body, knocking him senseless for a few moments. The rumor quickly spread that he was dead. But he soon revived somewhat, and pluckily insisted upon being placed on his horse to show the men that he was all right. The pain was so great, however, that after he had ridden but a short distance to the rear (north), he was laid upon a blanket on the ground and given some brandy. He was then helped back on his mount, and just as he vacated the blanket, an enemy solid shot struck the center of it, exactly where he had been lying seconds before. Hooker was taken to his new headquarters near Chandler's, where he lay down for a time in a tent filled with whiskey bottles and officers who were using them. He was able, with great will power, to ride around a bit later in the day and show himself to the troops; but, although he looked fairly normal, he was suffering severe paroxysms of pain. Throughout the day, and for the next several days, he alternated between moving in a

[34] 39 O.R., 851; B. & L., III, 166; Edward K. Gould, *Major General Hiram G. Berry* (Rockland, Maine, 1899), 267; *The Equestrian Statue of Major General Joseph Hooker*, 164.

semi-stupor and sleeping a great deal. In later life, the General's right side was paralyzed.[35]

Immediately after Hooker had reached the tent near Chandler's and was lying down, he was visited by Reynolds and Meade, who eagerly requested permission to attack the exposed Confederate left flank with their 37,000 fresh troops; but the Union commander unwisely refused this entreaty. At approximately 10:00 A.M., Hooker's second in command, Couch, was called to his tent. As Couch describes the incident, "Raising himself a little as I entered, he said: 'Couch, I turn the command of the army over to you. You will withdraw it and place it in the position designated on this map,' indicating a prepared line to the north of Chancellorsville." It was obvious that Hooker was unfit to exercise command, but as Colonel William R. Livermore rather cruelly remarks, "There is, in fact, no reason to suppose that his orders would have been wise, even if he had not been struck." [36]

By about noon, after some five hours of heavy fighting, the Federals had been pushed back a bit on most parts of their line. The Chancellor mansion—now a smoking ruin, fired by artillery shells—was relinquished by the Nationals at 10:00 A.M., soon after they had lost Fairview. Shortly after noon on May 3, Lee was preparing to resume the offensive with his 34,000 bone-weary soldiers against Hooker's 75,000 troops, strongly ensconced behind formidable fieldworks, when his attention was called to his rear, where, it was learned, Sedgwick had carried Marye's Heights at 11:00 A.M. and was about to advance westward along the turn-pike toward the Confederate rear. So Lee determined to turn back, defeat Sedgwick first, and then return to deal with Hooker. And Sedgwick aided Lee by delaying his march toward Salem Church

[35] Bigelow, *Chancellorsville*, 363–65; B. & L., III, 167, 215, 220–21; C.C.W. (1865), I, 36, 70; Frank Allaban, *John Watts De Peyster* (New York, 1908), II, 133.

[36] Doubleday, *Chancellorsville*, 53–54; 39 O.R., 307, 508; C.C.W. (1865), I, 46; B. & L., III, 167–70; Livermore, *Story of the Civil War*, I, 211–12.

until 3:00 P.M., thereby giving the enemy time to place troops in position at the church to check him. The Federals attacked at 4:00 P.M., and although the battle raged until dark, Sedgwick could make little progress, though it had cost him almost 25 per cent of his men since morning. Hooker, later, was angry at Sedgwick's alleged dilatoriness. The Union commander sent Gouverneur K. Warren back to Sedgwick during the night of May 3–4 with the brusque message that he would have to rely upon himself, and not upon Hooker and the main body, for deliverance from his predicament.[37]

At 1:45 on the afternoon of May 3, Hooker, still in great pain, had telegraphed Lincoln somewhat vaguely as follows: "We have had a desperate fight yesterday and today which has resulted in no success to us, having lost a portion of two lines, which had been selected for our defense. . . . We may have another turn at it this P.M. I do not despair of success. . . . We will endeavor to do our best. My troops are in good spirits. We have fought desperately today. No general ever commanded a more devoted army."[38]

May 4 was a hot day, and it passed without action on Hooker's part. Seeing that Fighting Joe would remain listless, Lee went with additional troops to attack Sedgwick at Salem Church, leaving Stuart—who had taken over from Jackson—with 25,000 men to contain Hooker's 75,000 north of Chancellorsville. At midday the Union commander informed Sedgwick that he expected "to advance tomorrow." Since Lee was not ready to attack until 6:00 P.M. on the fourth, Sedgwick crossed to safety at Banks's Ford.[39]

At midnight on the night of May 4–5, Hooker convened a council of war of most of his corps commanders. After voicing his preference for retreating to the north side of the river, he and Butterfield left the room. Three of the Federal corps commanders

[37] 39 O.R., 203, 560, 801, 826, 844, 888; B. & L., III, 222; C.C.W. (1865), I, 48.
[38] C.C.W. (1865), I, 225.
[39] 40 O.R., 379, 418–19; B. & L., III, 223 n, 231; C.C.W. (1865), I, 148.

voted to advance and attack; two, to retreat. When Hooker re-entered the room and was told the vote, he nonetheless said he would assume the responsibility to withdraw across the river. Meade wrote his wife that "poor Hooker himself, after he had determined to withdraw, said to me, in the most desponding manner, that he was ready to turn over to me the Army of the Potomac; that he had had enough of it, and almost wished he had never been born." Later, Hooker sneered unfairly and erroneously at his corps commanders for lack of intestinal fortitude at this time. But it was his own decision to give up the game and retreat back to the north side of the river from a very strong position which Lee was about to attack—and it was one of Hooker's most fateful and grievous errors in a campaign filled with blunders on his part. Late on May 5, despite heavy rain, Hooker, leaving behind him fourteen guns, 20,000 stand of arms, and his dead and wounded, began crossing his army to the north side. The Army of the Potomac moved to take up its old position again at Falmouth.[40]

On the afternoon of May 6 Hooker tried to explain his defeat to Lincoln. He said that he had recrossed the river to the north bank because the army had none of its supply trains with it. Inaccurately, he continued: "Above, I saw no way of giving the enemy a general battle with the prospect of success which I desire. Not to exceed three corps, all told, of my troops have been engaged. For the whole to go in, there is a better place at hand." But the President saw through Hooker's alibis. When he received the news of the withdrawal, he was in the greatest despair, and, with ashen face, cried out, "My God, my God, what will the country say! What will the country say!"[41]

When the Union army had retired to Falmouth, Hooker issued an order, claiming falsely that he had captured 5,000 prisoners (the

[40] B. & L., III, 171, 182; Doubleday, Chancellorsville, 67–68; C.C.W. (1865), I, 134; Meade, Life and Letters of Meade, I, 373; Walker, Second Corps, 250–51.

[41] Bigelow, Chancellorsville, 435; Brooks, Washington in Lincoln's Time, 57.

actual number was less than 2,000) and had inflicted 18,000 other casualties on Lee. Actually, the casualties suffered by Lee in the campaign and battle of Chancellorsville, where he was on the offensive most of the time, amounted to 1,649 killed; 9,106 wounded; 1,708 missing—a total casualty figure of 12,463. Hooker lost 1,606 men killed; 9,762 wounded; 5,919 missing—a total loss of 17,287. This shows that the fighting was close and hard, and that, so far as the armies and soldiers themselves were concerned, it was not too uneven a contest.[42]

After Chancellorsville, Hooker and Lincoln exchanged a number of messages. On May 7 the General declared that he preferred to operate on the line of the Rapahannock, that he had a plan which he would reveal only if Lincoln requested it, and that the merit of his new scheme was that the movements of all his corps would be directly under his own personal supervision—in other words, within his own field of vision. He said later to the President that he planned to cross the Rapahannock on May 14. But, in a conference in Washington, Lincoln stated that, since the Confederates had consolidated their position and communications at Fredericksburg, he was not now eager for Hooker to begin a general offensive. Also, the Union commander was losing the support, not only of the men in the ranks, but also of many of his highest-ranking subordinates, as well as of members of the cabinet. He was, ironically, beginning to reap the harvest he had sowed against Burnside. "If Hooker had been killed by the shot which knocked over the pillar that stunned him," said Lincoln, "we should have been successful." The President, however, apparently agreed to give the General one more chance.[43]

By late May, 1863, Hooker correctly perceived and predicted that Lee was about to embark on a second invasion of the North.

[42] 39 O.R., 171; Bigelow, *Chancellorsville*, 473 ff.; B. & L., III, 237, 238.
[43] Meade, *Life and Letters of Meade*, I, 373–85; J. G. Nicolay to T. Bates, May 10, 1863, Nicolay Papers, Div. of MSS, Library of Congress; 40 O.R., 438, 505; C.C.W. (1865), I, 50; Morse (ed.), *Welles's Diary*, I, 336.

He had 100,000 men as against the gray leader's 75,000. Seeing by June 5 that a major enemy advance was underway, Hooker suggested to the President the amalgamation of the several small, scattered Union forces in northern Virginia, in Maryland, and in the Potomac region. He urged that he be permitted to cross the Rappahannock and assail Lee's rear at Fredericksburg. But Lincoln recommended that Hooker stay on the north side of the river and fight defensively there. Halleck concurred in the President's suggestion. Actually, with Lee's army strung out from the Valley to Fredericksburg, Hooker's scheme had much to recommend it. The cavalry arms of the two hosts clashed indecisively at Brandy Station on June 9 in the greatest cavalry battle of the war. On the following day, Hooker foolishly proposed to Lincoln to ignore Lee's developing invasion of the North for awhile, and move the Army of the Potomac directly to Richmond, while the administration collected a force to contain Lee's thrust. Then, Hooker would bring his army *back* from Richmond, cross the Potomac, and capture Lee's army! Lincoln wisely rejected this hare-brained idea, and urged the General to concentrate on Lee's army and not Richmond.[44]

Finally, on June 13, Hooker began moving northward from Falmouth, keeping his army roughly between Lee and Washington. The President urged him to assail the elongated Confederate army at some point, but Hooker doubted the wisdom of such a move, and would do it only if Lincoln gave him a positive order to do so. Meanwhile, the incompetent Major General Robert H. Milroy, in command of 10,000 Federals, was crushed at Winchester by Confederate Richard S. Ewell, and lost 4,000 men captured, plus much equipment. Ewell crossed the Potomac and seized Sharpsburg and Hagerstown. By the seventeenth, the Shenandoah Valley had been cleared of Union troops. Fortunately, the National garrison of 11,000 men under John C. French had been moved out of the town

[44] Doubleday, *Chancellorsville*, 78; 40 *O.R.*, 543; *B. & L.*, III, 241 n, 263, 269, 440; 43 *O.R.*, 30, 34–35; *C.C.W.* (1865), I, 158 ff.; Basler (ed.), *Collected Works of Lincoln*, VI, 257.

of Harper's Ferry—itself a death-trap—and assembled on Maryland Heights, overlooking the ferry.[45]

Another sore point for the National military effort was the enmity existing between Hooker and Halleck. Reflecting on this, the
Army of the Potomac commander said in a telegram, "You have
long been aware, Mr. President, that I have not enjoyed the confidence of [Halleck] . . . and I can assure you so long as this
continues we may look in vain for success, especially as future
operations will require our relations to be more dependent upon
each other than heretofore." Lincoln's reply on June 16 must have
chilled Hooker to the marrow: "To remove all misunderstanding,
I now place you in the strict military relation to General Halleck of
a commander of one of the armies to the general-in-chief of all the
armies. I have not intended differently, but as it seems to be differently understood I shall direct him to give you orders, and you to
obey them." In a private covering letter, the President tried to convince Hooker that Halleck was not hostile to him and would support him. Perhaps unknown to Hooker, the President was being
bombarded at this time with requests to supersede him with
McClellan.[46]

On June 22 and 23 Hooker went to Washington for a conference
with Lincoln, Stanton, and Halleck. Apparently, the status of the
Federal garrison near Harper's Ferry was discussed, with Halleck
and Lincoln wanting to keep the garrison there, and Hooker wishing it to be attached to his field army. Returning to his command,
Hooker, in a preposterous telegram to Washington on June 24,
asserted, "The yeomanry of [Maryland and Pennsylvania] should
be able to check any extended advance of that column [Ewell's],
and protect themselves from their aggression." On June 25 the
army commenced crossing the Potomac at Edward's Ferry. But
Hooker had been angered when, about this time, he had to refute

[45] Doubleday, *Chancellorsville*, 94–97; 43 *O.R.*, 45; *C.C.W.* (1865), I,
163.
[46] 43 *O.R.*, 45; *C.C.W.* (1865), I, 163; Basler (ed.), *Collected Works of
Lincoln*, VI, 276, 280–82; 45 *O.R.*, 391, 409, 436.

a rumor, called to his attention by Lincoln, that he had sneaked back into Washington, ostensibly for some drinks at his usual loitering spots.[47]

On June 26 Hooker had his headquarters at Frederick, where three of his corps were concentrated; his other units were at Boonsboro and Middleton. His plan now was to move forward with his units fanwise toward the Susquehanna, with his left wing under Reynolds covering the Federal flank in the event that A. P. Hill's or Longstreet's corps turned eastward, while Slocum with his Twelfth Corps and the garrison of Harper's Ferry menaced Lee's rear. The wisdom of Hooker's policy in desiring to assail the enemy's communications is shown by the fact that, when apprised by a scout on the late evening of June 28 that the Union army was at Frederick in a threatening position to his rear, and not south of the Potomac as believed, Lee immediately turned back from Carlisle, Harrisburg, and York to concentrate at Cashtown, at the eastern foot of the South Mountain range.[48]

Thus far, on the whole, Hooker's march northward had been ably conducted. Yet he was despondent, probably feeling that Washington expected too much of him with the force he then had. So, on June 27 he asked permission to add the garrison of some 11,000 at Harper's Ferry to his mobile army, accurately warning of its danger of capture there. The General was then with French's garrison near Harper's Ferry, awaiting Halleck's reply to French in consequence of some orders which Hooker had given to the latter. Halleck's telegram arrived, and it instructed French to "pay no attention to General Hooker's orders." Fighting Joe was humiliated at the tone of the General-in-Chief's message, and remarked to an officer at the ferry who had said that a combat seemed imminent, "Yes, but I shall not fight the battle. Halleck's dispatch severs my connection with the Army of the Potomac." [49]

[47] Morse (ed.), *Welles's Diary*, I, 340; 45 *O.R.*, 271; 43 *O.R.*, 55–56; *C.C.W.* (1865), I, 290–91.

[48] Doubleday, *Chancellorsville*, 115, 116, 221.

[49] *C.C.W.* (1865), I, 173, 292; 43 *O.R.*, 58–60; Swinton, *Army of the Potomac*, 321–23.

Meantime, in Washington, Lincoln and others had decided that the army should not be permitted to fight another general battle under Hooker's leadership. But to appease the Radical faction, which was pro-Hooker, only a voluntary resignation from the General would be accepted, so "severe measures had to be resorted to in order to wring from him that tender of resignation." And Hooker co-operated. He appealed to Lincoln and Stanton over Halleck's head to get them to reverse the decision and let him annex the Harper's Ferry garrison, but to no avail. So, believing that he was not being allowed to maneuver his army as he felt proper, Hooker submitted his resignation as commander of the Army of the Potomac on June 27, telling Lincoln that Halleck was undermining his plans and operations. Chase, and perhaps Stanton, vainly beseeched him to reconsider and remain in command.[50]

Although Nicolay and Hay doubt whether Hooker, in his request to be relieved, intended to be taken at his word, Colonel Theodore B. Gates perhaps comes closer to the truth when he writes, "It is by no means improbable that General Hooker made use of the refusal of Halleck to extend his authority over French, to relieve himself of a command that he felt he was unequal to. A commander who believed himself entirely able to handle his army would not have resigned for so paltry a reason, on the eve of a battle which presented an opportunity to wipe out the stigma of a recent disgraceful defeat." And it is difficult not to agree with Swinton's assessment of Hooker's deportment: "Provoking as was the behavior of General Halleck, the conduct of General Hooker cannot be accounted noble or high-minded. A truly lofty sense of duty would have dictated much long-suffering, in a conjuncture of circumstances amid which the success of the campaign might be seriously compromised by the sudden change of commanders." [51]

[50] See Geer, *Campaigns of the Civil War*, 236–37; 43 *O.R.*, 59; *C.C.W.* (1865), I, 150–51, 176–78; Pierce, *Sumner*, IV, 142; *B. & L.*, III, 270.
[51] Nicolay and Hay, *Abraham Lincoln*, VII, 226; Gates, *Ulster Guard*, 404; Swinton, *Army of the Potomac*, 323.

While Hooker was waiting on June 28 for the reaction to his letter of resignation, he directed Slocum to move with his Twelfth Corps to Harper's Ferry, unite there with the Union force on Maryland Heights, cut Lee's communications, and, in co-operation with Reynolds' force, operate on Lee's rear. But Lincoln had made the decision to accept Hooker's resignation, and to supplant him with Meade, of whom the President had thought highly ever since Chancellorsville. Meade was a Pennsylvanian who, said Lincoln to Stanton, "will fight well on his own dunghill." [52]

On the night of June 27–28, Lieutenant Colonel James A. Hardie was sent from Washington with the orders announcing the change of command. Going first to Meade's headquarters, Hardie delivered the orders to that general, who was not only astonished, but who protested loudly that it was unfair to his esteemed senior, Reynolds, whom Meade felt was a better man for the job. Hardie and Meade then went to Hooker's tent. Meade and his predecessor had not been on good terms since Chancellorsville, but the meeting was fairly cordial. There was one flare-up from Hooker when Meade voiced surprise at Hooker's announcement of the dispositions of his units, Meade thinking the corps too scattered. Hooker was a bit chagrined, having construed favorably the delay in the administration's answering his letter of resignation; and Meade's nerves were overstrung. However, in the company of Butterfield and Hardie, the two men made the switch in command rather smoothly. In the main, both behaved well in this trying moment. [53]

On the evening of the twenty-eighth, Hooker took leave of his generals and some of the troops drawn up near his headquarters. He shook hands with his chief officers and staff, "laboring in vain to stifle his emotions. The tears rolled down his cheeks." Many of his subordinates were deeply moved. "Amid many a 'God bless you, General,'" Hooker got into a wagon with Hardie and rode off to the railroad depot, the first step of his trip to Baltimore,

[52] Heintzelman's Journal, June 28, 1863; George C. Gorham, *Life and Public Services of Edwin M. Stanton* (Boston, 1899), II, 98–100.

[53] *B. & L.,* III, 240–42; Meade, *Life and Letters of Meade,* II, 3.

where he was to report for orders. Hooker's farewell address to the army was one of his finest orders of the war, and assisted in the smooth transition of the command from himself to Meade, whom Hooker praised highly. As Hunt comments, "Many welcomed [Meade's] advent—some regretted Hooker's departure. All thought the time for the change unfortunate, but accepted loyally." [54]

As directed, Hooker went to Baltimore for orders. After waiting there three days, with no orders forthcoming, he took a trip to Washington. In the capital, Halleck had him arrested—an act which, while technically legal, was most shabby and ungracious, and showed Halleck's true feelings toward Hooker. The latter was soon released. [55]

From June 28, 1863, to September 24, 1863, Hooker was in Baltimore awaiting orders. Now that he was no longer to be an army commander during the war, his usefulness as primarily a combat officer once more asserted itself. In the fall of 1863 the Union Eleventh and Twelfth corps were consolidated into the Twentieth Corps, and Hooker was named to lead it. He participated quite ably in the hard fighting around Chattanooga—especially at Lookout Mountain—and in Sherman's 1864 campaign for Atlanta. He was brevetted major general in the regular army for his services at Chattanooga. However, upon the death of Major General James B. McPherson and the naming of Howard, Hooker's junior, to succeed McPherson on July 27, 1864, in command of the Army of the Tennessee, Fighting Joe asked to be relieved of duty, declaring, "Justice and self-respect alike require my removal from an army in which rank and service are ignored." [56]

From September 28, 1864, to July 5, 1865, Hooker commanded the Northern Department, with headquarters at Cincinnati. He then headed the Department of the East, with headquarters at New York, from July 8, 1865, to August 6, 1866. In 1865 he had been married to Olivia Groesbeck. From August 23, 1866, to June 1,

---

[54] B. & L., III, 241–43, 270; Stine, Army of the Potomac, 445.
[55] See Nicolay and Hay, Abraham Lincoln, VII, 227 n.
[56] 76 O.R., 273; Cullum, Biographical Register, I, 537–38.

1867, Hooker was in Detroit as commander of the Department of the Lakes. He retired from the army as a major general on October 15, 1868, due to partial paralysis stemming from his injury received at Chancellorsville. He died at Garden City, New York, on October 31, 1879.[57]

[57] Cullum, *Biographical Register*, I, 538; *D.A.B.*, IX, 198.

CHAPTER SEVEN

George G. Meade

> There is probably no other battle of
> which men are so prone to think and
> speak without a conscious reference to
> the commanding general of the victori-
> ous party, as they are regarding Gettys-
> burg.
>
> —*General Francis A. Walker*

MAJOR GENERAL GEORGE GORDON MEADE MIGHT WELL BE
called the "Old Reliable" of the Army of the Potomac, and his appearance would not belie that sobriquet. Had he been dressed in
civilian clothes, he would have passed for a college professor or a
clergyman. He was tall and spare, standing about six feet in height,
and, though slightly stooped, was nonetheless graceful and soldierly
in appearance. His sad eyes, although slightly sunken, were full and
large and swift in their movements. A frequent frown helped cause
the bagginess under his eyes. Since he generally wore spectacles, for
near-sightedness, he was known as "Old Four Eyes." His slightly
curling dark brown hair was, in 1863, heavily streaked with gray,
and he was balding. Meade had skin as white and antique-looking
as parchment. His head was small, his forehead high, and his voice
refined. He usually wore the regulation wide-brimmed army officers' black hat, but with the crown uncreased and the brim pulled
down all around. Mounted astride "Baldy," his favorite charger,
the General was recognized as a fine horseman.[1]

[1] George H. Gordon, *A War Diary of . . . the Great Rebellion . . .*
(Boston, 1882), 141; Meade, *Life and Letters of Meade*, I, 227 n; Isaac R.
Pennypacker, *General Meade* (New York, 1901), 2, 3; Gates, *Ulster
Guard*, 404–405.

The pre-Civil War career of Meade was largely that of army service. Cadiz, Spain, was the scene of his birth on December 31, 1815. He was the eighth in a family of ten children, his father being an American citizen and businessman. His early education was gained in Philadelphia, Washington, and Baltimore. In 1831 Meade entered West Point, and graduated nineteenth in the 1835 class of fifty-six cadets. He served for one year as a lieutenant in the Florida War, and then resigned from the army in October, 1836, to accept a job as assistant engineer of the Alabama, Florida, and Georgia Railroad. Meade then served as an assistant engineer for the government, and was engaged in surveying work. In 1840 he was married to Margaretta Sergeant, who bore him six children.[2]

In 1842 Meade rejoined the army as a lieutenant. In the Mexican War he participated in the campaign of Zachary Taylor, and won a brevet at Monterey. Except for the siege of Vera Cruz, he did not participate in Winfield Scott's campaign for Mexico City. Routine army assignments followed, except for service in the Seminole War. In 1856 Meade was promoted to captain, for fourteen years of continuous service. From then until the Civil War he worked on surveys for the army along the lakes and northern border. When the war came Meade was named a brigadier general of volunteers, and commanded one of the brigades in the famed Pennsylvania Reserves. In this capacity he participated in McClellan's Peninsula campaign, and was severely wounded in the arm, side, and back at Glendale—an injury which kept him away from the army for forty-two days. He returned in time to fight with Pope at Second Manassas and, as a division and temporary corps commander, with McClellan at South Mountain and Antietam. In November, 1862, Meade was named major general of volunteers, and was engaged as a division commander with Burnside at Fredericksburg, and as a corps commander in Hooker's Chancellorsville campaign.[3]

Meade's personal traits and characteristics added up to a fairly

[2] Cullum, *Biographical Register*, I, 472; *D.A.B.*, XII, 474–76.
[3] *D.A.B.*, XII, 474–76; Meade, *Life and Letters of Meade*, I, 298–300.

impressive sum total. As Nicolay and Hay state, "He had none of the genial gifts and graces which were in different ways possessed by all of those who had preceded him in command." He was not by nature, but rather by diligence to duty, a soldier. Politically, he was a conservative; but he kept out of politics, and had few powerful political friends. Meade was prone, on occasion, to self-pity and self-deprecation. Just before the Chancellorsville campaign, he even indulged in an uncharacteristic and amateurish attempt to curry favor with the Lincolns during their visit to the army in camp, "in view of the vacant brigadier-ship in the regular army." [4]

Meade was quite touchy and concerned with getting his just rewards and positions. He was nervous, dyspeptic, and irascible. Commented Grant: "He was unfortunately of a temper that would get beyond his control, at times, and make him speak to officers of high [and low] rank in the most offensive manner. No one saw this fault more plainly than he himself, and no one regretted it more. This made it unpleasant at times, even in battle, for those around him to approach him even with information." He was quick to make amends, however. Nonetheless, some of his troops called him "a damned old goggle-eyed snapping turtle." Then, too, Meade allowed responsibility to weigh him down and make him impatient and careworn. At times, in his rage at malefactors, he could deal out corporal punishment with his own hands, but he was usually just. He lacked the ability to win and inspire his soldiers with his personality, although he was a man of commanding presence. [5]

In the big picture, however, these were but petty and usually insignificant shortcomings in a character that was essentially fine and

[4] Nicolay and Hay, *Abraham Lincoln*, VII, 226–27; John P. Nicholson (ed.), *Pennsylvania at Gettysburg* . . . (Harrisburg, 1914), II, 953; Glenn Tucker, *High Tide at Gettysburg* . . . (Indianapolis, 1958), 74; Meade, *Life and Letters of Meade*, I, 241, 265, 364.

[5] Pennypacker, *General Meade*, 7; Meade, *Life and Letters of Meade*, I, 278, 308, 310–11; Grant, *Memoirs*, II, 538–39; Young, *Around the World with Grant*, II, 299; A. F. Hill, *Our Boys* . . . (Philadelphia, 1864), 368, 391–93; Joseph Warren Keifer, *Slavery and Four Years of War* (New York, 1908), II, 25; Bradford, *Union Portraits*, 84–85.

useful. "Few men," writes Gamaliel Bradford of Meade, "have built their lives upon a broader foundation of dignity, of purity, of courage, of faithful devotion to duty." Cecil Battine declares that Meade "was just, modest, and courteous; determined though cautious, and a good judge of men. He was personally brave and had the moral courage which is so often lacking to men who never fear for their own safety." Major General David M. Gregg asserts that "in his intercourse with those he knew but slightly, [Meade] was reserved; with his intimates he was pleasantly familiar. . . . For the rights of others he had the highest regard, and would not brook interference with his own." Another point that bears noting is the one that Bradford elucidates: "What is most of all attractive about Meade's intellectual make-up is his absolute candor. There is no bluff, no swagger, no pretension, no attempt to throw dust in the eyes of posterity. He debates and analyzes his own mistakes just as freely and frankly as he would those of another." "General Meade was emphatically a Christian soldier," comments another Union officer, "and never forgot his responsibility to a higher power. Caring more for the approval of his conscience than for the applause of his countrymen, no consideration could ever swerve him from the course he knew to be right; and on more than one occasion he deliberately chose to endanger his own reputation, rather than risk unnecessarily the lives of his men." He was quick to praise others who were deserving, while he seldom blew his own horn. McClellan thought Meade, above all, "an honest man." [6]

Meade impressed people as having a great deal of brains and a well-balanced mind. He was a lover of music and the arts. Charles A. Dana writes that "he was an intellectual man, and agreeable to talk with when his mind was free, but silent and indifferent to everybody when he was occupied with that which interested him."

[6] Bradford, *Union Portraits*, 76–77, 93; Cecil Battine, *The Crisis of the Confederacy* . . . (London, 1905), 148; Nicholson (ed.), *Pennsylvania at Gettysburg*, II, 962; James Grant Wilson and Titus Munson Coan (eds.), *Personal Recollections of the War of the Rebellion* . . . (New York, 1891), 1; Pennypacker, *General Meade*, 6–7; Meade, *Life and Letters of Meade*, I, 276–77, 311, 328, 337, 363; *M.O.S.*, 140.

As Meade said of himself, "I am a *juste milieu* man [a middle-of-the-roader]." Welles reports that, while Meade's brother officers "speak well of him . . . he is considered rather a 'smooth-bore' than a rifle." He was a master of logistics—a field in which a number of Civil War commanders were not proficient. Another strong point of Meade's is that described by Isaac Pennypacker: "With the exception possibly of General Humphreys, he was the only officer connected with the Army of the Potomac who, awakened at any hour of the night . . . could tell on the instant from the sound of the firing exactly what troops were engaged. . . . He had an extraordinary eye for topography. He saw a whole section of country from an indication." [7]

But what opinion did the great Confederate captain opposed to him hold of the new Union leader? Lee believed that Meade was abler than Hooker, but thought that this might be counterbalanced by the danger and difficulty of changing commanders at such a crucial and awkward moment. At the time that Meade took command, a man at Lee's headquarters spoke of the "Old Snapping Turtle" as a mediocre soldier. But the gray leader instantly contradicted this opinion. Meade, he said, was a general of ability and intelligence, who was conscientious and painstaking. Lee thought that the National commander would not make any major blunders when facing the Southern army, and that he would convert any mistakes committed by Lee into Federal advantages. This, then, was the two-star general on whose shoulders squarely rested the Union cause. As J. G. Randall expresses it simply, "Accepting extraordinary prerogatives conferred by the President, [Meade] prepared to fulfill a responsibility unexcelled, unless by Washington [and one is impelled to add, also, McClellan], in previous American history." [8]

[7] Bradford, *Union Portraits*, 73, 74; Meade, *Life and Letters of Meade*, I, 162, 361; Dana, *Recollections*, 189–90; Morse (ed.), *Welles's Diary*, I, 349; Pennypacker, *General Meade*, 5–6, 8.

[8] Long, *Memoirs of Lee*, 274; Robert Stiles, *Four Years Under Marse Robert* (New York, 1903), 227–28; Randall, *Lincoln the President*, II, 275.

When Hardie arrived at Meade's headquarters on the night of July 27–28, 1863, he found the forty-seven-year-old general half-dressed, sleeping on an army cot. Meade's first reaction to Hardie's unexpected appearance at his tent was that he was about to be placed under arrest, since he and Hooker had not been on good terms since Chancellorsville. When Hardie informed him of his elevation to the army command, Meade, as noted previously, did everything but show elation at the promotion. Then, accompanied by his staff and Hardie, Meade rode through the darkness to Hooker's headquarters. When the group arrived there near dawn, Hooker was found inside his tent, awake and in full uniform, and the change in command was made. So little did the North, in general, know about Meade that one New York paper referred to him as an "official accident." However, upon learning of Meade's promotion, Reynolds declared emphatically that the command had "fallen where it belongs." [9]

"There were few better soldiers in that army than Meade," writes Samuel Adams Drake; "none, perhaps, so capable of uniting it at this particular juncture, when unity was so all-important and yet so lamentably deficient." The same writer goes on to say that "it is difficult to see how a better selection could have been made, all things considered. In point of fact, there was no one of commanding ability to appoint; but every man in the army felt that Meade would do his best, and that Meade at his best would not fall far behind the best in the field. Meade could not become the idol of his soldiers, like Lee, because he was not gifted by nature with that personal magnetism which attracts men without their knowing why; but he could and did command unhesitating obedience and respect." [10]

Immediately upon being named to the command, the ill-at-ease

[9] Frederick W. Seward, *Reminiscences of a War-Time Statesman* . . . (New York, 1916), 238–41; Pennypacker, *General Meade*, 130–31; Nicolay and Hay, *Abraham Lincoln*, VII, 226; New York *Independent*, July 9, 1863; *B. & L.*, III, 242.

[10] Samuel Adams Drake, *The Battle of Gettysburg, 1863* (Boston, 1892), 42, 43.

Meade received instructions from Halleck which granted him a much wider latitude of discretion and autonomy than Hooker had been given. "All forces within the sphere of your operations," wrote the General-in-Chief, "will be held subject to your orders. Harper's Ferry and its garrison are under your direct orders." While Meade would not receive detailed directions from the administration as to how to maneuver his army, he must, said Halleck, remember always that the Army of the Potomac was not only an offensive sword but was also a defensive shield that must ever cover Washington and Baltimore, even while operating aggressively against Lee.[11]

The able and trusted Reynolds joined Meade shortly after the latter had taken over from Hooker near Frederick, and helped the new commander work out the plans for the next few days. When Meade took over, on June 28, his corps were in and around Frederick. Lee's divisions were at York and Carlisle, and between Chambersburg and Cashtown; while Stuart's cavalry corps was off on an ill-advised raid around the Union army. Meade showed sagacity in concluding that Lee would soon be found concentrated on the eastern side of the South Mountains, but he could still not determine whether the Southern leader intended to move against Harrisburg, Philadelphia, or Baltimore and Washington. The Union commander determined to act prudently. He later testified that "General Hooker left the camp in a very few hours after I relieved him. I received from him no intimation of any plan, or any views that he may have had up to that moment. And I am not aware that he had any, but was waiting for the exigencies of the occasion to govern him, just as I had to be subsequently." In his official report, he declared that, when he took command, "the Confederate army . . . [was] estimated at over 100,000 strong of all arms," while his own Army of the Potomac aggregated "a little over 100,000" present for duty.[12]

[11] 43 O.R., 61.
[12] McClure (ed.), *Annals of the War*, 62, 207; Doubleday, *Chancellorsville*, 114; Meade, *Life and Letters of Meade*, II, 28, 355; *C.C.W.* (1865), I, 329–30.

Meade spent most of June 28 in familiarizing himself with the dispositions of his army units and in bringing forward his cavalry divisions of John Buford, David M. Gregg, and Judson Kilpatrick. He retained Butterfield—who was to prove more loyal to Hooker's memory than to the interests of his new superior—as chief of staff because the latter possessed, necessarily, a great deal of information about the army which Meade or a new staff chief could not have time to acquire for some time.[13]

"Though Hooker's plan," writes Drake, "promised excellent results here, Meade was fearful lest Lee should cross the Susquehanna and take Harrisburg before he could be stopped. To prevent this the army must be pushed forward. Meade, therefore, at once drew back the left wing toward Frederick, thus giving up that plan in favor of one which he himself had formed; namely, of throwing the army out more to the northeast, the better to cover Baltimore from attack, should that be Lee's purpose, as Meade more than suspected. Selecting Westminster, therefore, as his base from this time forth, and the line of Big Pipe Creek, a little to the north of that as his battleground, Meade now set most of the army in motion in that direction, leaving Frederick to the protection of a rear-guard." It might be contended that Meade's scheme was a more menacing one to Lee than Hooker's, and, by following his own plan, the new Federal commander could still shift to a movement against Lee's communications via Mechanicstown and Hagerstown.[14]

Near midnight on June 28, learning that the National army was north of the Potomac, Lee issued orders recalling Ewell and directing a concentration at the eastern foot of the South Mountains at Cashtown—eight miles west of the roadhub of Gettysburg—where he hoped Meade would be induced to attack him. Lee had the advantage in that he had no less than seven roads upon which to concentrate his forces, while Meade had but three. At 10:00 A.M. on June 29, Meade telegraphed Halleck, "My endeavor will

[13] B. & L., III, 270; Pennypacker, General Meade, 136–37; 45 O.R., 462.
[14] Drake, Battle of Gettysburg, 48–49; B. & L., III, 407.

be in my movements to hold my force well together, with the hope of falling upon some portion of Lee's army in detail." On the thirtieth, he said he had "received information that the enemy are advancing, probably in strong force, on Gettysburg. . . . It is the intention to hold this army pretty nearly in the position it now occupies until the plans of the enemy shall have been more fully developed." So the initiative remained with Lee.[15]

In order to cover his contemplated occupation of the Pipe Creek line, just north of the Mason and Dixon line, Meade ordered Buford's cavalry division to Gettysburg on June 30, with the First and Eleventh corps to follow there a day later. The Third Corps was ordered to Emmitsburg. Reynolds was placed in command of the Left Wing of the army, comprising the First, Eleventh, and Third corps; Slocum was named to command the Right Wing, made up of the Twelfth and Fifth corps. Buford took his cavalry division through Gettysburg on the thirtieth, and deployed his two brigades about one mile west of town along McPherson Ridge, facing west. His appreciation of the terrain about the town had a far-reaching effect in precipitating the battle at Gettysburg. And Gettysburg was important for Lee because it was the first point in his eastward march across the South Mountains where roads led southward toward Baltimore and Washington. About midday of the thirtieth, one of Harry Heth's Confederate brigades, in search of shoes, approached Gettysburg along the Chambersburg pike from the west, spotted Buford's blue riders entering the town from the south, and withdrew westward some five miles.[16] It is surprising, however, that Meade had received no information, until late on the thirtieth, of Lee's position. It was not in Meade's power now to concentrate his army in one day at Gettysburg. As Drake declares, "By endeavoring to cover too much ground his army had been

[15] Alexander, *Military Memoirs*, 378–79; 43 *O.R.*, 66–68; see Warren W. Hassler, Jr., "The First Day's Battle of Gettysburg . . ." (Master's thesis, University of Pennsylvania, 1951), 27 n; 45 *O.R.*, 414–17.

[16] 45 *O.R.*, 414–17, 420; William F. Fox, *New York at Gettysburg* (Albany, 1900), I, 9; Nicholson (ed.), *Pennsylvania at Gettysburg*, I, 24.

dangerously scattered." But Meade correctly assumed that, if confronted by the entire Federal army, Lee, being on hostile soil, would have to attack if Meade stayed on the defensive.[17]

On the night of the thirtieth, with his headquarters at Taneytown, Meade ordered the First and Eleventh corps to march to Gettysburg on July 1 and the Third Corps to move to within supporting distance. Except for the Sixth Corps, which was to remain far in the rear at Manchester, the other Federal units were to march northward in the general direction of Gettysburg. In this missive, issued on the evening of June 30, Meade stated that the Confederate "movements indicate a disposition to advance from Chambersburg to Gettysburg." Therefore, believing that Lee was moving to the latter point, and knowing that several of his own corps were moving there also, it is possible that Meade really suspected that a battle could well take place at that point. From Taneytown he wrote to his wife at this time, "All is going well. . . . I continue well, but much oppressed with a sense of responsibility and the magnitude of the great interests entrusted to me. Of course, in time I will become accustomed to this. . . . Pray for me." [18]

The first day of July, 1863, dawned misty and rainy, but as the morning advanced, the sun was to come out and the weather to become intensely hot and humid. A gentle wind blew from south to north. About 8:00 A.M. or a little later, Buford's 3,200 Union cavalrymen on McPherson Ridge, a mile west of Gettysburg, encountered the first attacks of Heth's 7,500 graycoats coming from the west along the Chambersburg pike. An extremely stubborn contest, which varied in fortune, ensued until late afternoon, with fresh troops arriving on both sides. Ignoring his earlier message which had stated that Gettysburg was indicated as Lee's point of concentration, Meade sent the following dispatch to Halleck at 7:00 A.M. on July 1: "The point of Lee's concentration and the nature of the country, when ascertained, will determine whether I

[17] 45 O.R., 420; Drake, Battle of Gettysburg, 53; B. & L., III, 273.
[18] 45 O.R., 416, 418; Meade, Life and Letters of Meade, II, 15–16, 18.

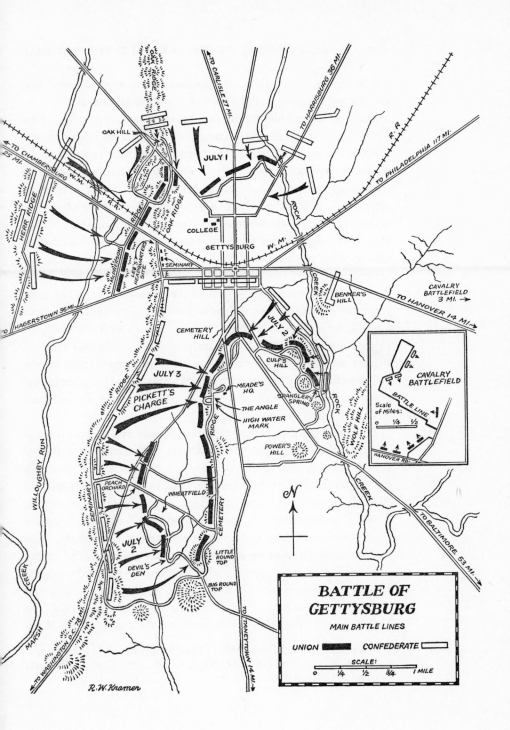

TO CARLISLE 27 MI.

TO HARRISBURG 36 MI.

R. R.

TO PHILADELPHIA 117 MI.

OAK HILL

JULY 1

OAK RIDGE

TO CHAMBERSBURG 25 MI.

W. M.

R. R.

HERR RIDGE

McPHERSON

OAK RIDGE

ROCK

COLLEGE

LEE'S HEADQUARTERS SITE

GETTYSBURG

W. M.

SEMINARY

CREEK

BENNER'S HILL

CAVALRY BATTLEFIELD 3 MI. →

TO HAGERSTOWN 36 MI.

TO HANOVER 14 MI.

CEMETERY HILL

JULY 2

CULP'S HILL

CAVALRY BATTLEFIELD

BATTLE LINE

JULY 3

RIDGE

PICKETT'S CHARGE

MEADE'S HQ

THE ANGLE

HIGH WATER MARK

SPANGLER'S SPRING

ROCK

WOLF HILL

Scale of Miles

0   ¼   ½

PEACH ORCHARD

WHEATFIELD

SEMINARY

POWER'S HILL

HANOVER RD.

WILLOUGHBY RUN

RIDGE

JULY 2

DEVIL'S DEN

CEMETERY

LITTLE ROUND TOP

BIG ROUND TOP

N

CREEK

TO BALTIMORE 53 MI.

MARSH

CREEK

TO WASHINGTON D.C. 78 MI.

TO TANEYTOWN 14 MI.

BATTLE OF GETTYSBURG

MAIN BATTLE LINES

UNION ▬▬▬   CONFEDERATE ▭▭▭

SCALE:

0   ¼   ½   ¾   1 MILE

R. W. Kramer

attack or not. Shall advise you further today, when satisfied that the enemy are fully withdrawn from the Susquehanna." [19]

Early on the morning of the first, Meade issued his so-called "Pipe Creek Circular" to his corps commanders. "It is no longer my intention," he said, "to assume the offensive until the enemy's movements or position renders such an operation certain of success. If the enemy assume the offensive, and attack, it is [my] intention, after holding them in check sufficiently long, to withdraw the trains and other *impedimenta*," and to pull the army back to the Pipe Creek line. About the same time that he issued this circular, Meade wrote privately to Reynolds, saying that if the Confederates concentrated north or west of Gettysburg, he was not sufficiently versed with the nature of the ground there "to judge of its character for either an offensive or defensive position." Reynolds left Marsh Creek after 6:00 A.M. on July 1 for Gettysburg with the vanguard of the First Corps, and it is quite probable that he had received neither the Pipe Creek Circular nor the private note from Meade. As he rode along the Emmitsburg road near Gettysburg, Reynolds' trained military eye could not have helped but notice the dominant Cemetery Ridge heights south of the town.[20]

Owing to the direction of the wind, Meade at Taneytown could not hear the firing from the field west of Gettysburg as Buford contended with the enemy. At 9:00 A.M. or a little later, Reynolds arrived on the field at the Seminary. His first infantry units relieved Buford's hard-pressed cavalrymen at approximately ten o'clock. About this time Reynolds sent to Meade the latter's first positive information of Confederate movements about Gettysburg. This communiqué, received by Meade about noon, stated, "The enemy is advancing in strong force, and I fear he will get to the heights beyond the town before I can. I will fight him inch by inch, and if driven into the town I will barricade the streets, and hold him back as long as possible." Upon receiving the message, Meade ex-

[19] See Hassler, "First Day's Battle of Gettysburg," *passim;* 43 *O.R.,* 70.
[20] 45 *O.R.,* 458–60; *C.C.W.* (1865), I, 348, 355; *B. & L.,* III, 290; Doubleday, *Chancellorsville,* 124–25.

GENERAL IRVIN McDOWELL

GENERAL GEORGE B. MCCLELLAN

GENERAL JOHN POPE

GENERAL AMBROSE E. BURNSIDE

GENERAL JOSEPH HOOKER

GENERAL GEORGE G. MEADE

General Ulysses S. Grant

THE ARMY OF THE POTOMAC IN TRIUMPHAL MARCH

claimed, "Good! that is just like Reynolds; he will hold on to the bitter end." But at approximately 10:15 A.M., the Union forces suffered a grievous loss when Reynolds was killed instantly in McPherson Grove. Perhaps an hour later, Howard, next in rank to Reynolds on the field, assumed command of the battle and of the Left Wing from the skillful Abner Doubleday, who had temporarily taken over when Reynolds fell. Meade later termed his friend Reynolds his "noblest" and "bravest" general.[21]

Just before receiving Reynolds' last message from the field, Meade had sent the following dispatch to Halleck: "The news proves my advance has answered its purpose. I shall not advance any, but prepare to receive an attack, in case Lee makes one," at Pipe Creek. "If I am not attacked, and I can from reliable intelligence have reason to believe I can attack with reasonable degree of success, I will do so; but at present, having relieved the pressure on the Susquehanna, I am now looking to the protection of Washington and fighting my army to the best advantage." But, receiving Reynolds' message a few moments later, Meade wired Halleck at 1:00 P.M., "The enemy are advancing in force on Gettysburg, and I expect the battle will begin today."[22]

The timely arrival of the First Corps held the Confederates in check to the west and northwest of Gettysburg, in bitter fighting, well into the afternoon. Howard himself arrived on the field about 11:15 A.M., and the bulk of his Eleventh Corps at 12:30 P.M. The Eleventh Corps was clumsily posted in a weak position on the plain to the north of the town, facing northward. However, Howard was unable to connect the left of the Eleventh Corps with the right of the First Corps on Oak Ridge. His deployment was completed by 2:00 P.M. Then the Eleventh Corps soldiers were soon struck in front and, irresistibly, on their right flank by Jubal Early, who arrived before 3:00 P.M. from the northeast.[23]

[21] McClure (ed.), *Annals of the War,* 210; Meade, *Life and Letters of Meade,* II, 35–36; Hassler, "First Day's Battle of Gettysburg," 62, 65, 67.
[22] 43 *O.R.,* 70–72.
[23] Hassler, "First Day's Battle of Gettysburg," *passim.*

Meanwhile, at Taneytown, Meade had received, between noon and 1:00 P.M., information of the death of the esteemed Reynolds and of the serious nature of the Federal situation on the field. At 1.10 P.M. the Union commander directed Hancock to go himself to Gettysburg to assume command of the National forces there. The orders given Hancock were, "If you think the ground and position there a better one to fight a battle under existing circumstances, you will so advise the General [Meade], and he will order all the troops up." Meade's decision to send Hancock to Gettysburg while he himself stayed at Taneytown shows perhaps that he had not as yet given up completely his intention to fight at Pipe Creek, and for this reason, probably, he held the Second Corps at Taneytown when it arrived there at 11:00 A.M. During the afternoon Howard had sent two messages to Meade in which he had stated, in a shockingly careless and erroneous way, that Doubleday's First Corps had given way and was retreating; and, without bothering to verify these allegations, Meade unfortunately relieved Doubleday of that command, and placed Newton at the head of the "Black Hats" on July 2.[24]

Back at Gettysburg, the Eleventh Corps, placed in a hopeless position, was defeated by 4:00 P.M. and forced to retreat through the streets of the town toward Cemetery Hill. The First Corps was still making its magnificent fight on McPherson Ridge and Oak Ridge, but the collapse of the Eleventh Corps exposed the flank and rear of Doubleday's men to enemy attack. After a stand at the Seminary, they too were obliged near 4:30 P.M. to fall back through Gettysburg to the heights south of town. Several thousand Federals were captured in the streets.[25]

Hancock arrived at Cemetery Hill near 4:30 P.M., just as the disorganized Federals began to reach this strategic height in their retreat through town. After an unfortunate public altercation with

[24] Meade, *Life and Letters of Meade,* II, 36–37, 55; 45 *O.R.,* 461; *B. & L.,* III, 288.

[25] Hassler, "First Day's Battle of Gettysburg," 118 ff.; 44 *O.R.,* 317, 445.

Howard over who was in command—in which Howard did not behave well—Hancock, with Howard's assistance, helped to rally the defeated troops. By 5:00 P.M. the bulk of these soldiers were posted on Cemetery Hill and, soon after, on Culp's Hill on the Union right. By 6:00 P.M. the Twelfth and Third corps had arrived in the area. Not until this time was a Confederate attack possible, and now it was too late to be made successfully because the Federal position was manned and secure. Then, with Howard's concurrence, Hancock selected the field as a most suitable one in which to contest the remainder of the decisive battle. He sent two aides to Meade with word of his determination to hold the field until dark, thereby allowing Meade to make the big decision as to whether to order up the whole army or pull the troops at Gettysburg back to Pipe Creek. Hancock himself left Cemetery Hill at dark (about 8:00 P.M.) for Taneytown to report in person to Meade.[26]

When Hancock arrived, Meade informed him that, having received reports from others at the front, he had already ordered all his troops to Gettysburg even *before* the delivery of Hancock's message via the two orderlies. Before Hancock's arrival at Taneytown, Meade had sent him this message at 6:00 P.M.: "It seems to me that we have so concentrated, that a battle at Gettysburg is now forced on us, and that if we can get up our people and attack with our whole force, tomorrow, we ought to defeat the force the enemy has." At 6:00 P.M. Meade had wired the General-in-Chief in Washington, ". . . I see no other course than to hazard a general battle" at Gettysburg, although "circumstances during the night may alter this decision." General Walker states that Meade's determination to risk battle on July 2, with the Fifth and Sixth corps still distant, with the First and Eleventh corps badly shattered, and in the face of Lee's swifter concentration, was "as brave as it proved fortunate; and his inspired rashness, like that of

[26] Doubleday, *Chancellorsville*, 143; B. & L., III, 284, 285, 288.

Reynolds in the morning, was of the kind which wins battles and saves states." [27]

The fighting at Gettysburg on July 1, 1863, was as desperate as any of the war. A total of some 18,000 Federal effectives had been pitted against approximately 28,000 Confederates. Total Union casualties amounted to over 9,000, while Lee—who had himself arrived near the battlefield in mid-afternoon—suffered losses of about 8,000 men. As Confederate General E. P. Alexander states, "Whether from discipline, or the inspiration of home, the fighting done by the Federal brigades was of the best type." "They gave way, it is true, after hard fighting," reports Howard, "yet they secured and held the remarkable position which . . . contributed to the grand results of July 2d and 3d." Many of the Southern brigades were so decimated from the ferocious fighting on the first that they were of little use to Lee on the second or third. [28]

At approximately 11:00 P.M. on July 1, Meade, accompanied by Hunt, rode forth from Taneytown toward Gettysburg. The Union commander arrived at the cemetery gate at approximately 1:00 A.M. on July 2. There, under the full moon and the tall pines surrounding the cemetery, he conferred with Slocum, Howard, Warren, and Sickles. It was noted that the army commander was gaunt and hollow-eyed from anxiety, responsibility, and loss of sleep. Meade was informed by these generals that the position then held by the Federal units on the field was quite strong, to which "he replied that he was glad to hear it, for it was now too late to leave it." Then, accompanied by Hunt, Howard, and others, Meade toured his lines by moonlight, posted troops, and issued orders to alter some dispositions. This activity took up the whole night, and was still going on at daybreak. [29]

[27] Meade, *Life and Letters of Meade*, II, 37–41; 43 *O.R.*, 71–72; *B. & L.*, III, 291, 409.

[28] Hassler, "First Day's Battle of Gettysburg," 187, 195–96; Alexander, *Military Memoirs*, 384; *B. & L.*, III, 289.

[29] *B. & L.*, III, 291, 293, 294; Meade, *Life and Letters of Meade*, II, 62, 392; Howard's *Autobiography*, I, 424; McClure (ed.), *Annals of the War*, 211.

The crucial day of the Battle of Gettysburg—July 2—dawned sultry and hot. By noon all of Meade's army would be on the field except the Sixth Corps, which would not arrive until near mid-afternoon. "The rapidity with which the army was assembled," writes Hunt, "was creditable to it and to its commander." As to Meade's own activities until late morning, the same commentator declares that the General "was busily engaged personally or by his staff in rectifying his lines, assigning positions to the commands as they came up, watching the enemy, and studying the field." Schurz was struck that morning by the army commander's "long-bearded, haggard face, his care-worn and tired look." "His mind," Schurz continues, "was evidently absorbed by a hard problem. But this simple, cold, serious soldier with his business-like air did inspire confidence. The officers and men, as much as was permitted crowded around and looked up to him with curious eyes and then turned away not enthusiastic but clearly satisfied." Meade personally placed the Second Corps in position, about 6:00 A.M., on Cemetery Ridge, to the left of the First Corps remnants, south of Cemetery Hill.[30]

On the left of the Union line, John W. Geary's division, which had occupied the lower-lying part of the ridge just north of Little Round Top and the slope of this hill itself, was withdrawn at 5:00 A.M. and moved to Culp's Hill on the Federal right, there to join the rest of the Twelfth Corps. About an hour later, Sickles was directed to move his Third Corps into the position evacuated by Geary. However, the orders from Meade were somewhat vague, Geary did not leave any of his officers behind to point out the position he had occupied, and Sickles was somewhat dense in compre-hending the purport of Meade's orders. The Union commander, preoccupied with his right, unfortunately did not visit his left during the morning of the second, and Sickles was left to his own mediocre devices. At approximately 7:00 A.M., Sickles' troops began oc-cupying the ground on lower Cemetery Ridge. The left of the Third Corps rested at the northern foot of Little Round Top, and the

[30] B. & L., III, 294, 295; Schurz, *Reminiscences*, III, 20.

right of the corps connected with the left of the Second Corps. Meade's qualified orders to Sickles as to Little Round Top were that he should occupy it "if practicable." [31]

Meade was so convinced that Lee meant to attack the Federal right that he spent most of the morning in that area and refused to give much credence to warnings that the enemy was massing to assail the Union left. The Federal left was Meade's strategic flank —should the Confederates turn it they would be between the Army of the Potomac and Baltimore-Washington—and he should have paid more attention to it. The National commander wanted to beat Lee to the punch and attack from his right with his own Twelfth, Fifth, and possibly Sixth, corps. But when Slocum and Warren, after a personal reconnaissance, reported the ground unfavorable for such an enterprise, Meade reluctantly agreed, and then considered shifting his Fifth Corps from its position on the Baltimore pike near his right over to the Union left, and attacking from that wing. Meade apparently was not anxious to fight defensively on the Cemetery Ridge position, and seemed to fear an enemy turning or flanking movement against it. He even went so far as to have Butterfield collect information about roads, communications, and so forth, in the event that a Federal retreat after a battlefield defeat would be necessary. Butterfield later erroneously stated that Meade wanted to retreat before the battle began in earnest on the second.[32]

Sickles was dissatisfied with the low, wooded nature of Cemetery Ridge just to the north of Little Round Top, but he failed to station even a small unit of his Third Corps on the hill itself, where he could better observe the enemy's movements. Before noon he went to Meade's headquarters to ask about his position. Meade repeated to him that he expected him to occupy the ground held the night before by Geary, and claims that he pointed out Little Round

[31] Livermore, *Story of the Civil War,* II, 434 n; Meade, *Life and Letters of Meade,* II, 63–64; *B. & L.,* III, 416 ff.; Powell, *Fifth Corps,* 517–19.
[32] Swinton, *Army of the Potomac,* 343; *C.C.W.* (1865), I, 377, 424 ff.; Meade, *Life and Letters of Meade,* II, 181; *B. & L.,* III, 297, 416.

Top as the point where Sickles was to station his left. Near noon a scouting force which Sickles had sent out into the Pitzer Woods to the west of Little Round Top reported that heavy lines of gray-clad infantry had been seen some 300 yards west of Seminary Ridge. Hunt then accompanied Sickles to the higher ground at the Peach Orchard, west of Little Round Top on the Emmitsburg road, where the Third Corps commander now wanted to station his troops. Hunt noted the strong and weak points of the proposed new position, but suggested to Sickles that he secure Meade's authority first before moving his troops out to it. Hunt returned to Meade's headquarters and told the General that he should himself examine the Peach Orchard area before allowing Sickles to move out to it. Meade agreed to do so.[33]

At two o'clock in the afternoon, however, on his own authority, Sickles left his old and shorter line on Cemetery Ridge, where both of his flanks had been secure, and moved his corps of some 10,000 men out to a new and longer line at the Peach Orchard, where his flanks would be in the air. Part of his corps, between the Devil's Den and the Peach Orchard, faced southward, while the other part, stretching northward from the orchard along the Emmitsburg road, faced westward—leaving a weak point at the salient at the Peach Orchard. Sickles did not even notify Hancock, originally on his immediate right, of his movement. He "failed," notes Walker, "properly to subordinate his views and acts to the instructions of his commander." However, Sickles' dubious advance to the Emmitsburg road did impel Lee to attack him directly instead of undertaking solely a turning movement against the Round Tops which might well have been more dangerous to the Federals than a more direct assault. Also, Longstreet would be obliged to expend time and casualties in driving the Nationals back from this advanced position before he could launch an attack on the main Union line on Cemetery Ridge—which line the Federals had to hold at all costs.[34]

[33] Powell, *Fifth Corps,* 519, 556–57; *B. & L.,* III, 301–303.
[34] Meade, *Life and Letters of Meade,* II, 75, 77, 78.

Just before convening a council of war of his corps commanders at his headquarters, Meade sent this dispatch to Halleck at 3:00 P.M.: "The army is fatigued. I have today, up to this hour, awaited the attack of the enemy, I having a strong position for defensive. I am not determined on attacking him till his position is more developed. . . . If not attacked, and I can get any positive information of the position of the enemy which will justify me in so doing, I shall attack. If I find it hazardous to do so, or am satisfied the enemy is endeavoring to move to my rear and interpose between me and Washington, I shall fall back to my supplies at Westminster. . . . I feel fully the responsibility resting upon me, but will endeavor to act with caution." [35]

At the corps commanders' conference in mid-afternoon, Meade directed Major General George Sykes to move his Fifth Corps to the left, since the Sixth Corps was arriving and could be held in the rear on the Baltimore pike as a reserve. The conclave was ending when Sickles rode up. Hearing the sudden barking of Longstreet's guns opposite the Peach Orchard, Meade excused Sickles from dismounting, told him to return to his corps, and said that he would join him shortly. Then the Union commander rode to his left for the first time that day to see about the posting of the Fifth Corps, and to inspect Sickles' lines. [36]

Meade arrived near 4:00 P.M. at the Third Corps position. He had sent Warren to Little Round Top to investigate the situation from that point. Meade was surprised and pained to see that Sickles was out at the Peach Orchard and not back on Cemetery Ridge, and told him that he was too far out. Sickles said that his new position could be reinforced by Meade, and that it was on elevated ground. "General Sickles," replied Meade, "this is in some respects higher ground than that to the rear; but there is still higher ground in front of you, and if you keep on advancing you will find constantly higher ground all the way to the mountains." When the Third

[35] *Ibid.*, 72; *B. & L.*, III, 349.
[36] 43 *O.R.*, 592; "Historicus," in New York *Herald*, Mar. 12, 1864; *B. & L.*, III, 416.

Corps leader said he would be happy to move his corps back to Cemetery Ridge, Meade declared, "I wish to God you could, Sir, but you see those people do not intend to let you." As if to emphasize Meade's point, Longstreet's attack on Sickles' lines began at that very moment. Meade told Sickles that he would reinforce him with the Fifth Corps and a division of the Second Corps, and that he could call on the artillery reserve for additional batteries. Then Meade rode back to his headquarters.[37]

The Federal army commander now directed most of the Twelfth Corps to hasten from the Union right to succor the hard-pressed left. As Pennypacker notes, "From the varying distances between them and the scene of conflict, it was impossible that all the reenforcements called for should arrive at the same time, and it was possible that each body of fresh troops upon arriving would encounter a confident and victorious enemy and be defeated in detail." Meanwhile, Warren performed an inestimable service when he moved troops from the Fifth Corps, going to the aid of Sickles, to Little Round Top just in time to save that vital knob from capture. However, at 6:00 P.M. Sickles was badly wounded, his weak salient at the Peach Orchard crushed in, the Devil's Den lost, and his lines forced back. Meade promptly galloped from headquarters to the left, and placed Hancock in command of the Third Corps. Brigadier General John C. Caldwell's division of the Second Corps arrived in the vicinity of the Wheatfield at 6:40 P.M., but it, too, was roughly handled by the Confederates, as were units of the Fifth Corps which were also thrown into the maelstrom in the Wheatfield and the surrounding woods.[38]

By 7:15 or 7:30 the situation was, for a time, critical for the Federals. But Meade was now on the ground on the Union left, anxious that the reinforcements he had ordered up would be

[37] McClure (ed.), *Annals of the War*, 211; "Historicus," *loc. cit.;* Meade, *Life and Letters of Meade*, II, 78–79, 82; *C.C.W.* (1865), I, 298, 299, 332, 377; 43 *O.R.*, 369; Powell, *Fifth Corps*, 520–21; *B. & L.*, III, 307 n–309 n.

[38] Pennypacker, *General Meade*, 173; Powell, *Fifth Corps*, 521–24; *B. & L.*, III, 307, 311.

properly placed and not all defeated in detail. He personally led Brigadier General Henry H. Lockwood's brigade forward into a gap in the Union lines. In this action Meade had his horse "Baldy" shot out from under him—although the animal later recuperated. The General then returned quickly and briefly to his headquarters, and while there ordered Newton to rush Doubleday's and Robinson's divisions into the gap which still remained to the left of the Second Corps. He then rode back to this gap, anxiously awaiting the arrival of these First Corps units. While waiting impatiently there, a Confederate line of battle approached menacingly, and Meade, in a reflex motion, drew his sword as if to try to stave off the attackers himself until the expected blue reinforcements arrived —a motion that was emulated by the few members of his staff with him. At the last moment, one of the commander's aides, spotting the expected reinforcements rushing up, shouted, "Here they come General! Here they come!" Waving his hat, Meade exhorted the troops, "Come on gentlemen!" "This way! This way!" he called, and led them forward into the breach against the enemy. In reply to someone's saying that at one time things seemed rather desperate, Meade heartily assented, saying, "Yes, but it is all right now." This action by Meade helped to establish, finally, a firm line which held steady behind Plum Run.[39]

Returning near dusk to Cemetery Hill to find it about to be attacked by the famed Louisiana "Tigers," Meade implored his artillerymen there as follows: "You must hold this position if it costs every man." After a severe hand-to-hand fight amongst the guns, the Confederates were repelled. After dark, Johnson's division, moving cautiously against the Federal works on Culp's Hill, found only Brigadier General George S. Greene's brigade remaining there (the rest of the Twelfth Corps had been sent down to the Union left earlier in the day), and occupied some of the breast-

[39] Wilson and Coan (eds.), *Personal Recollections*, 25; 43 *O.R.*, 371; *B. & L.*, III, 409; Meade, *Life and Letters of Meade*, II, 88–89; Pennypacker, *General Meade*, 173.

works on the slope of the hill. Unfamiliar with the ground, and perhaps fearing an ambush, Johnson missed a chance to secure completely this important hill and threaten the supply trains and rear of the Federal position on Cemetery Ridge.[40]

"Thus ended the second day," comments Alexander, "and one is tempted to say that thus ended the battle of Gettysburg." Lee himself declared that, had he known that Meade could concentrate his entire army so effectively, he would never have assaulted the Union force, and he complimented Meade on this feat. General Walker writes of Meade that "few commanders ever showed more resolution in fighting a seemingly lost battle, advanced their reserves more promptly, or stripped other parts of their lines with less hesitation." "There was not," asserts Alexander, "during the war a finer example of efficient military command than that displayed by Meade on this occasion." Nonetheless, like its opponent, the Union army was badly wounded. Besides the First and Eleventh corps, the Third, Fifth, and parts of the Second and Twelfth corps had now been badly cut up, not to mention the fact that the Army of the Potomac had suffered some 10,000 casualties on the second, which, added to those of the first, totaled almost 20,000 men lost.[41]

In the famous council of war, held on the night of the second in the tiny front room of the Leister house, which was Meade's headquarters on the Taneytown road behind his center, the army commander said little as a general discussion ensued. Then a ballot was taken, and all the generals present voted to remain in position and await the attack of the enemy on the morrow. When the council was breaking up, Meade said to Brigadier General John Gibbon, then temporarily in command of the Second Corps, which occupied the Union center, "If Lee attacks tomorrow, it will be in *your front.*" When asked by Gibbon why he thought this, Meade

[40] Pennypacker, *General Meade,* 180; *B. & L.,* III, 317.

[41] Alexander, *Military Memoirs,* 393, 412; Fitzgerald Ross, *A Visit to Cities and Camps of the Confederacy* (Edinburgh, 1865), 80–83; *B. & L.,* III, 409, 410.

answered, "Because he has made attacks on both our flanks and failed, and if he concludes to try it again it will be on our center." [42]

The morning of July 3, 1863—the forenoon of one of the most momentous days in American history—dawned sunny and hot. At approximately 4:00 A.M., both sides advanced simultaneously on Culp's Hill and jousted with each other in a seven-hour battle for possession of the works on that important elevation. The Federal units involved were two divisions of the Twelfth Corps, and one brigade of the Sixth Corps. By 11:00 A.M. the Confederates were thrown back and retreated across Rock Creek, thereby ending the threat to that flank. This success on the Federal right, declare Wood and Edmonds, "broke up the plan of a combined attack and threw the whole burden of the fight on the [Confederate] central column [Pickett's force]." [43]

"During the morning," writes Meade's grandson, "while the attack . . . [at Culp's Hill] was in progress, General Meade remained on the far right of the line, occasionally riding to various parts of the field, reforming the troops and strengthening their positions." But the General had undergone a change of mind since he had talked with Gibbon at the council of war on the previous night. Now, at mid-morning of the third, he told Hancock that the foe would *not* attack his center, because Lee had seldom before assailed the center of a Federal army, because of the open field of fire there for the Union guns, and because Meade could quickly send reinforcements to his center from both wings. Rather, Meade felt now that Lee would again attack his left, where sizeable National forces—the Fifth, Sixth, and Third corps—were massed. However, only some eighty-eight Federal guns were in position from the Cemetery to Little Round Top to reply effectively to approximately 138 Confederate cannon which had been posted by Lee to prepare the way for the great infantry charge to be made by

[42] B. & L., III, 313–14, 412; C.C.W. (1865), I, 350–51; John Gibbon, *Personal Recollections of the Civil War* (New York, 1928), 140–45; 43 O.R., 13–14, 124–27; Doubleday, *Chancellorsville*, 185 n.

[43] B. & L., III, 369–70; Wood and Edmonds, *The Civil War*, 244.

15,000 troops under the leadership of Major General George E. Pickett.[44]

At a little after noon, Hancock, Alfred Pleasonton, Gibbon, and Newton, seated on stools, were consuming a luncheon of toasted bread, butter, potatoes, stewed chicken, cucumber pickle, coffee, and tea, when they were joined by Meade, who was provided with a cracker box on which to sit. The army leader declared again that if an enemy attack came, it would be against the Union left. By 1:00 P.M. Meade had returned to his headquarters at the Leister house when the greatest artillery bombardment ever seen on this continent was unleashed, and continued on the Confederate side for one hour and fifty minutes. The enemy fire was directed at the Federal center, and, while some damage was done, the Confederate gunners in general aimed too high. The result was that most of the projectiles passed over Cemetery Ridge and burst in the rear, with the area around Meade's headquarters being swept with a devastating fire which killed men and horses. According to Pennypacker, Meade "stood in the doorway as a cannon shot, almost grazing his legs, buried itself in a box standing on the portico by the door." Owing to the fear of flying splinters, Meade and his staff moved out of the tiny house, but only into the fenced yard between the building and the Taneytown road. There, Meade joked with his staff officers, who were edging their way around behind the shelter of the building. Then the General and his aides moved a few hundred yards south of the Taneytown road to a barn (where Butterfield was wounded by a shell fragment), because couriers could scarcely get through the hail of shot and shell to the old headquarters. Later, the army headquarters were moved to Powers Hill, where Slocum had his command post.[45]

Then came Pickett's immortal charge across nearly a mile of open fields. The Union center at the Angle near the copse of trees, held by Brigadier General Alexander S. Webb's Philadelphia Brigade,

[44] Meade, *Life and Letters of Meade*, II, 102–104; *B. & L.*, III, 362.
[45] Pennypacker, *General Meade*, 188; Meade, *Life and Letters of Meade*, II, 106–108.

was temporarily breached at about 3:15 P.M. by a few hundred men led by Brigadier General Lewis A. Armistead. But Federal reinforcements rushed up from left and right, and the gallant gray remnants were compelled to fall back to Seminary Ridge after suffering casualties of over 50 per cent. It was a sight scarcely seen before—a large segment of Lee's army in full, breathless, disorganized retreat. At about the same time that Pickett was being repulsed in front, a Confederate cavalry sweep three miles to the rear (east) of the Union position was also being thrown back.[46]

Just as Pickett was repulsed, Meade rode up from the rear to the crest of Cemetery Ridge. Near Woodruff's battery, the General was surrounded by a howling mob of Confederate prisoners who beseeched him, as an officer of rank, to direct them to a haven of safety from the fire of their own guns. Frank A. Haskell described Meade at this moment as "a plain man, dressed in a serviceable summer suit of dark blue cloth, without badge or ornament save the shoulder straps of his grade, and a light, straight sword. He wore heavy, high top boots and buff gauntlets, and his soft black felt hat was slouched down over his eyes; his face was very white and pale, and the lines were marked and earnest and full of care." To Haskell he "asked in a sharp eager voice, 'How is it going here?'" When Haskell replied, "I believe, General, the enemy's attack is repulsed," Meade exclaimed, *"What! Is the assault already repulsed?"* When Haskell answered in the affirmative, Meade declared fervently, "Thank God!"[47]

Meade then rode to Cemetery Hill—where a large number of officers surrounded him to offer congratulations—to make sure that the Confederates were not about to renew their assaults of the previous evening there. He then decided to attack the enemy's right, and began to ride down the entire length of his lines on Cemetery Ridge. No sooner had he reached Ziegler's Grove than

[46] See G. Moxley Sorrel, *Recollections of a Confederate Staff Officer* (New York, 1905), 172; Tucker, *High Tide at Gettysburg*, 378–79.

[47] Frank Aretas Haskell, *The Battle of Gettysburg* (Madison, 1908), 136; Pennypacker, *General Meade*, 195.

his soldiers began to cheer him lustily. The effect upon the troops of this dramatic ride to Little Round Top "was electrical." Arriving on the summit of Little Round Top, Meade ordered an attack to be mounted against the enemy's right; but the fact was that his soldiers were practically out on their feet after three blistering hot days of marching and fighting. Then, too, the units were widely scattered about, and darkness—hastened by a thunderstorm at 6:30 P.M.—approached before any kind of a large, well-organized, sustained offensive could be made. It seems quite likely that had Meade been able to launch an attack it would have suffered the same fate as Pickett's. But Hancock, severely wounded in the thigh, voiced hope that Meade would take the offensive anyway.[48]

At 8:45 that evening, the Union commander telegraphed Halleck of the day's operations, claiming only that he had achieved "a handsome repulse" of the enemy. One of his staff officers said to Meade, "You ought to boast a little more, General, for the country will not appreciate what you have done, unless you do so." Replied the Old Snapping Turtle, "I would rather understate our success than claim greater results than I have accomplished." Because his old headquarters house had been damaged by artillery fire, and was being used as a hospital, Meade and his staff rode that night a quarter of a mile southward on the Taneytown road, where the exhausted commander and his aides lay down to sleep on the ground amongst some rocks. But after only an hour's sleep, the General was awakened by a heavy rain, upon which he arose and seated himself on a rock, quickly becoming soaked as the downpour continued. And so he spent the night which followed the greatest battle ever fought on American soil—a pivotal combat which the Union and its cause could not have afforded to lose.[49]

Of the total number of about 95,000 men which Meade had

[48] Jacob Hoke, *The Great Invasion of 1863* . . . (Dayton, 1887), 437–41; *B. & L.,* III, 375–76; Pennypacker, *General Meade,* 197–98; Meade, *Life and Letters of Meade,* II, 109–11, 249; McClure (ed.), *Annals of the War,* 214–16, 455–56; 43 *O.R.,* 74.

[49] 43 *O.R.,* 74; McClure (ed.), *Annals of the War,* 217; Meade, *Life and Letters of Meade,* II, 112; Pennypacker, *General Meade,* 200–201.

available, he employed some 88,000 effectives at Gettysburg, as against Lee's 75,000 troops. Meade suffered the following casualties: 3,155 killed; 14,529 wounded; 5,365 missing—a total loss of 23,049. Lee lost 2,592 killed; 12,709 wounded; 12,227 missing (including many wounded prisoners)—total casualties of 27,528.[50]

The anniversary of the nation's birth—July 4, 1863—was a day of steady rain, as the two bone-weary armies lay facing each other across the valley between the two ridges. On the evening of the fourth, Lee began his skillful retreat from Gettysburg to the Potomac via the Hagerstown and Chambersburg roads, while Meade felt obliged to pursue carefully by the more circuitous route of the lower mountain passes. The Union commander had been named brigadier general in the regular army on July 3.[51]

Immediately after the battle of Gettysburg, even the Radicals joined in the chorus hailing Meade for his triumph. On the fourth the General issued an order to his army, praising the soldiers for having "baffled" the supposedly superior-numbered invading army. He added that there remained yet the task of driving "from our soil every vestige of the invader." Lincoln was overjoyed after learning of the repulse of Pickett's charge; but when he read Meade's congratulatory order to the army, the President dropped his hands to his knees in anguish, and cried, "Drive the invader from our soil! My God! Is that all?"[52]

There is much controversy as to whether Meade's pursuit of Lee to the Potomac was made with adequate rapidity or with excessive caution. The Union commander's fears and state of thinking were shown in a telegram he sent to Halleck on July 6, in which he said that he would attack Lee if he got a chance, and that if a calamity engulfed him, splinters from his army could be nursed back into the defenses of Washington to aid in fighting for the capital against

[50] Livermore, *Numbers and Losses,* 102–103; B. & L., III, 440; 43 O.R., 65, 114.

[51] Powell, *Fifth Corps,* 563; B. & L., III, 379.

[52] New York *Tribune,* July 7, 1863; David H. Bates, *Lincoln in the Telegraph Office* . . . (New York, 1907), 155–56; Allen T. Rice (ed.), *Reminiscences of Abraham Lincoln* . . . (New York, 1886), 402.

the triumphant foe. The day before, after reading dispatches from the front, Lincoln asserted to Halleck, "These things all appear to me to be connected with a purpose to . . . get the enemy across the river again without a further collision. . . ." [53]

Finding the Potomac River unfordable, owing to heavy rains, Lee took up and entrenched on July 6 a very strong defensive position running from Falling Waters to Williamsport. Halleck, although he agreed with Meade's caution in approaching Lee, subordinated his views to Lincoln's and, on July 7 and 8, urged Meade to strike the Confederates before they crossed the Potomac. In reply Meade shot back this message to the General-in-Chief on the eighth: "I expect to find the enemy in a strong position well covered with artillery, and I do not desire to imitate his example at Gettysburg and assault a position where the chances were so greatly against success. I wish in advance to moderate the expectations of those who in ignorance of the difficulties to be encountered may expect too much." [54]

As the Army of the Potomac neared Lee's powerful line on the north bank of the Potomac—described by some as stronger than the Confederate position at Fredericksburg or the Union one at Gettysburg—Meade received these significant directions from the General-in-Chief on July 10: "Do not be influenced by any despatch from here against your own judgment. Regard them as suggestions only. Our information here is not always correct." Halleck said further, "I think it will be best for you to postpone a general battle till you can concentrate all your forces and get up your reserves and re-enforcements. . . . Beware of partial combats. Bring up and hurl upon the enemy all your forces, good and bad." [55]

On the night of July 12, Meade had decided, in answer to new appeals from Halleck, to attack Lee. He called a council of war, but

[53] 43 *O.R.*, 80–81; Bates, *Lincoln in the Telegraph Office*, 156.

[54] *B. & L.*, III, 380; Morse (ed.), *Welles's Diary*, I, 363–64; 45 *O.R.*, 498; 43 *O.R.*, 84.

[55] Pennypacker, *General Meade*, 203, 209; 43 *O.R.*, 88, 89; *B. & L.*, III, 380.

five of his six corps commanders voted against an assault, and Meade reluctantly acceded to their wishes. He made as thorough a reconnaissance on the thirteenth as the misty weather would permit, and decided, on his own authority, to launch an attack on the fourteenth, come what might. But during the night of July 13–14, Lee crossed his army safely over the Potomac into Virginia. It is the concensus of those who were there that any Federal assault—which the Confederates hoped would be made—on Lee's impregnable position would have been hurled back with fearful losses.[56]

When word reached Lincoln of Lee's escape, the President was furious as well as downcast. "We had them within our grasp," he cried; "we had only to stretch forth our hands and they were ours, and nothing I could say or do could make the army move." Lincoln was angered also at Meade's statement that he had driven the foe from Northern soil, and exclaimed, "Will our generals never get that idea out of their heads? The whole country is our soil." On July 14, in the depths of his depression, the Chief Executive went too far when he trumpeted to Welles, "And that, my God, is the last of this Army of the Potomac! There is bad faith somewhere. . . . What does it mean, Mr. Welles? Great God! what does it mean?" Stanton, too, was livid with rage at Meade's conduct at this time.[57]

The ire of Washington officialdom was duly passed on to the army head. When Halleck, on July 14, wired Meade that the President was dissatisfied with his having permitted Lee to cross the Potomac, Meade hurled back this rejoinder: "Having performed my duty, conscientiously and to the best of my ability, the censure of the President . . . is, in my judgment, so undeserved, that I feel compelled, most respectfully, to ask to be immediately

[56] Powell, *Fifth Corps*, 564–65; 43 *O.R.*, 91; *C.C.W.* (1865), I, 381; DeTrobriand, *Army of the Potomac*, 522–23; Gordon, *War Diary*, 143; B. & L., III, 367, 382; A. A. Humphreys, *Gettysburg to the Rapidan* (New York, 1883), 8; Swinton, *Army of the Potomac*, 370–71.

[57] Dennett (ed.), *Diaries and Letters of Hay*, 66–67; Nicolay and Hay, *Abraham Lincoln*, VII, 278; Morse (ed.), *Welles's Diary*, I, 370; McClure, *Lincoln and Men of War-Times*, 360.

relieved from the command of this Army." Halleck replied that
no censure was intended, but only "a stimulus to an active pursuit.
It is not deemed a sufficient cause for your application to be relieved." Later, on the night of the fourteenth, Meade described to
his wife the criticism of the President and the exchange of messages with Halleck. "This is exactly what I expected," asserted the
disgusted General; "unless I did impracticable things, fault would
be found with me." "My army (men and animals) is exhausted,"
he wrote two days later; yet, he said, the administration insisted
he press on without proper rest and reorganization. "This has been
the history of my predecessors, and I clearly saw that in time their
fate would be mine." [58]

In the ensuing days Lee moved up the Shenandoah Valley, while
Meade, adopting McClellan's scheme, marched southward, parallel
to Lee, along the eastern side of the Blue Ridge Mountains. "Another
great trouble with me," Meade bemoaned, "is the want of active
and energetic subordinate officers, men upon whom I can depend
and rely upon taking care of themselves and commands. The loss of
Reynolds and Hancock is most serious; their places are not to be
supplied." By the end of July Lee's army had crossed the Rapidan
and moved to Orange Court House, while the Federal army
stopped on the north bank of that river. Meade determined "to
hold my force well together, with the hope of falling upon some
portion of Lee's army in detail." But on July 29, showing little
confidence in his army commander, Lincoln told Halleck that he
did not think a showdown battle should then be fought by Meade.[59]

August and September, 1863, were, in general, months of rest
for Meade's army and for Lee's. Two brigades of the Fifth Corps
had been sent to New York City to help quell the draft riots. Then,
the Eleventh and Twelfth corps, under Hooker's command, entrained for the West to bolster Rosecrans. On the Confederate side,
Longstreet and two of his divisions were sent also to the West to

[58] 43 O.R., 92–94; Meade, Life and Letters of Meade, II, 134, 135.
[59] Meade, Life and Letters of Meade, II, 136; C.C.W. (1865), I, 480;
43 O.R., 104–107; Basler (ed.), Collected Works of Lincoln, VI, 354.

augment Bragg's army. On September 21, however, Lincoln let
go to Welles this blast at the army, its commanders, and generals:
"It is the same old story of this Army of the Potomac. Imbecility,
inefficiency—don't want to *do*—is defending the Capital. . . . Oh,
it is terrible, terrible, this weakness, this indifference of our Potomac generals, with such armies of good and brave men." When
asked by Welles why he did not get rid of Meade, Lincoln replied, "What can I do with such generals as we have? Who among
them is any better than Meade?" [60]

With the Army of the Potomac reduced to some 68,000 men,
Lee outflanked Meade's right on October 9 and forced him to fall
back to the north side of the Rappahannock. Then ensued a race
toward the old Bull Run battle area in which Meade got the better
of Lee, arriving at Centreville before him, and inflicting, under
Warren, a sharp repulse upon assaulting Confederate troops on the
fourteenth at Bristoe (Broad Run). This check forced Lee, in turn,
to fall back rapidly, first to Culpeper, and then, by November 7, to
his former position on the south bank of the Rapidan. In repeated
reports to Davis, Lee spoke highly of the rapidity of Meade's
movements. But during this maneuvering in northern Virginia in
October, Meade felt that he was being heckled by the General-in-
Chief, and when Halleck replied to one of his dispatches by
quoting one of Napoleon's maxims, Meade exploded to his superior,
"If you have any orders to give me I am prepared to receive and
obey them, but I must insist on being spared the infliction of such
truisms in the guise of opinions as you have recently honored me
with, particularly as they were not asked for." Halleck apologized.[61]

Meanwhile, the Radicals were speeding up the tempo of their
attacks on Meade. The General stated, on October 21, that the
army should go into winter quarters closer to Washington, and
visited the capital to discuss the matter. "The President was, as he

[60] Nicolay and Hay, *Abraham Lincoln*, VIII, 233–34; Morse (ed.),
Welles's Diary, I, 439–40.

[61] Swinton, *Army of the Potomac*, 376 ff.; 49 O.R., 228, 328, 334, 345,
346; Meade, *Life and Letters of Meade*, II, 153–54; 48 O.R., 408.

always is, very considerate and kind," wrote Meade to his wife on the twenty-second. "He found no fault with my operations, although it was very evident he was disappointed that I had not got a battle out of Lee." However, as the good fall weather continued, Lincoln changed his mind and urged Meade to fight a battle; but the latter was reluctant. In early November Meade did suggest that the army's line of operations be shifted from the vulnerable Orange & Alexandria to the R. F. & P., and that, after a rapid march, the heights back of Fredericksburg be seized. But his superiors in Washington, for no worthy reasons, rather curtly rejected this plan, even though it was well known that every commanding general of the army (and this would later include Grant) had had to cut loose from the Orange & Alexandria the moment the army crossed the Rapidan. While Meade felt that, consequently, he should be superseded, Lincoln disagreed, and complimented him on his operations. All in all, Meade had about held his own in the autumn maneuvering campaign with Lee.[62]

Then, in the last days of November, hoping to surprise Lee at Orange Court House, Meade crossed the Rapidan at Germanna Ford. The Confederate leader, however, was warned by his cavalry of the Federal approach, and entrenched himself in an impregnable position along the western bank of Mine Run, astride the Orange Turnpike and Plank Road. Despite the bitter cold weather, Meade was hopeful that an attack could be successfully launched. But after the trusted Warren reversed himself and asserted positively that an assault would fail, Meade reluctantly agreed with him and withdrew the army to its position on the north bank of the Rapidan. The two armies now remained quiescent until the following May— Meade's near Culpeper Court House and Lee's in the vicinity of Orange Court House.[63]

[62] Morse (ed.), *Welles's Diary*, I, 472–73; 49 *O.R.*, 361–63, 375–77, 409–10, 412; Basler (ed.), *Collected Works of Lincoln*, VI, 534; Meade, *Life and Letters of Meade*, II, 154–56.

[63] Swinton, *Army of the Potomac*, 390 ff.; George R. Agassiz (ed.), *Meade's Headquarters, 1863–65* . . . (Boston, 1922), 60–61; *C.C.W* (1865), I, 474–75; *B. & L.*, IV, 89.

During the winter Meade reorganized the Army of the Potomac. He broke up the shattered First and Third corps, and distributed their units into the remaining three corps. Whether this was wise, considering the morale of the soldiers and their love for their old outfits, is debatable. Then, too, reducing the army to just three corps would make these latter units quite large and unwieldy. At any rate, when the campaign season opened in the spring of 1864, there were but three infantry corps: Hancock's Second Corps, Warren's Fifth Corps, and Sedgwick's Sixth Corps. By December 28 Hancock had recovered sufficiently from his painful and serious groin wound to rejoin the army. Wrote Meade to Mrs. Meade on the twenty-eighth: Hancock "says it was undoubtedly intended at first to relieve me, and it was, as I surmised, intimated to him that he would be placed in command. Such was his impression till the day before he came down, when, on reporting to Halleck, he was told the design was abandoned, and that he could go down to his old corps. Hancock further says that Halleck declares he saved me," and that Meade's official report and the almost unanimously good opinions of officers going up to Washington changed the picture.[64]

In January and February, 1864, Meade visited his home in Philadelphia, where he was taken ill for some time. Upon recuperating, and on his way back to the army in mid-February, he visited Washington, where his superiors expressed confidence in him and treated him kindly. But in January and February the Radicals began in earnest their renewed efforts to discredit Meade and to have him and other Conservative generals removed. Late in February, the nefarious Committee on the Conduct of the War began a series of hearings designed to ruin Meade. Radical generals, such as Sickles, Doubleday, and A. P. Howe were called upon to testify, and they scored Meade severely for his handling of the army at Gettysburg as well as for his alleged disloyalty to the government. Even in March, when Grant arrived East and at first refused to have anything to do with the Jacobins, the latter group

[64] Meade, *Life and Letters of Meade,* II, 163–64.

continued to shriek for Meade's ouster. Meade himself testified during the first week of March, and, seeing through the Radicals' scheme, confounded Benjamin F. Wade and the committee with his straightforward and honest testimony. The General, of course, was incensed at his treatment, especially by his former subordinates. But the President refused to buckle in late March when badgered by Wade and Zachariah Chandler to fire Meade.[65]

In early March, 1864, Meade and the country were informed that Grant was to be brought East as lieutenant general and General-in-Chief of all the Union armies, and that he would establish his headquarters with the Army of the Potomac. In a letter to his wife on March 8, Meade gave his views before the newcomer had arrived and joined the army in the field: "Grant is to be in Washington tonight, and as he is to be commander in chief and responsible for the doings of the Army of the Potomac, he may desire to have his own man in command, particularly as I understand he is indoctrinated with the notion of the superiority of the Western armies, and that the failure of the Army of the Potomac to accomplish anything is due to their [sic] commanders." In that frame of mind, George G. Meade spent the last few days of his really independent command of the army, awaiting the arrival of the taciturn Westerner who had won such a great name throughout the North by his capture of Vicksburg on July 4, 1863, just one day after Meade had repulsed the last desperate assault of Lee at Gettysburg.[66]

Meade's performance under Grant in directing the operations of the Army of the Potomac from March, 1864, to April, 1865, will be considered briefly in the following chapter dealing primarily with Grant. In the three years immediately after Appomattox, Meade commanded the Military Division of the Atlantic,

[65] Pennypacker, *General Meade*, 257–58; *Congressional Globe*, 38th Cong., 1st Sess., 897–98; Williams, *Lincoln and the Radicals*, 336; *C.C.W.* (1865), I, xix, 295 ff.; Meade, *Life and Letters of Meade*, II, 165, 169, 170, 172–73.
[66] Meade, *Life and Letters of Meade*, II, 176.

and the Department of the East, with headquarters in Philadelphia. From 1868 to 1869, at Atlanta, he headed the Third Military District of the Department of the South, comprising the "reconstructing" states of Georgia, Alabama, and Florida; and he was liked and respected by most Southerners during the occupation. In 1869 he was back in Philadelphia as commander of the Military Division of the Atlantic. From 1866 until his death, he served as commissioner of Fairmount Park in Philadelphia. On October 31, 1872, while taking his daily walk from his office with his wife, he was stricken with a terrible pain in his back, in the area of his old Glendale wound. Pneumonia set in, and led to his death on November 6, 1872.[67]

[67] Cullum, *Biographical Register*, I, 473; D.A.B., XII, 475–76.

CHAPTER EIGHT

Ulysses S. Grant

> [Grant's] is a strange character.
> Nothing like it is portrayed by Plutarch
> or the many who have striven to portray
> the great men of ancient or modern
> times. I knew him as a cadet at West
> Point, as a lieutenant of the Fourth In-
> fantry, as a citizen of St. Louis, and as a
> growing general all through the bloody
> Civil War. Yet to me he is a mystery,
> and I believe he is a mystery to himself.
> —*General William T. Sherman*

AN "ORDINARY, SCRUBBY-LOOKING MAN, WITH A SLIGHTY SEEDY
look, as if he was out of office and on half-pay and nothing to do but
hang around"—these were words used to describe forty-one-year-
old Lieutenant General Ulysses S. Grant in April, 1864. To those
who looked more closely, the new General-in-Chief of all the
Union armies appeared as "a short, round-shouldered man, in a
very tarnished uniform," who usually stood with his left hand in his
trousers pocket. He was five feet eight inches in height, "never
carried himself erect except when on horseback, and his walk
and appearance were unmilitary. He seldom buttoned his military
coat, and his outward appearance gave an impression of carelessness." He had a well-formed head; high forehead, with several
horizontal creases; short-clipped brown hair and beard; slightly
sunken, piercing, blue-gray eyes, the left one of which was a trifle
lower than the right; a firm mouth; a stubborn chin; and a reddish-
brown complexion. An ever-present cigar was a part of his square-
cut visage. "His countenance was rarely free from a certain anxious
and careworn expression." "He possessed a melodious voice, which
he rarely raised even in the excitement of battle." He wore a size

seven and one-half regulation black felt military hat directly on the top of his head; its crown was high and the sides were pressed in. "He had . . . the look of a man who did, or once did, take a little too much to drink." As to his gait, an eyewitness reports that "he gets over the ground queerly. He does not march, nor quite walk, but pitches along as if the next step would bring him on his nose." [1]

Grant's history up to the Civil War is largely a story of failure, with few bright episodes to enrich it. He was born of Puritan stock in Point Pleasant, Ohio, on April 27, 1822. As a boy, his greatest talent was his handling of horses. Despite his qualms as to his abilities, Grant entered West Point in 1839 and graduated in 1843. He stood twenty-first in the class of thirty-nine. Although born Hiram Ulysses Grant, an error in registration at the Military Academy listed him as Ulysses Simpson Grant, or just U. S. Grant. His fellow cadets nicknamed him "United States Grant," "Uncle Sam Grant," or, more frequently, just plain "Sam Grant." After routine duty, the Mexican War came, and although opposed to it, Grant served with distinction with both Taylor and Scott, and won two brevets. Then followed more monotonous assignments. He was married in 1848 to Julia Dent, but poverty prevented him from having her with him at army posts on the West Coast. Finally, alcohol proved his undoing, and he was obliged to resign from the army in 1854. From then until the attack at Fort Sumter, Grant worked unsuccessfully as a farmer, a real estate agent, a candidate for county engineer, and a clerk in a customs house. Finally, he was taken in as a clerk in his brothers' leather-goods store in Galena, Illinois. [2]

---

[1] Morse (ed.), *Welles's Diary*, I, 538–39; Frank Moore (ed.), *Rebellion Record* (New York, 1862–1871), XI, 560–61; Louis A. Coolidge, *Ulysses S. Grant* (Boston, 1917), 4; Horace Porter, *Campaigning with Grant* (New York, 1897), 14–16; James Grant Wilson, *General Grant* (New York, 1897), 119, 369–78.

[2] Cullum, *Biographical Register*, II, 85–86; Coolidge, *Grant*, 4, 18, 27–29, 33–35; Lloyd Lewis, *Captain Sam Grant* (Boston, 1950), 324, 327, 336.

When the Civil War broke out, Grant declared for the Union. He tried to get a job on McClellan's staff—which, had he been successful, would probably have reduced him to military oblivion for the war—but was kept from this fate only because McClellan chanced to be absent from his headquarters for a few days on an inspection trip. Grant then received command of an Illinois regiment, and, on May 17, 1861, was named a brigadier general of volunteers. Assisted by the navy, Grant's land forces captured Forts Henry and Donelson in February, 1862. On the sixteenth of that month he was made a major general of volunteers. Then, in early April, Grant was caught unprepared and almost defeated at Shiloh by Albert Sidney Johnston—only the timely arrival of preponderant reinforcements saving the day for the careless, almost reckless, Union commander. He was in command of the Department of the Tennessee from October, 1862, to October, 1863. From November, 1862, Grant was engaged in the operations against Vicksburg, which bastion finally fell on July 4, 1863, after a number of earlier movements against it had failed. Grant's Vicksburg campaign was his finest operation of the war—a masterpiece—and he was named major general in the regular army on the day the great Confederate stronghold fell. Now supreme commander in the West, Grant, after Rosecrans' defeat at Chickamauga in September, 1863, went himself to Chattanooga. In November, in a skillful operation, he defeated Bragg's army there, and cleared the way for Sherman's later advance on Atlanta.[3]

In early March, 1863, Grant had pledged on his honor to John A. Rawlins, his close friend and staff officer, that he would drink no more liquor during the war. But just before the battle of Chattanooga, Grant resumed his drinking, and only Rawlins or Grant's wife could "stay it." This habit was to plague him later, on occasion, when he was with the Army of the Potomac. Shortly after the capture of Vicksburg, Grant's influential friend in Congress, Elihu B. Washburne, sounded him out on his being sent to command the

[3] Cullum, *Biographical Register*, II, 85–86; 36 *O.R.*, 63; Adam Badeau, *Military History of Ulysses S. Grant* . . . (New York, 1868–81), I, 285.

Army of the Potomac. Grant replied, "My going could do no possible good. They have there able officers who have been brought up with that army; and to import a commander to place over them, certainly could produce no good." In early August of 1863, learning that Stanton and Halleck were trying to arrange it for him to supersede Meade, Grant opposed this, and wrote to Charles A. Dana, assistant secretary of war, "Whilst I would disobey no order I should beg very hard to be excused before accepting that command." [4]

Perhaps feeling his reputation to be heightened even more after his victory at Chattanooga, and conceivably making a bid for the post of General-in-Chief, Grant sent to the War Department during the winter of 1863–1864 several sweeping plans of grand strategy—not free from flaws—designed to win the war, and including movements of all the Federal armies. Grant also indicated that Meade should be replaced in command of the Army of the Potomac by either Sherman or William F. Smith. But when the administration seemed about to name the latter to supersede Meade, Grant suddenly did an about-face. He thought highly of Smith, but perhaps saw now that he was too prone to be touchy and engage in controversy. Also, probably to ease Lincoln's fears, Grant stated that he had no political interests or desires to become President. As to this latter contingency, Grant declared, "This is the last thing in the world I desire. I would regard such a consummation as highly unfortunate for myself if not for the country." [5]

In December, 1863, the Radicals threw their full weight behind Grant, adopting him as one of their own. Lyman Trumbull intro-

---

[4] William Farrar Smith, *From Chattanooga to Petersburg* . . . (Boston, 1893), 179; Grant to Dana, Aug. 5, 1863, Charles A. Dana Papers, Div. of MSS, Library of Congress; *McClure's Magazine*, Jan., 1898, pp. 254, 258.

[5] 55 *O.R.*, 72–73; 56 *O.R.*, 349–50, 457–58; 58 *O.R.*, 41, 99–101, 126–27, 411–13; 60 *O.R.*, 394–95; A. L. Conger, *The Rise of U. S. Grant* (New York, 1931), 311; W. F. Smith to W. B. Franklin, Apr. 28, 1864, William B. Franklin Papers, Div. of MSS, Library of Congress; James H. Wilson, *Life of John A. Rawlins* (New York, 1916), 206–208; Coolidge, *Grant*, 141, 142.

duced a bill to recreate the grade of lieutenant general—the highest in the service—so that Grant could be named to it. The bill became law on February 29, 1864. This three-star rank had been held previously by only two men in American history—George Washington and Winfield Scott, and the latter had held it by brevet only. The man to be named to it now in 1864 would, of course, become General-in-Chief. On March 3, 1864, Grant received an order from Stanton to repair to Washington as soon as possible to receive the lieutenant general's commission. On the following day he departed, after writing his close friend, Sherman, that he would accept the position only if he were permitted to station himself outside of the Federal capital.[6]

Grant's characteristics and personal traits were, on the whole, simple and direct. He was rather tight-lipped, and was known by some as the "Great Unspeakable," "Ulysses the Silent," and the "American Sphinx." While "certainly natural, and clear of all appearance of self-consciousness," "he had no gait, no *station*, no manner." Grant's features, says Regis DeTrobriand, show "an expression of tranquil firmness, something like the consciousness of force in repose." At other times, reports one of his staff officers, Grant looked like a determined man about to try to ram his head through a brick wall. At first glance, he was most unimpressive, almost comical, and he was dynamic in neither personality nor appearance. His soldiers seldom responded with wild adulation or boisterous cheers when he rode among them. Grant "seemed always preoccupied." He "would gaze at any one who approached him with an inquiring air, followed by a glance of recollection and a grave nod of recognition." [7]

Basically, as he himself acknowledged, Grant did not like to

[6] Pierce, *Letters of Sumner*, IV, 172; J. Palmer to L. Trumbull, Jan. 24, 1864, Lyman Trumbull Papers, Div. of MSS, Library of Congress; *Congressional Globe*, 38th Cong., 1st Sess., pt. 1, 586–94, Appendix, Feb. 29, 1864, p. 142; 59 *O.R.*, 18; Sherman, *Memoirs*, I, 399–400.

[7] Agassiz (ed.), *Meade's Headquarters*, 80–83; Porter, *Campaigning with Grant*, 14–16, 196; Rusling, *Men and Things*, 135–36; DeTrobriand, *Army of the Potomac*, 563.

work; but, when obliged to, he could perform prodigies of mental and physical labor. He had a knack for handling horses and animals, and was a good swimmer and diver. He never hunted or used firearms for sport, and he abhorred bloodshed and killing. He liked to ride, walk, and observe grain growing, and he was an expert on trees. He was clean-minded and clean-spoken, and would not tolerate uncouth stories in his presence. He did not have an ear for music, and never kept in step with a band or with others walking with him. In conversation, Grant would stroke his chin beard with his left hand, while he would raise and lower his right hand (with closed fingers forming an "L" with the back of his hand) and occasionally rest it on a table or his knee. He was usually slow in his bodily movements, but in moments of crisis he could move and work rapidly. In the presence of people, "he was civil to all." [8]

According to his military secretary, Adam Badeau, Grant "was always careless about his papers, and private or semi-official ones were often thrust into his pockets, where they remained for months." A staff officer, Horace Porter, relates that Grant was "the most difficult man to cater to in the whole army." The only meat he really liked was beef, very well done (no blood!). He was partial to fruit and oysters, buckwheat cakes and corn, pork and beans, and cucumbers; but he disliked game, fowl, and mutton. Though somewhat slight in build, he was possessed of a rugged physique. Although speaking ungrammatically on occasion, the General was not a poor conversationalist. His temperament was naturally buoyant and optimistic, and he usually kept his strong temper curbed. [9]

Under fire, Grant had unflinching courage, and he was unusual in that he never blinked or moved a muscle. He hated two kinds of people only—liars and cowards. He was accustomed to calling Sherman, Sheridan, and Rawlins by just their last names, although he would add the word "General" when speaking to Meade or other high-ranking officers with whom he was not so well acquainted.

[8] Coolidge, *Grant*, 8–15; Porter, *Campaigning with Grant*, 14–15.
[9] *B. & L.*, IV, 113; Porter, *Campaigning with Grant*, 213–14.

"He never criticized an officer harshly in the presence of others," notes Porter. "If fault had to be found with him, it was never made an occasion to humiliate or wound his feelings. . . . The fact that he never 'nagged' his officers, but treated them all with consideration, led them to communicate with him freely and intimately." Colonel Theodore Lyman, of Meade's staff, asserts that Grant never did anything without a specific reason. "His reasons may be good or bad, but they are reasons." James Ford Rhodes comments of the General, "He was not a man who assimilated a variety of knowledge; he had, in fact, a mind the reverse of encyclopaedic, but by careful observation and systematic thinking he made certain truths his own; these became ingrained in the fibre of his brain, guiding his action in the supreme moment of opportunity." On only two recorded occasions during the war did Grant allow his high temper to master him: once when he had a man lashed to a tree for six hours for whipping a horse, and once when he smashed a Union rapist over the head with a clubbed musket, dropping him horizontal.[10]

Sherman once stated that Grant had "in an eminent degree that peculiar and high attribute of using various men to produce a common result." "The chief characteristic of your nature," Sherman said to Grant after the latter's promotion to three star rank, "is the simple faith in success you have always manifested, which I can liken to nothing else than the faith a Christian has in his Saviour." Badeau admitted that he and other staff officers did not know why Grant succeeded; they believed in him "because of his success." Charles Francis Adams, Jr., said to his father of Grant that "in a crisis he is one against whom all around, whether few in number or a great army . . . would instinctively lean."[11]

Grant had, as do all men, a few shortcomings and several hostile

[10] Rhodes, *History of the United States*, III, 595–98; Military Historical Society of Massachusetts, . . . *Petersburg, Chancellorsville, Gettysburg* . . . (Boston, 1906), V, 4; Agassiz (ed.), *Meade's Headquarters*, 359; Porter, *Campaigning with Grant*, 164–65, 249, 340.

[11] Lew Wallace, *Lew Wallace: an Autobiography* (New York, 1906), 662–64; Channing, *History*, VI, 546 n.

critics. (His drinking proclivities will be touched on later). He was, as were many in that period, anti-Semitic, and an order of his in December, 1862, ousting all "Israelites" from his department, had to be countermanded by Lincoln. At times he hesitated to deal firmly with his subordinates lest he hurt their feelings. He lacked political sagacity, and was occasionally taken advantage of by the shrewd civilian. On occasion his mind would lay torpid. Hooker once asserted that Grant had "no more moral sense than a dog," and Rosecrans referred to him as "that puppy" Grant. Major General William F. Smith assesses Grant in this fashion: "Ability, ordinary; sense of responsibility, utterly wanting, except so far as his personal interests were concerned; professional acquirements absolutely wanting, so far as related to the direction of movements and conduct of battles. . . . He was malignant in his hatred, but would forgive for a consideration; *vide* Butler, while Grant was president; also Lew Wallace. Utter disregard for truth where his own interests were concerned; the moral qualities drowned in rotgut whisky." Three months before Grant was elevated to the lieutenant generalcy, Meade wrote to his wife that he had known Grant "as a young man in the Mexican War, at which time he was considered a clever young officer, but nothing extraordinary. . . . I think his great characteristic is indomitable energy and great tenacity of purpose." [12]

A somewhat shabby-looking little man, in a crusty blue uniform, accompanied by his fourteen-year-old son, arrived on the 5:00 P.M. train at the Washington depot on March 8, 1864. No one met them at the station, so the two went to Willard's Hotel, where, in the crowd of other room-seekers, they were the last to come up to the desk. "The plainly attired and unassuming officer, who looked as if he might be a captain or major," signed the guest register "U. S. Grant and son—Galena, Illinois." Not recognizing the General and his little charge, the desk clerk assigned them to a small

[12] 25 *O.R.*, 424, 530; Macartney, *Grant and His Generals*, x, xi, 88–89, 221–22, 304; Meade, *Life and Letters of Meade*, II, 162–63.

room on the fifth floor, and they walked away uncomplainingly. Then, glancing at the name on the register, the clerk became panic-stricken, rushed after them, and promptly installed them in the famous hotel's best rooms on the second floor.[13]

That evening Grant attended a reception at the White House. The President and the General had never met before, and when the soldier was ushered into one of the small rooms of the Executive Mansion, Lincoln's first words were, "This is General Grant, is it?" Said Grant, "Yes." A brief chat ensued, with Seward and Mrs. Lincoln joining the conclave. Then Grant was taken into the large East Room, where scores of palpitating guests were awaiting his arrival. A buzz of excitement greeted the drab little man as he entered the room. "His presence," declare Hay and Nicolay, "excited a feeling which burst the bonds of etiquette, and cheer after cheer rose from the assembled crowd. Hot and blushing with embarrassment he was forced to mount a sofa from which he could shake hands with the eager admirers who rushed upon him from all sides of the great room." This continued for an hour before Grant could break away and go into the Blue Room, where Lincoln, Stanton, and Nicolay were awaiting him. Here, Grant was told that on the following day, in a little ceremony, the President would give him his commission, the two of them to make a few appropriate remarks from manuscripts. Grant was asked by Lincoln to emphasize in his short speech of acceptance two points: first, to say something in the way of balm to the Army of the Potomac; and, second, to reassure the other generals that they had no reason to be envious or jealous of him.[14]

At 1:00 P.M. on March 9, 1864, a group including Lincoln, Grant, Halleck, the cabinet, and a few others, gathered in the Cabinet Room of the White House. The President read a very brief

[13] Wilson, *General Grant*, 212; Coolidge, *Grant*, 145; Morse (ed.), *Welles's Diary*, I, 538–39.

[14] Nicolay and Hay, *Abraham Lincoln*, VIII, 339–43; J. G. Nicolay's Memorandum, Mar. 8, 1864, Nicolay Papers; Morse (ed.), *Welles's Diary*, I, 538–39.

and fitting address, and handed Grant his commission as lieutenant general. The soldier responded, reading from lead-pencil notes written on a half-sheet of paper. He had difficulty in making out his own handwriting, and stumbled badly over the words; "his embarrassment was evident and extreme." "The President," said Grant in his memoirs, "told me he did not want to know what I proposed to do." "I did not communicate my plans to the President, nor did I to the Secretary of War or to General Halleck." [15]

Grant was formally elevated to the position of General-in-Chief of all the Federal armies on March 10, Halleck gracefully asking for orders to be issued to relieve him of this top post. Halleck was then named by Grant to fill a new post—that of Chief of Staff, in Washington—and he did quite well in this important, non-policy-making position. He had a happy faculty of being able skillfully to put Lincoln's thoughts and words into good military parlance. The new command system was certainly more modern and streamlined than anything the United States had had up to that time, and it was not surpassed in Europe until Helmuth Von Moltke created the high command of the Prussian Army in 1866–1871. "In point of reality," wrote Lyman toward the end of March, 1864, "the whole is Grant's: he directs all, and his subordinates are only . . . executive officers having more or less unimportant functions." [16]

Grant paid a quick visit to Meade at Brandy Station on March 10. Wrote the latter to his wife of Grant, "He has been very civil, and said nothing about superseding me." At this first conference, Meade offered to step down if Grant wanted Sherman or someone from the West to take over as commander of the Army of the Potomac. "He urged," reports Grant, "that the work before us was of such vast importance to the whole nation that the feelings or wishes of no

[15] Morse (ed.), *Welles's Diary*, I, 538–39; Grant, *Memoirs*, II, 122–23.
[16] Halleck to Stanton, Mar. 9, 1864, Lincoln Papers; 60 *O.R.*, 663; Williams, *Lincoln and His Generals*, 302; Agassiz (ed.), *Meade's Headquarters*, 224.

one person should stand in the way of selecting the right man for all positions. For himself, he would serve to the best of his ability wherever placed." Grant refused, however, to replace Meade, and said, "This incident gave me even a more favorable opinion of Meade than did his great victory at Gettysburg the July before." At another time Grant remarked, "Sedgwick and Meade were men so finely formed that if ordered to resign their generals' commissions and take service as corporals, they would have fallen into the ranks without a murmur." He declared that even if Meade did not agree with another's plan, he would carry it out as conscientiously as if it were his own. The two generals each had their own separate staffs and headquarters, which did not allow for a very intimate friendship to grow between them.[17]

A few days after receiving his commission and visiting Meade, Grant entrained for Nashville to confer with Sherman, who was now in command in the West. "We reached the satisfactory conclusion," recalls Sherman, "that, as soon as the season would permit, all the armies of the Union would assume the 'bold offensive' by 'concentric lines' on the common enemy, and would finish up the job in a single campaign if possible." Grant returned to Washington on March 23, and, on the twenty-sixth, set up his headquarters at Culpeper Court House. His own staff consisted of but fourteen officers, headed by Brigadier General John A. Rawlins as chief of staff. Meade wrote home that "Grant is emphatically an executive man, whose only place is in the field. One object in coming here is to avoid Washington and its entourage. I intend to give him heartiest cooperation, and so far as I am able do just the same when he is present that I would do were he absent. . . . He was as affable as ever, and seems not at all disposed to interfere with my army in any details. . . . He . . . at once adopts all my suggestions. I believe Grant is honest and fair, and I have no doubt he will give me full credit for anything I may do." But in one of their

[17] Meade, *Life and Letters of Meade*, II, 177; Grant, *Memoirs*, II, 117; Coolidge, *Grant*, 154, 155, 156.

early confabulations, Grant told Meade, "I want it distinctly understood beforehand that after we cross the [Rapidan] river there is to
be no maneuvering with this army for position." [18]

In April, 1864, Grant evolved his plan of grand strategy for the
movements of his various armies. Meade's Army of the Potomac
was to press Lee's army relentlessly in northern Virginia. Major
General Benjamin F. Butler's Army of the James was to move up
the river for which it was named, from Fortress Monroe, and
threaten or seize Richmond—which would prevent Lee from falling back before Meade into the forts of the Confederate capital.
Another task of Butler's was to sever the rail lines leading southward from Richmond. Major General Franz Sigel was to move a
force up the Valley via Staunton and Lynchburg, destroy the railroads around Gordonsville, and then link up with the Army of the
Potomac. In concert with the Eastern armies, Sherman's army at
Chattanooga was to drive deeply into Georgia, annihilate Johnston's
army, and then wreak havoc upon the enemy's economic resources
in the Atlanta area. While these operations were in progress, Major General Nathaniel P. Banks's army was to move from New
Orleans against Mobile. The Federal armies would advance simultaneously, with continuous blows to be rained on all fronts. This
would prevent the enemy from using his interior lines to reinforce
first one threatened area and then another. The Nationals would
triumph eventually by sheer attrition if in no other way. All in
all, it was a most sound and comprehensive strategic program.[19]

At the end of April, Grant made his last visit to Washington before active campaigning began. He said to Lincoln, "I have an impression that the Army of the Potomac has never been fought to
its capacity—until its military effectiveness was exhausted. This

[18] Grant, Memoirs, II, 118, 121; B. & L., IV, 247; Meade, Life and Letters of Meade, II, 182, 183.

[19] B. & L., IV, 206; 61 O.R., 8–9, 13–14; 60 O.R., 794–95, 804–805,
827–29; 59 O.R., 245–46; 63 O.R., passim; Andrew A. Humphreys, Virginia Campaign of '64 and '65 (New York, 1883), 6.

time it will be." At the same time, the Lieutenant General wisely cautioned the President against any hopes for a quick, overwhelming victory. He said that the two rival armies were about equal, man for man, and that victory, as in other wars, would come only when the weaker side was exhausted of its men and resources. On April 30 Lincoln told Grant that he was satisfied up to this time with the General's conduct. The Chief Executive continued, "The particulars of your plan I neither know nor seek to know. You are vigilant and self-reliant; and, pleased with this, I wish not to obtrude any constraints or restraints upon you. While I am very anxious that any great disaster or capture of our men in great numbers should be avoided, I know these points are less likely to escape your attention than they would be mine." This fine attitude of the President should be compared with that of the administration toward McClellan two years previous, when there was far too much amateur meddling in the details of campaign plans and operations by the Lincoln government.[20]

With Lee's army of some 62,000 men posted near Orange Court House on the south bank of the Rapidan, Grant had three alternatives in moving the Army of the Potomac (numbering 118,000) offensively: first, to move the army amphibiously down the Chesapeake Bay, as McClellan had done in 1862; second, to move around Lee's left flank; and third, to move around Lee's right flank. Despite his denials, there is some evidence that Grant had, at one time, preferred the water route, which William F. Smith had favored, and this seems to have been the best possible alternative. Nonetheless, owing possibly in part to political reasons, Grant chose the overland route, and attempted to move past Lee's right. However, as the overland campaign unfolded, Grant found himself, whether consciously or not, coming ever closer to adopting McClellan's line of approach to Richmond.[21]

[20] Lincoln to Grant, Apr. 30, 1864, Lincoln Papers.
[21] Grant, *Memoirs*, II, 134–37; Swinton, *Army of the Potomac*, 406–10; Humphreys, *Campaign of '64 & '65*, pp. 9–11.

With his plans well matured by the first of May, Grant hoped to move into the Wilderness past Lee's right flank, and, by speed and concealment, get through that tangled forest before the Confederate general could do anything about it. This was unrealistic, however, as the Federal movement would be easily seen by the enemy signal station on Clark's Mountain—and this proved to be the case. Despite Grant's later claims that his movement took Lee by surprise, the exact opposite is true. Lee, on Clark's Mountain, predicted on May 2—two days before the Union army began to move—that, instead of crossing the river by the upper fords against his left, Grant would cross at Germanna Ford or Ely's Ford in an advance against his right.[22]

The Army of the Potomac began its forward movement on May 4. But after successfully crossing the Rapidan at Germanna and Ely's fords, Grant halted the army at Chancellorsville and Wilderness Tavern to allow his wagon train of over 4,000 vehicles to pass through. General Francis A. Walker declares that he "has never been able to regard this early halt on the 4th of May otherwise than as the first misfortune of the campaign." He states that the bulk of the army could have been deployed facing west almost anywhere between the Wilderness and Mine Run by late on the fourth or by daylight on the fifth. Even though Grant correctly states that his unopposed crossing of the Rapidan was "a great success," he and Meade were unaware of the close proximity of the Confederate army, just a few miles to the west. Grant's handling of his cavalry at this time was not overly skillful, although the blue horsemen, under the command of Philip H. Sheridan, were to gain an ascendency over the Southern riders as the campaign progressed. Except at Shiloh—where he had certainly not shone—it must be remembered that Grant had never actually been in command of a large army in a desperately fought large-scale battle. Chattanooga was assuredly not in that category, nor were any of the combats fought during the Vicksburg campaign. Grant, therefore,

[22] Humphreys, *Campaign of '64 & '65*, p. 11; Grant, *Memoirs*, II, 191; *B. & L.*, IV, 118.

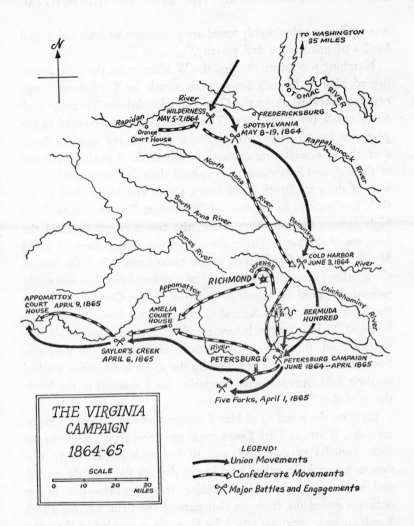

TO WASHINGTON
35 MILES

POTOMAC RIVER

N

FREDERICKSBURG

Rapidan River

WILDERNESS
MAY 5-7, 1864

SPOTSYLVANIA
MAY 8-19, 1864

Orange
Court House

Rappahannock River

North Anna River

South Anna River

James River

Pamunkey River

COLD HARBOR
JUNE 3, 1864

River

Chickahominy River

DEFENSE

RICHMOND

Appomattox

LINE

BERMUDA
HUNDRED

APPOMATTOX
COURT
HOUSE   APRIL 9, 1865

AMELIA
COURT
HOUSE

River

SAYLOR'S CREEK
APRIL 6, 1865

PETERSBURG

PETERSBURG CAMPAIGN
JUNE 1864-APRIL 1865

Five Forks, April 1, 1865

THE VIRGINIA
CAMPAIGN
1864-65

SCALE

0   10   20   30
                    MILES

LEGEND:

Union Movements

Confederate Movements

Major Battles and Engagements

was *really* not a thoroughly tested army commander who had waged battles of great scope and severity.[23]

Marching southward through the Wilderness on the early morning of May 5, Grant's forces were struck by Confederate units pressing eastward along the Orange-Fredericksburg Turnpike and, to the south, the Plank Road. The Federals turned westward to engage the foe on these two highways. After heavy fighting, however, the Nationals were checked sharply on both roads by the end of the day, and barely managed to hold their fieldworks just to the west of the vital Brock Road artery. Grant and Meade had set up their headquarers to the west of Wilderness Tavern, where, from high ground near the Lacy house, the two generals watched the progress of the battle. Grant for quite some time believed (as did Meade) that the Confederate attack came from only a fraction of the Southern army, and he was at first convinced that Lee was really retreating toward the North Anna River. Hence, Grant had allowed the bulk of Hancock's Second Corps to stand immobile for two hours at Todd's Tavern before recalling it to the battlefield, ten miles distant. Burnside's dilatoriness in marching to the field also hampered Union operations. During the night both armies worked on their field entrenchments, preparing for a renewal of the battle the next day.[24]

Early on the morning of May 6 the combat was resumed. On the turnpike, Warren's Fifth Corps could not drive Ewell, while to the right (north) of that road, part of Sedgwick's Sixth Corps was driven out of its trenches later in the day, its flank partly turned, and some 500 prisoners—including two generals—lost before darkness ended the strife on that part of the field. On the Plank Road, an early morning attack by Hancock succeeded in throwing Hill back some distance. But then Longstreet arrived on the field,

[23] 67 *O.R.*, 18, 188–89; Humphreys, *Campaign of '64 & '65*, pp. 9–11, 18–23; Walker, *Second Corps*, 409–10; Swinton, *Army of the Potomac*, 416, 419.

[24] 67 *O.R.*, 189–90; Humphreys, *Campaign of '64 & '65*, pp. 21–36; B. & L., IV, 145.

struck Hancock's left flank, and "rolled it up like a wet blanket." With fresh troops, Longstreet was preparing to complete his success when he was seriously wounded in the throat and neck by his own men, and was put out of action for five months. It was then rather late in the day for Lee to reorganize the Confederate lines, and he hesitated to resume the attack. The Unionists, however, had been barely able to hold their works along the western edge of the essential Brock Road, and it had cost them the life of General Wadsworth. The fighting was of the most sanguinary character, waged in the thick, tangled forest, where one could scarcely see what was going on twenty yards away. The Federals gave as good as they received. Wounded men were roasted alive when the woods caught fire. Only the coming of night brought an end to the bloody holocaust.[25]

During the second day of battle, Grant had been seated beneath the trees at his headquarters, receiving reports from the battle lines, and nervously whittling away at sticks until he had worn holes in the fingers of his buff-colored gloves. Throughout the long day the General met couriers bearing messages of Union successes and setbacks. He calmly received them and issued orders to cope with changing situations. Then he went into his tent, flung himself face downward on the cot, and wept uncontrollably. Never had his staff officers seen him moved so deeply in this manner.[26]

In the two-day battle of the Wilderness, Grant employed about 102,000 effectives as opposed to Lee's entire army of some 62,000 men. The Union commander lost 17,666 soldiers killed, wounded, and missing; Lee lost probably at least 8,000 men. Grant must have been impressed now with the fighting qualities of Meade's army and Lee's, for he expresses in his memoirs this opinion: "More desperate fighting has not been witnessed on this continent than that of the 5th and 6th of May." On the morning of May 7, 1864, he com-

[25] Morris Schaff, *Battle of the Wilderness* (Boston, 1910), *passim;* 67 *O.R.,* 190; *B. & L.,* IV, 123–26.
[26] Macartney, *Grant and His Generals,* 39, 93; Wilson, *Under the Old Flag,* I, 390.

mented, "Joe Johnston would have retreated after two days of such punishment." But Lee, too, had been badly battered.[27]

Grant had hoped to get through the Wilderness to the south before meeting Lee in battle, so that the superior Federal artillery could be used to best advantage on more open ground. While it is not true that the Union general fought the battle without plan, nonetheless everything did not go as planned. Opinion differs widely as to who came out ahead. General Webb contends that "Grant had been thoroughly defeated in his attempt to walk past General Lee on the way to Richmond." Edward Steere, on the other hand, points out that Lee had lost his offensive power as a result of the battle, and that Grant retained the initiative. "The advantage in the day's fighting," writes Colonel Spaulding, "was in general on the Confederate side. The Federal lines were pushed back, and ways were found to both their flanks, but they could not be forced across the Brock Road." Except for the losses he had inflicted on Lee, Grant had done little more than gain a tactical draw with an army only half as large as his own. "The Wilderness," proclaims Walter Geer, "is unique among battles as presenting the novel spectacle of an army of 60,000 enveloping the flanks of an army of 100,000!" Yet, as Steere mentions, Lee was unable to hold the line of the Rapidan-Rappahannock, as he believed he had to do.[28]

Like McClellan and Lee on the day after Antietam, and like Meade and Lee on the day following Gettysburg, so too Grant and Lee, on the day after the Wilderness, lay idle, the two exhausted armies facing each other behind their breastworks. On the evening of May 7, Grant determined to press on southward, despite his rough handling in the gloom of the Wilderness. This famous and vital decision of Grant's led Sherman to remark, "That was, in my judgment, the supreme moment of his life." Grant ordered the

[27] Livermore, *Numbers and Losses,* 110–11; Edward Steere, *The Wilderness Campaign* (Harrisburg, 1960), 463; *B. & L.,* IV, 182; Grant, *Memoirs,* II, 204; Channing, *History,* VI, 567 n.

[28] See Steere, *The Wilderness Campaign,* 297–302, 459, 461; *B. & L.,* IV, 161–62; Oliver L. Spaulding, *The United States Army . . .* (New York, 1937), 327; Geer, *Campaigns of the Civil War,* 343.

movement to be made by his left flank to Spotsylvania Court House in an effort to get around Lee's right flank and intervene between the gray army and Richmond, thereby compelling Lee to fight in open country on ground of Grant's choosing. When this "sliding" process was revealed to the Union troops on the night of May 7 as being in reality a movement toward Richmond, they wildly cheered Grant and Meade when the two generals rode through their midst.[29]

Although not aware at first of Grant's move, and believing for a time that the Union commander was retreating, Lee nonetheless had troops in position to cover the crossroads at Spotsylvania in time to check Warren's advance on the morning of May 8. More troops arrived on both sides. In subsequent attacks on the eighth, the Federals were repelled. But as late as 11:30 A.M. that day, Grant was saying to his staff, "It looks somewhat as if Lee intends to throw his army between us and Fredericksburg, in order to cut us off from our base of supplies." It was not until the afternoon of May 8 that the Lieutenant General would believe the unwelcome fact that Lee's army was already concentrating behind fieldworks covering Spotsylvania. Grant had prepared marching orders to push on southward from Spotsylvania Court House. He had also sent off Sheridan—after that fiery officer had had a run-in with Meade—with the bulk of the Union cavalry on a raid near Richmond which accomplished little save that it resulted in the death of the dashing Confederate cavalry leader, Jeb Stuart—killed in a clash at Yellow Tavern.[30]

Although the Spotsylvania battlefield was in itself of little strategic importance, Grant decided to fight there. "I shall take no backward step," he announced to Halleck. He determined to repeat his costly Wilderness experiment of attacking along his entire line. Walker avers that "to assault 'all along the line,' as was often done in the summer of 1864, is the very abdication of leadership." None-

[29] Porter, *Campaigning with Grant*, 74, 78–79; *B. & L.*, IV, 248; Grant, *Memoirs*, II, 210, 211; 67 *O.R.*, 64.

[30] See Steere, *The Wilderness Campaign*, 458, 462; 67 *O.R.*, 12, 19, 191, 773–81; *B. & L.*, IV, 118, 128, 189.

theless, this continual hammering process would steadily wear Lee down. Although "only a surprise attack had any chance of success against Lee's lines," Grant felt obliged to take the rest of the eighth and all of May 9 in preparing his forces to strike. Lee's line —stronger than that at the Wilderness—extended between the Po and Ny rivers. To turn this position, Grant would have to cross one of these streams, thus dividing his army and giving Lee a chance to defeat it in detail. Therefore, Grant relied chiefly on frontal assaults in the thickly wooded country. During some desultory firing on May 9, Grant suffered the loss of his able Sixth Corps commander, Sedgwick, who was killed by a sharpshooter. A competent officer, Major General Horatio G. Wright, succeeded the beloved "Uncle John." [31]

On the morning of May 10, Hancock, who had moved to a good position on the south side of the Po threatening the enemy left and enfilading his lines, was unfortunately ordered back to the north side of that stream by Grant, who had decided to attack in front. This proved to be an unwise move. The numerous Union attacks on May 10 were repulsed by the Confederates, including the skillful one made at 5:00 P.M. by Emory Upton's three picked brigades, which, after an initial success, was also hurled back. Grant lost over 4,000 men on this day, compared with light enemy losses. On the Union left, a forward movement by Burnside had, in effect, turned the Confederate right at the time the Union attacks in front were in progress; but neither Grant nor Burnside was aware of this, and a splendid opportunity was lost. [32]

Little action took place on the rainy eleventh. Grant believed that only lack of proper support had cost Upton a victory on the tenth, so he ordered a massive attack by the Second Corps, supported by the Ninth, against the northern apex of Lee's salient for

[31] Humphreys, *Campaign of '64 & '65*, p. 71; Walker, *Hancock*, 193.
[32] Swinton, *Army of the Potomac*, 449–50; Humphreys, *Campaign of '64 & '65*, pp. 81 ff.; *B. & L.*, IV, 129 ff., 167 ff.; Livermore, *Numbers and Losses*, 112; 67 *O.R.*, 665–68.

4:00 A.M. on May 12. On the eleventh Grant wired Halleck, "We have now ended the sixth day of very heavy fighting. . . . I . . . propose to fight it out on this line if it takes all summer." He asked for all the reinforcements possible. Lee's choice of wooded terrain in which to fight had so neutralized the powerful array of Union guns that Grant sent his entire artillery reserve back to Washington.[33]

When Hancock's brilliant dawn attack was made on May 12, it was aided by Lee's having just pulled twenty-two guns from the point under attack for service elsewhere. The assault was at first eminently successful, capturing some twenty of the returning guns, almost 4,000 prisoners, and Confederate Generals Johnson and George H. Steuart. Only Lee's prompt sending of reserves to man a trench line at the base of the salient prevented the Federals from exploiting this initial triumph. Other Union attacks on each flank were contained. Learning that Hancock had now been halted, Grant poured eight of Wright's brigades, followed soon by sixteen more, against a slight bend on the western face of the enemy salient known ever afterwards as the Bloody Angle. However, too many troops were used in such a cramped area, the attacking lines were too close together, and after some fourteen hours of vicious fighting the Federals had won the breastworks at the Angle, but little else, as Lee had manned a firm line in the rear. So competent, however, had been Meade's carrying out of Grant's orders that the Lieutenant General telegraphed Stanton, "General Meade has more than met my most sanguine expectations. He and Sherman are the fittest officers for large commands I have come in contact with." [34]

The day's operations cost Grant at least 6,820 men. But he had inflicted about 4,000 to 5,000 casualties in killed and wounded on the enemy, in addition to capturing approximately 4,000 additional Southerners. The Northern general had definitely come out ahead

[33] 67 O.R., 4; Nicolay and Hay, Abraham Lincoln, VIII, 378, 379.
[34] Grant, Memoirs, II, 134–38; Humphreys, Campaign of '64 & '65, pp. 88–106; B. & L., IV, 170–74; Meade, Life and Letters of Meade, II, 196.

in the day's fighting. Grant's losses from May 5 to May 12 inclusive totaled about 31,000.[35]

From May 13 through May 18, Grant maneuvered at Spotsylvania to strike first at Lee's right and then at his old center (now Lee's left) at the base of the muleshoe. However, rain hampered the operations, and a Union attack at the base of the salient on the eighteenth was repulsed with some 2,000 men killed and wounded. Actually, in all the actions at Spotsylvania Court House, Grant might have saved thousands of casualties by turning Lee's position, which was quite feasible. However, he seemed determined to carry the gray lines by direct assault.[36]

The eighteenth of May, 1864, was a black day for Grant. His own efforts at Spotsylvania had been frustrated. News arrived that Sigel had been thoroughly thrashed at New Market in the Valley; that Banks had failed utterly in his peripheral campaign up the Red River in Louisiana; and that Butler, with 36,000 men, had met ignominious defeat at the hands of Beauregard at Drewry's Bluff near Richmond. Missing a good chance to seize Petersburg, Butler had lost 3,500 men, and was now thoroughly bottled up at Bermuda Hundred Neck, where the Appomattox River joins the James.[37]

The battles at Spotsylvania Court House, from May 8 to May 19, cost Grant casualties amounting to 18,399 men. In the two battles of the Wilderness and Spotsylvania, Grant lost a total of approximately 36,000 men, while Lee's loss in these two combats has been estimated by Livermore at 17,250, not including the missing. Grant was reinforced during May by perhaps 30,000 men, while Lee received some 15,000 additional troops.[38]

Grant began to withdraw his army from Lee's front on the night of May 20, determining to try another swing around Lee's right.

[35] Livermore, *Numbers and Losses,* 112–13.
[36] Wood and Edmonds, *The Civil War,* 327–29; Swinton, *Army of the Potomac,* 454–57.
[37] Grant, *Memoirs,* II, 238; Humphreys, *Campaign of '64 & '65,* pp. 137, 139 ff.
[38] B. & L., IV, 182; Geer, *Campaigns of the Civil War,* 356–57.

Refusing to be distracted by a Federal feint toward Guinea Station, Lee arrived first at the North Anna River, despite a twelve-hour Union start. The Confederate leader thereby kept between Grant and Richmond, and covered the Virginia Central Railroad. Lee took up a powerful position with an umbrella-shaped front. As Swinton remarks, "The game of war seldom presents a more effectual checkmate than was here given by Lee; for after Grant had made the brilliantly successful passage of the North Anna, the Confederate commander, thrusting his centre between the two wings of the Army of the Potomac, put his antagonist at enormous disadvantage, and compelled him, for the reinforcement of one or the other wing, to make a double passage of the river." So, on the night of the twenty-sixth, Grant was impelled to withdraw the army to the north bank of the river and move once more by his left flank toward Hanover Town on the Pamunkey. He wisely issued orders at about this time to have bridging material available for a possible future crossing of the James.[39]

Learning that Grant, after some skirmishing, had pulled out from the North Anna, Lee once again guessed correctly the Union general's plans, and, by use of interior lines, once more won the race. He arrived in front of Grant at the Totopotomoy on May 28, and entrenched a position so strong that Grant sensibly decided not to attack it. Again some skirmishing ensued. Union casualties at the North Anna and the Totopotomoy amounted to almost 4,000 men.[40]

So once more Grant repeated the process of pulling out and moving by his left flank in an endeavor to get around Lee's right. He had optimistically wired Washington on May 26 that "Lee's army is really whipped. . . . I may be mistaken, but I feel that our success over Lee's army is already assured." But when he reached the vicinity of Cold Harbor, there was the enemy, awaiting his pleasure. Grant was already being censured as a butcher by the Northern press and public, and especially by the Radicals. At Cold Harbor

[39] Swinton, *Army of the Potomac*, 477; 67 *O.R.*, 21.
[40] Wood and Edmonds, *The Civil War*, 334; *B. & L.*, IV, 182.

the General launched several limited attacks on May 30 and June 1 which were partially successful in gaining some ground and prisoners. Casualties on each side amounted to 2,000 men. Grant had been reinforced by W. F. Smith's Eighteenth Corps from Butler's army. But fatigue and the intense heat forced the Union commander to postpone renewal of his attacks until 4:30 A.M. on June 3, when a massive assault was to be thrown directly at Lee's lines from across largely open ground. Grant had some 114,000 men available. Perhaps he was emboldened by his minor successes on May 30 and June 1. Seeing the hopelessness of the venture, the soldiers in blue fastened slips of paper to their backs giving their names and addresses. The hopeless attack was gallantly made, but was immediately hurled back with fearful losses in the first fifteen minutes. When Grant rashly ordered another desperate attack, his troops simply refused to move forward, and Meade assumed the responsibility of calling it off. The Federal casualties in the combats around Cold Harbor amounted to 12,737; Confederate losses on June 3 were about 1,700.[41]

James Ford Rhodes states that Grant had attacked at Cold Harbor "with unjustifiable precipitation," and terms the battle "the greatest blemish on his reputation as a general." But Grant was man enough to see and admit his blunder. "I have always regretted that the last assault at Cold Harbor was ever made," he wrote. "No advantage whatever was gained to compensate for the heavy loss we sustained." After one month of active campaigning against Lee, Grant acknowledged to Halleck, "Without a greater sacrifice of life than I am willing to make, all cannot be accomplished that I had designed north of Richmond." In effect, this was an admission of partial failure. However, with grim tenacity and dogged determination, Grant decided to cross to the south side of the James and seize

[41] Grant, *Memoirs*, II, 253; Humphreys, *Campaign of '64 & '65*, pp. 166–69, 176, 192; *Century Magazine*, Mar., 1897, 720; *B. & L.*, IV, 182, 187, 217–18; Livermore, *Numbers and Losses*, 114; Swinton, *Army of the Potomac*, 483, 485, 487, 488.

the rail-hub of Petersburg, which, he hoped, would force Lee to come out from behind his fieldworks and fight in the open.[42]

The New York *Times* war correspondent, William Swinton, in analyzing Grant's campaign which terminated with the repulse at Cold Harbor, believes that the coastal route was superior to the overland route. He goes on to say, "As the overland campaign was unsuccessful either in the destruction of Lee's army or the capture of Richmond, and as the line of operations was at length abandoned. . . . the balance was very much in favor of the enemy," since, by the time Grant was obliged to besiege Petersburg, he had lost some 60,000 men to Lee's 20,000. As to the argument that the Union had infinite resources as compared with those of the South, Swinton points out that only the morale of the people permits the employment of these resources, and that, after Cold Harbor, the morale of the North was sagging dangerously, and that there was "great danger of a collapse of the war." Only success elsewhere bolstered the Northern will to win at that time. However, Lee could ill afford to suffer the losses he did.[43]

"I think," wrote Meade on June 5, "Grant has had his eyes opened, and is willing to admit that Virginia and Lee's army is not Tennessee and Bragg's army." Grant himself correctly asserted to Congressman Washburne on June 9, "All the fight, except defensive and behind breastworks, is taken out of Lee's army. Unless my next move brings on a battle, the balance of the campaign will settle down to a siege." Despite the unfavorable signs, Lincoln had stated on June 3—the day of the great debacle at Cold Harbor—"My previous high estimate of General Grant has been maintained and heightened by what has occurred in the remarkable campaign he is now conducting." [44]

[42] Rhodes, *History of the United States*, IV, 445; 67 *O.R.*, 22; *B. & L.*, IV, 142–43, 213–20, 229; Grant, *Memoirs*, II, 276, 280 n; Young, *Around the World with Grant*, II, 304.

[43] Swinton, *Army of the Potomac*, 491–95.

[44] Meade, *Life and Letters of Meade*, II, 201, 202; Wilson, *General Grant*, 344; Nicolay and Hay, *Complete Works*, X, 112.

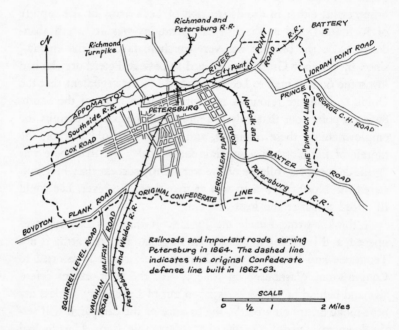

N

Richmond and
Petersburg R.R.

Richmond
Turnpike

BATTERY
5

RIVER

City Point

CITY POINT ROAD

R.R.

JORDAN POINT ROAD

APPOMATTOX

Southside R.R.

PETERSBURG

PRINCE

GEORGE C.H. ROAD

(THE "DIMMOCK LINE")

COX ROAD

Norfolk and

JERUSALEM PLANK ROAD

BAXTER

ROAD

Petersburg

R.R.

BOYDTON

PLANK ROAD

SQUIRREL LEVEL ROAD

VAUGHAN

HALIFAX

ROAD

Petersburg and Weldon R.R.

ORIGINAL CONFEDERATE

LINE

Railroads and important roads serving
Petersburg in 1864. The dashed line
indicates the original Confederate
defense line built in 1862-63.

SCALE

0   ½   1   2 Miles

R.W. Kramer

Grant's new plan was to seize Petersburg, turn the enemy works of Beauregard in front of Butler at Bermuda Hundred, and then advance on Richmond. On the night of June 12, the Federals began pulling out of Cold Harbor, and by the sixteenth Grant had his army safely across the James on the south bank. The operation was a brilliant success. This movement, declares Steele, "belongs to a class of strategical operations which are considered among the most hazardous and difficult in warfare. It was a flank movement involving the crossing of close and wooded country by narrow roads, and the passage of two difficult streams, the Chickahominy and the James, over which pontoon bridges had to be laid." The bridge across the James was over 2,000 feet in length—a feat of engineering in itself. On the thirteenth Lee discovered Grant's withdrawal from Cold Harbor, and on the same day he dispatched Early to the Shenandoah Valley.[45]

Grant visited Butler at Bermuda Hundred on June 14 and ordered him to capture Petersburg at once. The Lieutenant General earmarked Hancock's Second Corps to succor Butler's force under Smith. Grant failed, however, to notify Meade and Hancock of the intended attack on Petersburg. On the fifteenth Smith launched a brilliant assault which captured a mile and a half of Beauregard's trenches, many prisoners, and twenty guns. However, Grant's failure to inform Hancock until 5:00 P.M. that he was to assist in the attack kept him from reaching the field until after dark, and Smith hesitated to attempt to press into Petersburg after nightfall. Only much later, when their friendship had changed to enmity, did Grant charge Smith with overcaution and slowness in attacking the city. Actually, perhaps, more than anyone else, Grant was to blame for the failure to take the place. The baffled Lee, with his army, was still at Malvern Hill on the north side of the James, and did not begin to move to Beauregard's assistance until June 16. By the morning of the sixteenth, Beauregard had increased his force

[45] Humphreys, *Campaign of '64 & '65*, p. 203; Steele, *American Campaigns*, 528.

to but 14,000 men—still not enough to man properly his line of entrenchments.[46]

Grant arrived on the field to the east of Petersburg during the forenoon of June 16. At 6:00 P.M. he threw Hancock at both flanks of Beauregard's line and captured a few redoubts, with the result that the Confederates began to work on a new line a little to the rear. "Sheridan was, during this whole movement," notes Ropes, "on one of those useless raids which General Grant seems to have greatly favored. Had he accompanied the army to Petersburg, it is not too much to say that the defenceless state of the enemy's southern line would have been promptly ascertained, and Petersburg captured." On the morning of the seventeenth, new Federal assaults, chiefly by the Ninth Corps, gained a bit of ground, but cost Grant 4,000 more casualties. Beauregard pulled his force back a little to the newly constructed line closer to the city. Then, Grant launched a general attack, by most of his army, all along the line on the morning of June 18. After slight initial gains, the heavy assaults were repelled with severe loss, and the somewhat demoralized Federals dug in. The two armies were to remain essentially in these positions, with some changes on the southern flanks, for the next nine and one-half months during the siege of Petersburg. Since crossing the James River on June 15, Grant had lost approximately 10,000 men before Petersburg. Since the crossing of the Rapidan, he had lost about 62,000 soldiers, not counting Butler's 7,000 casualties.[47]

Quite unhappy with the state of affairs, and perhaps with some qualms as to the generalship of Grant, Lincoln visited the army at City Point for several days around June 21. The President talked with Grant and his top officers, and inspected the troops. The Lieutenant General apparently convinced Lincoln that he had been

[46] 67 *O.R.*, 25; 81 *O.R.*, 36; *Petersburg, Chancellorsville, Gettysburg*, V, 36–73, 77–115, 133, 195; W. F. Smith to S. Foot, Dec. 12, 1864, Lincoln Papers; Humphreys, *Campaign of '64 & '65*, p. 202–15.

[47] *Petersburg, Chancellorsville, Gettysburg*, V, 161–64; Livermore, *Numbers and Losses*, 115.

stymied only for the time being and that victory for the Nationals was inevitable. The President said to one of the staff officers, "When Grant once gets possession of a place, he holds on to it as if he had inherited it." Perhaps as a slight rebuke to the General for his heavy losses, the Chief Executive said to him, "I cannot pretend to advise, but I do sincerely hope that all may be accomplished with as little bloodshed as possible." [48]

Beginning on June 21, Grant attempted a movement on his left aimed at the important, enemy-held Weldon and Southside railroads to the south of Petersburg. But on the twenty-second of June, the Second Corps, after only slight gains, and with the nearer rail line still a mile away, was checked with the loss of four guns and 1,700 prisoners. Then, from June 22 to July 2, Brigadier General James H. Wilson and 5,500 Federal cavalrymen went off on a raid ordered by Grant—but opposed by Meade—against these same railroads. After tearing up some track (which was soon repaired by the enemy), Wilson was crushed by Lee at Ream's Station, and lost twelve guns, 1,500 men, and his entire wagon train. [49]

Then, another unfortunate incident befell the Union General-in-Chief. About the end of June, Grant became inebriated—possibly because of Butler's contrivance—and visited several generals' headquarters in this condition. Butler threatened to make use of this episode against the Lieutenant General. When Butler and Smith got into a row, Grant telegraphed Halleck that Butler should be shelved to an administrative department post at Fortress Monroe, and succeeded in actual command of his field army by Smith, Franklin, or Joseph J. Reynolds. Lincoln at first issued such an order in his own name, placing Smith in field command; but on second thought, the President remembered Butler's political influence and had the order recalled and reissued without the phrase, "by order of the President." [50]

[48] Morse (ed.), *Welles's Diary*, II, 55; Porter, *Campaigning with Grant*, 216–24.

[49] Humphreys, *Campaign of '64 & '65*, p. 227–29, 236–41.

[50] Macartney, *Grant and His Generals*, 215–16; 80 *O.R.*, 28; 81 *O.R.*, 558–59, 598; 82 *O.R.*, 31, 59, 69.

Seeing that, in essence, he was being superseded by Smith, Butler charged up to City Point to remonstrate with Grant. He held out a copy of the directive and demanded, "General Grant, did you issue this order?" Glancing at the missive, the Lieutenant General stammered, and finally replied hesitatingly, "No, no; not in that form." Butler then moved into a room alone with Grant, and apparently threatened to expose him for drinking if Grant did not have the order rescinded. For perhaps the only time in his military career, Grant was cowed. He backed down and told Butler the order was a mistake, and then communicated with Halleck and had it canceled. Butler now crowed that he would receive a command of greater prestige, and that he was stronger than ever before. The aftermath was that when Smith—whom Grant had before extolled —returned to the army from a leave, he was removed from his command and shipped to New York. This was done, possibly, to separate Smith and Butler. But another factor, perhaps, was that Smith earlier had urged Grant to move via the water route instead of the overland route. Also, in a private talk with Grant, Smith had sharply criticized Meade's movements with the army, especially at Cold Harbor, and the Lieutenant General, knowing well that he (Grant) was responsible for the army's movements and for the Cold Harbor fiasco, possibly resented Smith's censuring him over Meade's shoulder. Grant's explanations of his cave-in to Butler are rather feeble evasions.[51]

But Grant's attention was diverted from such semi-political affairs to strictly military matters at the beginning of July, when Lee sent Early to the Valley for a raid toward the Potomac. Grant's actions in attempting to cope with this last Confederate foray form one of the less creditable pages in his military career. He was poorly versed on affairs in the Valley, and at first refused to believe that anything serious was developing. Nicolay and Hay write that

[51] Smith, *From Chattanooga to Petersburg*, 32–59, 174–78; Williams, *Lincoln and His Generals*, 323–24; 82 *O.R.*, 114, 122–23, 334, 577; *B. & L.*, IV, 107 n, 229; Benjamin F. Butler, . . . *Butler's Book* (Boston, 1892), 685 ff.

"after Early had seized Martinsburg, so late as the 3d of July, Grant insisted that he was at Petersburg, and that it was impossible he could be threatening Hunter's department." The inept Hunter retreated off into a limbo in West Virginia. Not until the fifth was Grant convinced of the enemy threat. As Rhodes states, "It was . . . little to the credit of Grant that Washington should be in so imminent danger, while Richmond was in none, and that the measures for its safety should have been so tardily taken. During these days the commander seemed to be stunned." [52]

On July 6 Grant dispatched 5,000 men of the Sixth Corps to Washington and 3,000 cavalrymen (of whom 2,496 were sick!) to Baltimore. The General actually believed, and stated, that these troops, plus those of the far-removed Hunter, might "succeed in nearly annihilating Early and Breckinridge." Inexplicably supporting the incompetent Hunter, Grant declared, somewhat flippantly, to Dana, "If the enemy has left Maryland, as I suppose he has [Early, after reaching the outskirts of the capital, retired on July 12], he should have on his heels veterans, militiamen, men on horseback, and everything that can be got to follow to eat out Virginia clear and clean as far as they go, so that crows flying over it for the balance of the season will have to carry their provender with them." After first offering to come himself to Washington, Grant reversed himself when the President accepted this suggestion, and remained at City Point. As the sequel proved, Grant erred in not proceeding at once to the capital. [53]

The General soon cooled in his desire to press Early closely. He at first wanted the Sixth and Sixteenth corps returned to him at Petersburg, but desisted when Halleck correctly protested. The latter became embittered and flailed out at Grant, excoriating his crossing of the James, his leaving Washington insecure, and his

[52] Nicolay and Hay, *Abraham Lincoln*, IX, 164; Rhodes, *History of the United States*, IV, 499–500.

[53] Lincoln to Grant, July 10, 1864, Basler (ed.), *Collected Works of Lincoln*, VII, 437; Grant to Lincoln, July 10, 1864, Lincoln Papers; 71 *O.R.*, 80, 134, 156, 223, 300–301, 332, 365.

failure to accomplish anything at Petersburg. Grant's suggestion on July 18 that Franklin be placed in command of a new military division embracing the four separate commands near the Potomac met with a cool reception in Washington. There were even overtures made—unsuccessfully—by the administration to McClellan to return to a high command position. Later in the month of July, the Federals were caught flat-footed when a detachment of Early's under the command of John McCausland invaded Pennsylvania and burned Chambersburg. When Grant then urged Meade as the commander of the new military division, Lincoln came down to Fortress Monroe and conferred with the General. The results of this conclave will be noted shortly. During this critical period, Rawlins noticed that, while he had been away for a few days, Grant had resumed his drinking.[54]

Meanwhile, just to the east of Petersburg, work had been proceeding since June 25 on a 511-foot Union mine which reached to a point under the Confederate lines. By July 28 the mine was finished and charged with 8,000 pounds of powder. As a feint, Grant had sent Hancock's Second Corps and three of Sheridan's cavalry divisions across the James on a mission to the north of Richmond; and, while Lee successfully countered this threat to the Virginia Central and R. F. & P. railroads, he had to draw troops away from his lines at Petersburg to do so. Despite adequate orders from Grant, and very explicit orders from Meade as to how the attack was to be made early on the morning of July 30, following the detonation of the mine, Burnside fouled up the whole enterprise in a remarkably large number of ways. Grant had high hopes that the attack would be successful in breaching the enemy lines and capturing Petersburg, but Meade was "not sanguine of success." [55]

[54] Badeau, *Grant*, II, 446–51; Nicolay and Hay, *Abraham Lincoln*, IX, 175, 178; J. G. Randall and Richard N. Current, *Lincoln the President* . . . (New York, 1955), IV, 218; 71 *O.R.*, 300–301, 350, 374, 408, 444, 463; 74 *O.R.*, 150–51; 82 *O.R.*, 676.

[55] Grant, *Memoirs*, II, 310–12; C.C.W. (1865), I, 110; Humphreys, *Campaign of '64 & '65*, pp. 247–54; Meade, *Life and Letters of Meade*, II, 217; B. & L., IV, 549.

The mine was touched off at 4:30 A.M. on the thirtieth, and, until 2:00 P.M., Burnside poured regiment after regiment into the seething cauldron. Actually, he threw forward too many troops; they got in each other's way, and piled up in the 150-foot-long crater itself instead of going forward to capture the ridge and city beyond. Then, too, Burnside did not follow Meade's orders in a number of other particulars. To make matters worse, two of Burnside's division commanders stayed behind in the safety of a bunker, entertaining John Barleycorn. The result was that Lee, quickly sending in reinforcements, checked the Federal attackers, who were finally ordered by Meade to fall back. Over 4,000 casualties were suffered by Grant in the mine debacle, while Lee lost but 1,200 men. To round out the unfortunate day for the Nationals, Generals Meade and Burnside got into a heated altercation during the battle.[56]

The responsibility for the "miserable failure," as Grant called it, rests largely on Burnside's broad shoulders. A military court so found, and Burnside resigned from the service. Grant's views as to the cause of the mine failure were, first, "allowing Ledlie to lead the assaulting column"; "then . . . the neglect of Burnside to prepare the parapets"; and finally, "the absence of the corps and division commanders from their troops." Said the General-in-Chief further: "I think the cause of the disaster was simply leaving the passage of orders from one to another down to an inefficient man. I blame his seniors also for not seeing that he did his duty, all the way up to myself." Grant remarked to Halleck, "It was the saddest affair I have witnessed in the war."[57]

On August 1, 1864, after conferring briefly with Lincoln at Old Point Comfort, Grant formed the West Virginia, Susquehanna, Middle, and Washington departments into a new military division, headed nominally by Hunter as chief administrator, but with

[56] Humphreys, *Campaign of '64 & '65*, pp. 250–65; Meade, *Life and Letters of Meade*, II, 217 n; Livermore, *Numbers and Losses*, 116; *B. & L.*, IV, 560 n, 564.

[57] Badeau, *Grant*, II, 484, 486; *C.C.W.* (1865) I, 110, 111.

Grant's favorite, Sheridan, in actual field command. Upon Lincoln's urging, Grant reluctantly journeyed up to Monocacy Junction on August 5 to inaugurate and give initial impetus to the movement of the gathering Union forces designed to pursue Early. Believing that Halleck had lost confidence in him, Hunter conveniently stepped down, and Sheridan was named to command the new military division. In his memoirs "Little Phil" misstates the facts when he claims that the President had opposed the amalgamation of the four departments into the new division, but he was more accurate when he states that Stanton was not too happy with the small, thirty-three-year-old Sheridan's receiving this new command. Actually, although not proving to be a mental giant as a strategist in planning and conducting operations against Early's outnumbered force, Sheridan was pugnacious, a good tactician on the field, and an aggressive man in a fight.[58]

When he got back to the army at Petersburg on August 7, Grant found the Old Snapping Turtle angry at Sheridan's getting the new post. Meade said that Grant had promised *him* a new military division when one was created. Then, on August 24, when he learned that Sherman, Hancock, and Sheridan had been promoted and that he had not, Meade asked Grant for an explanation. The General-in-Chief frankly stated that it was done, in effect, to forward his favorites, Sherman and Sheridan. "It is the same old story," remarked Meade in disgust to his wife, "an inability to appreciate the sensitiveness of a man of character and honor. Grant really thinks he is one of my best friends, and can't conceive why I should complain of a little delay in giving me what he tells me I am certainly to have." Meade later came to Grant complaining about newspaper criticisms of him, and even threatening to resign. Grant soothed him and talked him out of such drastic action. Not only was the General angered at these smears against Meade, but he wrote the latter,

[58] 71 *O.R.*, 558; 88 *O.R.*, 38; Grant, *Memoirs*, II, 317–21; P. H. Sheridan, *Personal Memoirs of P. H. Sheridan* (New York, 1888), I, 346–47; Bates, *Lincoln in the Telegraph Office*, 67.

"I have never expressed dissatisfaction at any portion of your services." [59]

When, on August 18, the Confederates offered to exchange prisoners of war with Grant on a man-for-man basis, Grant refused, saying, "It is hard on our men held in Southern prisons not to exchange them, but it is humanity to those left in the ranks to fight our battles. . . . If we hold those [Confederates] caught they amount to no more than dead men. At this particular time to release all rebel prisoners North would insure Sherman's defeat and would compromise our safety here." When Halleck unwisely suggested to Grant that he send north a large portion of his forces at Petersburg to quell expected draft riots, Grant firmly rejected this advice, and was strongly backed by the President. Apparently miffed at Halleck for this, as well as for the former's rather open criticism of him earlier, Grant, showing that on occasion he could be shifty and devious, told Stanton, with obvious duplicity, that McDowell, on the West Coast, was inefficient (this was blatantly untrue) and that the Chief of Staff should be sent there to replace him. Recognizing this sly plan to shelve Halleck, the Secretary of War wired back that Halleck was needed in Washington, and that, anyway, there had been no reports received of McDowell's inefficiency. Grant capitulated.[60]

Meanwhile, to favor Sheridan's operations in the Valley, Grant moved Warren's Fifth Corps, reinforced by the Ninth Corps, against Lee's right flank south of Petersburg. After tearing up some track on the Weldon Railroad near Globe Tavern, Warren received a check. In the end, however, he managed to throw back the Confederates and maintain his position. The operation had cost the Federals 4,455 casualties. Then, on August 24 and 25, trying to seize more of the railroad to the south, Hancock—not properly sup-

[59] Meade, *Life and Letters of Meade*, II, 220–21, 223–24, 236–37.
[60] 120 *O.R.*, 607; 121 *O.R.*, 811; 88 *O.R.*, 193–94, 243; Basler (ed.), *Collected Works of Lincoln*, VII, 499; 106 *O.R.*, 945, 949, 951; Wilson, *Rawlins*, 257.

ported—was defeated at Ream's Station by A. P. Hill, the Federals losing nine guns and 2,742 men as compared to Hill's acknowledged loss of 720 men.[61]

Atlanta fell to Sherman on September 2, thus saving Grant from further attacks by the Radicals. In the fall political campaign, Congressman Washburne asked Grant to allow the President to use one of the General's letters in answering the criticism made against Lincoln by the Democrats. Agreeing to this, Grant, in one of his rare flings at humor, added, "I think, however, for him to attempt to answer all the charges the opposition will bring against him will be like setting a maiden to work to prove her chastity." In early October Grant (and Lincoln) felt that Sherman should first defeat John B. Hood's army before embarking on his great march to the sea from Atlanta to Savannah; but Sherman disagreed, and Grant reluctantly allowed "Cump" to have his way.[62]

On September 15 Grant paid a quick visit to Sheridan. Seeing that the latter was eager to strike at Early, the General told him to "go in!" After scoring victories at Winchester and Fisher's Hill on September 19 and 20, and pursuing as far as Staunton, Sheridan, fearing for his long line of communications, pulled back. In his march northward he destroyed much of the economic resources of the Valley, as Grant had directed on August 26. Meanwhile, as a diversion, Grant moved Major General E. O. C. Ord to the north side of the James with 14,000 men on September 29 and 30. Ord skillfully attacked and captured Fort Harrison, but was repelled in his assaults on Fort Gilmer, losing, in all, 3,327 men to a probable enemy loss of 2,000. At the same time Lincoln warned Grant that Lee might send reinforcements to enable Early to turn on Sheridan. However, Grant replied overconfidently that his own pressure on Lee at Petersburg would prevent this from happening. As part of the co-operative movement at the end of September, Grant directed the Fifth and Ninth corps to swing south of Petersburg toward

[61] Humphreys, *Campaign of '64 & '65*, p. 272–83; Livermore, *Numbers and Losses*, 118.

[62] 88 *O.R.*, 934, 935; 79 *O.R.*, 202, 222, 239, 576, 594.

Lee's right flank. The Federals succeeded in moving west of the Weldon Railroad against the Boydton Plank Road. Though checked for a time, they did gain and hold some useful ground.[63]

Finally, back in the Valley, Early brilliantly attacked Sheridan's army at Cedar Creek at dawn on October 19, and drove it back in rout to Winchester. Sheridan, just returning after being absent from his command, rushed to the field in dramatic fashion, and helped to wrap up the successful counterattack which was already underway against the outnumbered enemy. "Old Jube" was forced to fall back. This practically terminated the operations in the Valley, Sheridan's army going into winter quarters at Kernstown. During his entire Valley campaign, Sheridan had lost 17,000 out of a total force of 43,000; Early's loss in his total command of less than 20,000 is unknown.[64]

Before the arrival of winter, Grant hoped to seize the vital Southside Railroad to the south-southwest of Petersburg, one of the last remaining Confederate supply lines into the city. He earmarked some 32,000 men for this movement in the vicinity of Hatcher's Run and the Boydton Plank Road. But once again Lee thwarted him, and the enterprise was largely unproductive. Before the firing had died down, both Grant and Meade had recklessly exposed themselves to a severe enemy artillery fire on the field. The General-in-Chief was rather quick to call off the action when it appeared to be futile, because of fear of hurting Lincoln in the approaching presidential election if the Federals suffered a large setback. Nonetheless, the venture of the Boydton Plank Road cost Grant losses of 1,758 men. A co-operative movement by Butler north of the James at the same time resulted only in defeat and 1,100 additional casualties. These two actions ended major operations at Petersburg and Richmond for 1864. For the five months from June through October, Grant had lost over 47,000 men. But at the end of the

[63] 67 O.R., 30; Grant, Memoirs, II, 583; Humphreys, Campaign of '64 & '65, pp. 285 ff.; Livermore, Numbers and Losses, 128; Basler (ed.), Collected Works of Lincoln, VIII, 29; 88 O.R., 1090–91.

[64] Geer, Campaigns of the Civil War, 411, 454–55; B. & L., IV, 500–32.

year, reinforcements had kept his army at 110,000, as compared to Lee's 47,000 men.[65]

In mid-November, Grant took a trip to visit his children in school in New Jersey, and went also to New York, Philadelphia, and Washington. When he returned to the army at Petersburg, Meade fell upon him regarding Sheridan's promotion. Meade reported that, in reply, Grant claimed to have had nothing to do with Sheridan's promotion, to have wanted Meade as commander of the Middle Division instead of Sheridan, and to have been remiss in not urging that Meade be advanced at the same time as Sherman. "Now I *believe* Grant," said Meade, but added that he was the only one among those recommended who had not been promoted. On the twenty-fifth of November, he was still proclaiming "Grant's truthfulness and sincerity. I am willing," he said, "to admit, as he does himself, that his omissions have resulted unfavorably to me, but I am satisfied he is really and truly friendly to me. I like Grant, and always have done so."

On the following day the army lost the services of one of its finest officers. Hancock, "The Superb," suffering from his old Gettysburg wound, was forced to leave the army for less strenuous duty in Washington, and his place as commander of the Second Corps was taken by the able Andrew A. Humphreys.[66]

In early December the center of military attention was shifted to the Western theater. A Union army under Major General George H. Thomas was bottled up inside Nashville by Hood's Confederate army, which had invaded Tennessee. Lincoln feared that Thomas would delay too long in attacking Hood's smaller force, and Grant sent three curt messages to the "Rock of Chickamauga" to strike out at Hood. Thomas replied that he would do so as soon as possible. But Grant apparently did not believe him, and committed an unfair act when he assailed Thomas' generalship in a letter

[65] *Petersburg, Chancellorsville, Gettysburg,* V, 327; Livermore, *Numbers and Losses,* 131; Humphreys, *Campaign of '64 & '65,* pp. 294 ff.; B. & L., IV, 593, 594.

[66] Porter, *Campaigning with Grant,* 325; Meade, *Life and Letters of Meade,* II, 244, 247, 248.

to Stanton, claiming that Thomas was unversed in offensive fighting and probably never would move against Hood. Grant stated that Thomas should be ousted and replaced by Major General John M. Schofield. Lincoln and Halleck were astounded at Grant's attitude, and said that since no one in Washington wanted Thomas fired, the General-in-Chief would have to do it himself. Despite the President's undisguised opposition, Grant refused to take the hint, and insisted on drawing up the removal order. Before it could be issued, however, Halleck wired Grant that Thomas was being delayed in attacking only by a terrible sleet storm at Nashville. The General gave Thomas a little more time, but bombarded him with vehement and ill-considered exhortations to do what Grant knew to be impossible. Grant then sent Major General John A. Logan to supersede Thomas, and left himself for Nashville to remove "Old Slow Trot." But just at this time, in mid-December, word arrived that Thomas had attacked and had, in effect, annihilated Hood's army as a further effective fighting force. Grant's only reaction was to compliment Thomas in a somewhat ungracious manner for his brilliant success. All in all, it was a rather shabby performance on Grant's part.[67]

The approaching holiday season was brightened by the news that Sherman had captured Savannah on December 21, 1864. However, at City Point, a black cloud appeared in the form of the Committee on the Conduct of the War—the Radicals hoping to whitewash Burnside and frame Meade for the mine disaster. Grant entertained the solons and, according to George W. Julian, got drunk. In his testimony, however, the General infuriated the Jacobins by stoutly defending Meade and censuring Burnside. Christmas was made more joyful for Grant by the arrival of his wife and two sons at City Point. Sticking pretty close to business, however, Grant exchanged telegrams with Sherman as to Cump's future course of action. The President refrained from intervening in these strategic

[67] Nicolay and Hay, *Abraham Lincoln*, X, 25, 28–29; 94 *O.R.*, 15–18, 70, 84, 96, 97, 114–16, 143, 195, 196; Basler (ed.), *Collected Works of Lincoln*, VIII, 169; Bates, *Lincoln in the Telegraph Office*, 315–17.

plannings. The two generals agreed that Sherman should press up from Savannah through the Carolinas, doing maximum damage to Confederate economic resources. Nor was the General-in-Chief too busy in January, 1865, to write several Congressmen regarding the delay in Meade's being promoted to major general in the regular army. "General Meade," asserted Grant to Washburne, "is one of our truest men and ablest officers. . . . I defy any man to name a commander who would do more than he had done with the same chances." And to Congressman Henry Wilson, Grant wrote, "I have been with General Meade during the whole campaign, and not only made the recommendation upon a conviction that this recognition of his services was fully won, but that he was eminently qualified for the command such rank would entitle him to." [68]

As to the Meade-Grant relationship and status, R. M. Johnston nicely summarizes the rapport of these two strong-willed soldiers: "He [Grant] was in character and education too unlike Meade to make friendship or sympathy between them possible. Yet it is infinitely to the credit of both men that, placed as they were, they should have co-operated so closely until the end of the war. . . . The arrangement was clumsy and occasionally of great disadvantage; Meade concurred in it as a matter of duty, and Grant because he would not do injustice to so good a soldier as Meade." As James Grant Wilson owns, Meade filled the responsible position as head of the Army of the Potomac "to the perfect satisfaction of his superior officer." And as Grant himself acknowledged to Admiral David D. Porter near the end of the war, "I esteem [Meade] highly, and second only to Sherman, and but for his quick temper he would have no superior; and yet with that quick temper goes his quick perception of what is required on the field of battle, and makes his judgment so unexceptionable. He seldom makes mistakes." [69]

[68] Julian, *Political Recollections*, 249; 92 *O.R.*, 636–37, 726–28, 740–41, 797–800, 820–21; 99 *O.R.*, 793–94; Meade, *Life and Letters of Meade*, II, 253–54, 343–44; *C.C.W.* (1865), I, xxviii, 109–12.

[69] R. M. Johnston, . . . *Leading American Soldiers* . . . (New York, 1907), 254; Wilson, *General Grant*, 214; Pennypacker, *Meade*, 4.

The winter was further enlivened for the Federals by the removal of Butler from his command. This was done, finally, on
Grant's insistence, after Butler had ruined the first assault by the
army and navy on Fort Fisher, at Wilmington, North Carolina. This
time, with the fall elections over, the re-elected Lincoln did not
stand in Grant's way in having the hopelessly incompetent political
general fired. The Radicals and Butler himself raised a big fuss, and
castigated Grant and "the West Point crowd." Perhaps in return for
this favor, Grant agreed in February, 1865, at Lincoln's request, to
appoint the President's eldest son to his staff. A Harvard gradu-
ate, Robert Todd Lincoln did pretty well as a staff officer, and was
"exceedingly popular" at headquarters.[70]

At the end of January, 1865, three Confederate peace commissioners—Alexander H. Stephens, R. M. T. Hunter, and John A.
Campbell—presented themselves at Grant's headquarters at City
Point for a discussion. Said Stephens of the General: "I was instantly struck with the great simplicity and perfect naturalness of
his manners, and the entire absence of everything like affectation,
show, or even the usual military air or *mien* of men in his position.
He was plainly attired, sitting in a log cabin, busily writing on a
small table, by a kerosene lamp. . . . There was nothing in his
appearance or surroundings which indicated his official rank.
There were neither guards nor aids about him." Perhaps the Confederate commissioners thought they could inveigle Grant to take
some extraordinary or even dictatorial step. "We had tried," wrote
Hunter, "to intimate to General Grant . . . that a settlement
generally satisfactory to both sides could be more easily effected
through him and General Lee by an armistice than in any other
way. The attempt was in vain." However, just before the three
Southerners had talked with him, Grant, probably forseeing the

[70] James R. Soley, *Admiral Porter* (New York, 1903), 414–23; Butler,
Butler's Book, 774–824; 89 *O.R.,* 1087; 84 *O.R.,* 26, 69; Chandler to his
wife, Jan. 16, 1865, Chandler Papers; Morse (ed.), *Welles's Diary,* II,
224; *C.C.W.* (1865), II, 1–35; Porter, *Campaigning with Grant,* 388–89;
Basler (ed.), *Collected Works of Lincoln,* VIII, 408; Macartney, *Grant
and His Generals,* 334–35.

end of the war, had agreed to a man-for-man prisoner exchange with the Confederates.[71]

With February, 1865, heralding the approach of the active campaign season, Grant drew up comprehensive plans for the movements of the armies of the Union. Never did the General-in-Chief show to better advantage his ability at grand strategy. Sheridan was to move up the Shenandoah Valley and destroy several rail lines and the James River Canal; Stoneman, with 4,000 men, was to raid Confederate communications from eastern Tennessee; Edward R. S. Canby, at New Orleans, was to move with 45,000 men against Mobile, Montgomery, and Selma; Thomas was to dispatch Wilson into Alabama with a large cavalry force; Sherman was to march on Columbia, Fayetteville, and Goldsborough; Schofield was to be brought by water to the North Carolina or Virginia littoral; and Meade's Army of the Potomac, aided by Ord's Army of the James, was to watch, strike, pursue, and crush Lee. The movements encompassed a theater of war greater than any in modern military history up to that time, and all of these movements were carried out successfully.[72]

Determining first to test the enemy before him, Grant, on February 5–7, tried again to swing around Lee's right to the south of Petersburg in the Hatcher's Run area. However, the Fifth Corps could make only a little headway, and suffered losses of over 1,500 men. During the long siege of Petersburg, in all of these many movements of the Federal left wing pivoting on the center and right wing, the only one that had not been checked with severe loss was that against the Weldon Railroad—and that was of a somewhat different nature. These failures were due to the fact that Grant did not adhere to an axiom of war which states that if a turning operation is worth making at all, then the turning column must

[71] Alexander H. Stephens, *A Constitutional View of the Late War Between the States* . . . (Philadelphia, 1868–70), II, 597; Alexander H. Stephens, *Recollections of Alexander H. Stephens* . . . (New York, 1910), 79, 80; *Southern Historical Society Papers*, III (April, 1897), 175.

[72] Porter, *Campaigning with Grant*, 386–87.

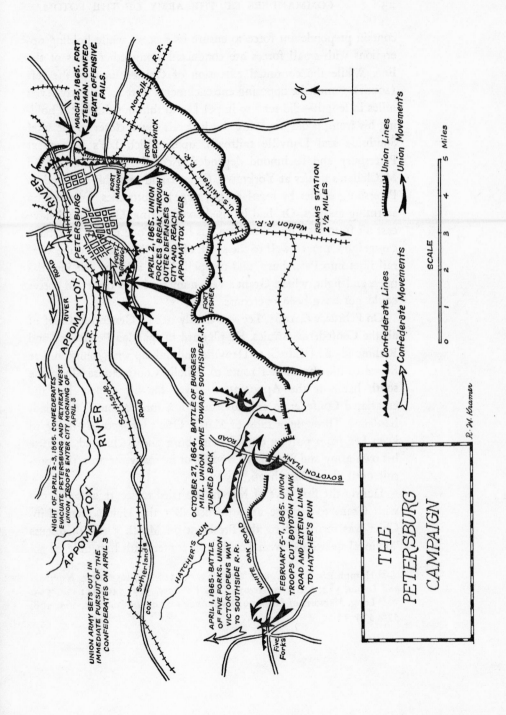

MARCH 25, 1865. FORT STEDMAN. CONFEDERATE OFFENSIVE FAILS.

NIGHT OF APRIL 2-3, 1865. CONFEDERATES EVACUATE PETERSBURG AND RETREAT WEST. UNION TROOPS ENTER CITY MORNING OF APRIL 3

UNION ARMY SETS OUT IN IMMEDIATE PURSUIT OF THE CONFEDERATES ON APRIL 3

APRIL 2, 1865. UNION FORCES BREAK THROUGH OUTER DEFENSES OF CITY AND REACH APPOMATTOX RIVER

OCTOBER 27, 1864. BATTLE OF BURGESS MILL. UNION DRIVE TOWARD SOUTHSIDE R.R. TURNED BACK

APRIL 1, 1865. BATTLE OF FIVE FORKS. UNION VICTORY OPENS WAY TO SOUTHSIDE R.R.

FEBRUARY 5-7, 1865. UNION TROOPS CUT BOYDTON PLANK ROAD AND EXTEND LINE TO HATCHER'S RUN

REAMS STATION 2½ MILES

Union Lines
Union Movements
Confederate Lines
Confederate Movements

SCALE
0 1 2 3 4 5 Miles

THE
PETERSBURG
CAMPAIGN

R. W. Kramer

contain preponderant force to ensure its success, while holding operations with small forces are conducted along other parts of the line. While the continual extension of Grant's lines to the left (south)—until the opposing entrenchments were some thirty-seven miles in length—did tend to impel Lee to thin out the forces holding his front, it did not bring the Federals much closer to the vital Southside and Danville railroads, upon which Lee's posture at Petersburg and Richmond depended. Actually, had he employed McClellan's tactics at Yorktown, Grant could probably have taken Petersburg earlier by regular (i.e., siege) approaches, followed by storming assaults. Or, had he used some daring, Grant could have cast off from his City Point base (as he had done in the Vicksburg campaign), moved well to the south of Lee's right, severed the vital rail lines into Petersburg, and compelled Lee to come out into the open and fight, where Grant's vast numerical superiority in forces could not have been overcome.[73]

On February 6, 1865, Lee was finally named General-in-Chief of all the Confederate armies. He planned to abandon Petersburg and Richmond and fall back to Danville and link up with Johnston. Lee hoped to use the shorter route to Amelia Court House along the south bank of the Appomattox River for his escape, but the emaciated Confederate animals could not function until the roads hardened. Throughout most of March, Grant was actually trying to keep Lee *from* pulling out of Petersburg and Richmond, because his own army and Sherman's would not be ready for an active pursuit until about March 26.[74]

During the first days of March, Lee tried to secure a conference with Grant to arrange an armistice. But the Union General-in-Chief was instructed by the President on March 3 not to discuss "political questions" with Lee, but to confer with him only to ac-

---

[73] Humphreys, *Campaign of '64 & '65*, pp. 312–15; Livermore, *Numbers and Losses*, 134; Swinton, *Army of the Potomac*, 547, 549, 551–52, 553.

[74] Long, *Memoirs of Lee*, 679; Swinton, *Army of the Potomac*, 565, 568, 570, 574–75.

cept the surrender of the Army of Northern Virginia. On March 24, at Grant's invitation, Lincoln, Mrs. Lincoln, and Tad arrived by the steamer *River Queen* at City Point for a visit with the army of nearly two weeks. The next day the President was treated to some action. Hoping to impel Grant to shift troops from the menacing Union left, Lee launched a skillful attack at Fort Stedman, toward the Federal right. But a Union counterattack—watched at a safe distance by Lincoln—recaptured Stedman, and inflicted casualties of 4,000 (including almost 2,000 prisoners) on the enemy as against 2,000 Federal losses.[75]

"Grant appears at his best," declares Rhodes, "in the final operations of his army. He is the Grant of Donelson, Vicksburg and Chattanooga with the judgment developed through larger experience and the discipline of adversity." By March 30, despite delaying rain, Lee had moved such a large number of his troops to his right—opposite which Grant had some 90,000 men—that the rest of his lines were weakly held. But Grant was so discouraged by the untimely rainfall that he might have called off the advance had not Rawlins and Sheridan encouraged him to press ahead. On the thirty-first, after being thrown back a little by a Confederate sortie, Warren repulsed the enemy on the Union left and gained the White Oak Road. Then, after being driven back in considerable confusion between Five Forks and Dinwiddie Court House, Sheridan was succored by Warren and, with the latter's invaluable assistance, succeeded in defeating Pickett at Five Forks on April 1, and capturing over 3,000 men. (In unseemly pique, Grant—who was prejudiced against the Fifth Corps commander—urged Sheridan to depose Warren, and Little Phil, unjustifiably, did precisely that to the illustrious hero of Little Round Top. It was not until 1879 that Warren could obtain a court of inquiry, which vindicated his conduct at Five Forks). Then, successful Union attacks

[75] Nicolay and Hay, *Abraham Lincoln*, X, 158, 214–15; 96 *O.R.*, 801–802, 841; 97 *O.R.*, 50; Basler (ed.), *Collected Works of Lincoln*, VIII, 372–73; Humphreys, *Campaign of '64 & '65*, pp. 317 ff.

elsewhere on Lee's lines caused the Confederates to evacuate Petersburg and Richmond on the night of April 2.[76]

Grant now strained every nerve to prevent Lee's escape to the southwest. He ordered Sheridan and the Fifth Corps to move ahead of Lee and block his movement via the Danville Railroad, while Meade—who, though ill, managed to keep to his post—pressed directly on the enemy's rear. Grant was now, for the first time in the East, using his cavalry to best advantage. Federal troops entered Petersburg and Richmond on April 3.[77]

Grant's relentless chase of Lee continued. An unavoidable but fatal Confederate delay occurred at Amelia Court House on April 4–5, and this enabled Sheridan's cavalry, supported by infantry, to assume a position ahead of Lee to the southwest and thereby cut off the retreat of the Army of Northern Virginia. Meade continued to pound along right on Lee's heels. At Sayler's Creek, the grayclads were badly cut up and lost several thousand prisoners, including Generals Ewell and Joseph B. Kershaw. Making one last but futile attempt to cut his way out of the cordon that surrounded him, Lee finally agreed, after an exchange of notes with Grant, to meet him on April 9. The message from the Confederate leader found Grant, on the night of the eighth, suffering terribly "from a severe headache, the result of fatigue, anxiety, scant fare, and loss of sleep," which even the application of mustard plasters failed to relieve. In this final Appomattox campaign, Grant had suffered 10,780 casualties, while Lee surrendered some 28,000 men on April 9.[78]

The story of the surrender meeting of Grant and Lee on the afternoon of April 9 in the little Appomattox Court House village has

[76] Rhodes, *History of the United States*, V, 110; Sheridan, *Memoirs*, II, 142–45; Grant, *Memoirs*, II, 444; B. & L., IV, 723–24; Swinton, *Army of the Potomac*, 601 n.

[77] Humphreys, *Campaign of '64 & '65*, p. 373; B. & L., IV, 718–20.

[78] Porter, *Campaigning with Grant*, 462; Humphreys, *Campaign of '64 & '65*, pp. 374 ff.; B. & L., IV, 722, 751; Livermore, *Numbers and Losses*, 136.

been told often. The account of the immaculately clad Southern knight meeting in the front parlor of McLean's house the stumpy, mud-bespattered Union General-in-Chief; the pleasant small talk of old army days before Sumter; Lee's rigorously bringing the conversation back each time to the unpleasant business at hand; the drafting, reading, and signing of the surrender documents; and the quiet farewell of Lee—these moving incidents are all well known. But one of the clauses of Grant's generous terms to Lee—which were approved by Lincoln—warrants attention, since it is of a political nature, and really an overstep by Grant beyond his authority. This was that, after each Confederate officer had sworn an oath not to take up arms again against the United States government, "each officer and man will be allowed to return to their [sic] homes, not to be disturbed by United States authority so long as they observe their parole and the laws in force where they may reside." By including this clause, which practically gave pardon and amnesty to everyone in Lee's army, Grant really assumed Executive authority denied to him by Lincoln's decree of March 3. Although Sherman, after Lincoln's assassination, was later unsupported by the government in his similarly magnanimous terms to Joe Johnston at Durham Station, Grant was backed by the administration in his April 9 action, so great was the rejoicing in the North over his signal triumph.[79]

And what were Grant's sensations during the surrender session with Lee at McLean's house? The Federal General writes in his memoirs, "What General Lee's feelings were I do not know. As he was a man of much dignity, with an impassible face, it is impossible to say whether he felt inwardly glad that the end had finally come, or felt sad over the result, and was too manly to show it. Whatever his feelings, they were entirely concealed from my observation; but my own feelings, which had been quite jubilant on the receipt of his letter, were sad and depressed. I felt like any-

[79] B. & L., IV, 734–43; Grant, *Memoirs*, II, 490; Nicolay and Hay, *Abraham Lincoln*, X, 196; Philadelphia *Public Ledger*, April 12, 1865.

thing rather than rejoicing at the downfall of a foe who had fought so long and valiantly, and had suffered so much for a cause. . . ." [80]

This final Appomattox campaign of Grant was one of his finest performances. Rhodes is convinced "that in these final operations he outgeneralled Lee." However, in all his military actions since May 4, 1864, against the Southern general, Grant had lost 124,000 men. After a final brief and pleasant conversation with Lee between the lines on April 10, Grant departed by rail for Washington. [81]

On April 14 Grant reached the capital and met with the President and the cabinet at the White House. Mrs. Lincoln invited the General and Mrs. Grant to accompany her and the President to Ford's Theater that evening to see a presentation of "Our American Cousin," starring Laura Keene. At first accepting, the Grants shortly afterward declined because of their anxiety to entrain for New Jersey to see their children. So instead of there being two major targets for John Wilkes Booth at Ford's that evening, there was only one tall one. Nine days after the dastardly deed had claimed its towering victim, his successor, Andrew Johnson, joined on the reviewing stand in front of the White House by Grant, watched breathlessly as the mighty Army of the Potomac, with Meade at its head, marched impressively down Pennsylvania Avenue into history. [82]

After the war Grant remained General-in-Chief of the armies of the United States until his inauguration as President, March 4, 1869. One of the saddest chapters in his postwar career was the estrangement with Meade. The latter resented Sheridan's crude pushiness and Grant's support of Little Phil. The incident that caused the break between the two occurred when Grant placed

[80] Grant Memoirs, II, 489.
[81] Rhodes, History of the United States, V, 130; Humphreys, Campaign of '64 & '65, p. 385; Grant, Memoirs, II, 495; B. & L., IV, 746.
[82] Nicolay and Hay, Abraham Lincoln, X, 281, 292, 331–34; Rhodes, History of the United States, V, 185.

Halleck in command of the new Military Division of the James, over Meade and Ord. In 1866 Congress created the four-star rank of general, and President Andrew Johnson immediately named Grant to that grade, Sherman becoming the lieutenant general. As James G. Wilson states, the rank of full general "never before existed under our Government. Washington was general of the Continental army and under the Confederation; but in the United States army he was only lieutenant general." On August 12, 1867, Grant assumed the duties of Secretary of War ad interim, and for the next five months was his own superior officer. But then, in the famous clash over the Tenure of Office Act, Grant, apparently breaking his promise and an understanding with Johnson, surrendered the office to Stanton. After Grant became President, Sherman, as was expected, succeeded him as General-in-Chief, with the rank of full general. But it came as a severe shock to Meade and others when Sheridan, instead of the hero of Gettysburg, was named to the now vacant lieutenant generalcy, Meade crying out that this "is the cruelest and meanest act of injustice." [83]

As President for two terms, Grant did not distinguish himself. He scored his chief successes in the field of foreign affairs, where he was blessed by having as his Secretary of State the astute Hamilton Fish. In one of the high points of his career, Grant dedicated the handsome monument over Lincoln's tomb at Springfield. On this occasion, with a eloquence that was rare for him, Grant said, "From March, 1864, to the day when the hand of the assassin opened a grave for Mr. Lincoln . . . my personal relations with him were as close and intimate as the nature of our respective duties would permit. To know him personally was to love and respect him for his great qualities of heart and head, and for his patience and patriotism. With all his disappointments from failures on the part of those to whom he had intrusted commands, and treachery on the part of those who had gained his confidence but to betray it, I never heard him utter a complaint, nor cast a censure, for bad conduct or

[83] Meade, *Life and Letters of Meade*, II, 271, 275, 276, 300; Wilson, *General Grant*, 293.

bad faith. It was his nature to find excuses for his adversaries. In his death the nation lost its greatest hero; in his death the South lost its most just friend." [84]

From 1877 to 1879, after his presidency, Grant took a two-year trip around the world, visiting most of the principal foreign capitals and heads of government. In 1880 he was defeated for the nomination for a third term, and in the following year he took up residence on East Sixty-sixth Street in New York City. Grant had saved little money while President, and he now lived on income from a fund of $250,000, placed in trust for him by his admirers; but this soon failed. He then went into business and was exploited; in 1884 the brokerage firm of Grant and Ward went under, and he was bankrupted. He yielded up his war swords and souvenirs as collateral for a loan. In March, 1885, the grade of general was revived by friends. President Chester A. Arthur signed the bill into law on his last day in office, and President Grover Cleveland delivered to Grant this commission, which carried with it a salary for life.[85]

Grant was now suffering from throat cancer, and his family and relatives were heavily in debt. To alleviate their misfortune, Grant wrote an article on Shiloh for the *Century Magazine* in 1884 which was well received. Then, in 1885, with his life ebbing away at Mt. McGregor, Grant fought his last and in many respects his most gallant battle, as he strove to finish his memoirs before death called him. He was just able to complete them; but they were fantastically successful, and netted his family royalties of $450,000. Perhaps his finest hour—and it is an unforgettable picture—was that when, seated on the porch at Mt. McGregor, wrapped in shawls and blankets, and wearing a woolen pull-over cap, he managed to win his last great struggle, finishing the final chapter of his now-classic memoirs a week before going to his Maker. He died on July 23, 1885, and was laid to rest in an imposing tomb on Riverside Drive along the Hudson.[86]

[84] Nicolay and Hay, *Abraham Lincoln*, X, 325.
[85] *D.A.B.*, VII, 497–501.
[86] *Ibid.*

CHAPTER NINE

Conclusion

> . . . We cannot escape history. We
> . . . will be remembered in spite of
> ourselves. No personal significance, or
> insignificance, can spare one or another
> of us. The fiery trial through which we
> pass, will light us down, in honor or
> dishonor, to the latest generation. . . .
> We . . . hold the power, and bear the
> responsibilities. We shall nobly save, or
> meanly lose, the last best, hope of earth.
> —*Abraham Lincoln*

BEFORE MAKING A COMPARATIVE AND GENERAL EVALUATION of the commanders of the Army of the Potomac, a separate appraisal of each is in order.

In any assessment of Irvin McDowell's campaign and of the man himself as a soldier and general, it must first be emphasized that a crude, Bull Run-type of campaign was possible only where military unprepardedness existed to the degree it did in the United States in 1861. As to the campaign, "one may fairly say," writes R. M. Johnston, "that it was foreordained to failure, and yet conclude that it came within inches of success." McDowell was terribly hampered by a lack of aides and staff officers. Many of the army's officers failed miserably, and the whole command structure broke down to such an extent that a civilian, Governor William Sprague of Rhode Island, was seen giving orders to troops on the field. Also, there was too much "nursing" of the Union infantry in their advances; too much lying down and firing at short range, and too little use of the bayonet charge, pressed home. But considering the actual number of troops engaged, the casualty figures show fairly hard fighting for green soldiers.[1]

As for McDowell himself, he was unfitted by training and experience for army command—but so too were his opponents at that time. It was his fate "ever to be involved in enterprises which his judgment condemned"; and, even though it may be asserted that a general makes his own luck, McDowell was certainly one of the unluckiest and least popular field commanders in American history. And, in addition, he had a number of serious shortcomings. He showed little tactical ability, and his handling of infantry and artillery on the field was weak, especially in the piecemeal attacks of July 21. He failed utterly, at every point, in doing the one thing essential to a success at Bull Run; namely, in moving with sufficient rapidity. Also, McDowell tried to do too much himself. Instead of controlling situations, he accepted them as they were. Then, too, he probably deferred too much to the opinions of his subordinates. As to strategic planning, he did not act like the commander of a large army, but rather performed the role of a staff officer or second in command to Scott.[2]

"The wonder . . . is not that [McDowell] should not have done more," states Swinton, "but that he did so much; and the spirit of forbearance and alacrity with which he entered upon and carried through his trying task, entitles him to great credit." Most authorities agree that he was a magnanimous man and a true soldier. This is shown by his official report, which, R. M. Johnston thinks, "is on the whole a straightforward and honest confession of failure, very little colored or distorted in an endeavor to evade responsibility." The final judgment of McDowell—perhaps a bit too cruelly blunt, but nonetheless accurate—might well be that presented by Johnston: "As a general he proved faithful to his duty, courageous, painstaking; but it cannot be said that his abilities extended further."[3]

[1] Johnston, *Bull Run*, 1–2, 269, 270–72; 2 *O.R.*, 407; *C.C.W.* (1863), II, 198, 215.

[2] Johnston, *Bull Run*, 269–70; Longstreet, *Manassas to Appomattox*, 56.

[3] Swinton, *Army of the Potomac*, 43–44; Johnston, *Bull Run*, 20, 273.

In considering George B. McClellan and his stewardship of the Army of the Potomac, one is struck immediately with the fact that, after the First Bull Run debacle, he was thrust to the fore at the real beginning of the long-haul mobilization of the Union's resources. It was he who was in the saddle while the complexion of the war was changing from that of a limited to a total war. Swinton points out that "to General McClellan personally it was a misfortune that he became so prominent a figure at the commencement of the contest; for it was inevitable that the first leaders should be sacrificed to the nation's ignorance of war." U. S. Grant stated this matter nicely as regards McClellan: "All my impressions are in his favor. . . . The test which was applied to him would be terrible to any man, being made a major-general at the beginning of the war. It has always seemed to me that the critics of McClellan do not consider this vast and cruel responsibility—the war, a new thing to all of us, the army new, everything to do from the outset, with a restless people and Congress. McClellan was a young man when this devolved upon him. . . . If [he] had gone into the war as Sherman, Thomas, or Meade, had fought his way along and up, I have no reason to suppose that he would not have won as high distinction as any of us." [4]

One of McClellan's chief troubles stemmed from the fact that he was somewhat cavalier in his dealings with politicians and with his civilian superiors. General Sir Frederick Maurice states on page 89 of his *Statesmen and Soldiers,*

the ultimate cause . . . of all McClellan's misfortunes was his incapacity to establish relations of trust and confidence with Lincoln. He never could free himself from the obsession that he and he alone was capable of conducting the war in all its aspects, and the many intrigues against him in Washington . . . tended to harden him in his opinion that all the politicians in Washington were dishonest schemers, and all the administrators incompetents. This was due in a great part to McClellan's character and mentality, but a little study on his part of

[4] Swinton, *Army of the Potomac,* 228; Young, *Around the World with Grant,* II, 216–17.

how to deal with a statesman in war, and on Lincoln's part of the principles of statecraft in the conduct of war, would almost certainly have overcome such difficulties as existed and have enabled McClellan to be a very valuable servant of the State.

Of course, it was difficult for any commander who was not of the Radical stamp to establish smooth relations with Stanton, Chase, and members of the Committee on the Conduct of the War. Yet, with most of his officers, and especially with the men in the ranks, it was demonstrated time and again that McClellan was one of the most popular generals ever to command American troops.

McClellan had real talent for devising sweeping plans of grand strategy. He would have made a good General-in-Chief if retained longer in that position. As a strategist in his own operations, he showed a sure grasp and appreciation of military realities and probabilities. He was less adept as a tactician, although when fighting on the defensive he had few peers. In offensive operations, his engineering training and background revealed itself, and made him extremely cautious. His hesitancy in committing troops to combat cost him dearly on a number of occasions. Yet, in a crisis, when pressed, he could act swiftly, and South Mountain and Antietam showed that he was improving in handling troops in offensive tactics. But McClellan frequently magnified difficulties confronting him, and failed to allow for similar problems facing the enemy. He should never have accepted as gospel the grossly exaggerated estimates of Confederate numbers made for him by Allan Pinkerton. But he was a brilliant organizer, administrator, drillmaster, and disciplinarian, as the future history of the Army of the Potomac shows. While not distinguished in directing cavalry operations, McClellan demonstrated considerable skill in his use of artillery, as was shown at Yorktown, Malvern Hill, and Antietam.

McClellan was called in to command the Army of the Potomac after two terrible Federal defeats at Bull Run, in moments of grave crisis to the Union cause both at home and abroad, and while he might have accomplished more, his achievements were nonetheless substantial—some of them masterly. General Palfrey, whose writings are far from complimentary to McCellan, acknowledges that "there are strong grounds for believing that he was the best commander the Army of the Potomac ever had. . . . While the Confederacy was young and fresh and rich, and its armies were numerous, McClellan fought a good, wary, damaging, respectable fight against it. . . . With longer possession of command, greater things might fairly have been expected of him. . . . In such a war . . . it would probably have been impossible to retain in command of the Army of the Potomac a man who was not only a Democrat, but the probable Democratic candidate for the Presidency at the next election, and that his removal was therefore only a question of time." [5]

General Walker says of McClellan, "Let military critics or political enemies say what they will, he who could so move upon the hearts of a great army, as the wind sways long rows of standing corn, was no ordinary man; nor was he who took such heavy toll of Joseph E. Johnston and Robert E. Lee an ordinary soldier." [6]

But probably the man best able to judge McClellan with authority as compared with the other generals in blue was the eminent Confederate commander who had faced them all. Lee wrote to a friend after the war, "As regards General McClellan, I have always entertained a high opinion of his capacity, and have no reason to think that he omitted to do anything that was in his power." One of Lee's daughters was quoted as stating that "Genl. McClellan was the only Genl. Father dreaded." After Appomattox, when asked to name the ablest Union general he had faced during the war, Lee, without a pause, declared emphatically, "McClellan by all odds!" [7]

If McClellan receives a fairly good grade as an army commander, John Pope is less fortunate. Despite the latter's obnoxious charac-

[5] Palfrey, *The Antietam*, 134–35.

[6] Walker, *Second Corps*, 138.

[7] Freeman, *R. E. Lee*, IV, 477; letter to McClellan from "A Friend," Washington, D. C., Mar. 28, 1863, McClellan Papers; Robert E. Lee [Jr.], *Recollections and Letters of General Robert E. Lee* (New York, 1905), 415–16.

ter, he is really one of the most pathetic figures of the Civil War on the Federal side. Neither his men nor his officers had any confidence in him. George T. Strong summed up the Union general in these words: "Pope is an imaginative chieftain and ranks next to Cooper as a writer of fiction." "As a tactician," asserts G. F. R. Henderson, "Pope was incapable. As a strategist, he lacked imagination, except in his dispatches." Theodore A. Dodge thinks that Pope "was utterly outgeneralled; he never knew where his enemy was; he fought to no purpose. But when he did fight, it was with a will beyond his discretion." George H. Gordon, a general in the campaign, assesses the "demented" Pope in this fashion: "What he should not have done he did with frightful energy, and what he should have done he culpably neglected to do." [8]

"In reviewing the campaign," writes Ropes, one of Pope's fairest critics, "we ought freely to accord to Gen. Pope the merit of courage, energy, and decision of character. It is impossible, however, to credit him with strategic skill." As to the tactical handling of his army, Pope was even less adroit than as a strategist. "In no action in Pope's campaign," notes Gordon, "were the troops properly handled. Attacking lines or columns were never properly supported. There was no want of troops. They lay idly around until the crisis had passed, when they were pressed forward to a useless sacrifice. . . . Whipped in detail should be Pope's epitaph. Neither in manoeuvring nor in fighting had Pope any strategy. He made no flanking movements; he displayed no threatening force to divert the enemy's attention from a real attack. It was all groping and murder in driblets." Also lamentable was the General's inability to keep a cool head in a crisis.[9]

In the use of his cavalry, Pope showed some dexterity and sense at the beginning of his campaign. There were frequent reconnais-

[8] Nevins and Thomas (eds.), *Strong's Diary,* III, 249; Theodore A. Dodge, *A Bird's-Eye View of Our Civil War* (Boston, 1883), 80; Gordon, *Campaign of the Army of Virginia,* 462.

[9] Dwight (ed.), *The Virginia Campaign of General Pope in 1862,* p. 95; Gordon, *Campaign of the Army of Virginia,* 462.

sances, and outposts were maintained well in advance of the army. However, in the later phases of the operations, Pope unwisely wore out his cavalry by excessive courier and escort service. He was inept in the use of artillery throughout his operations, although this was one of the Federals' strongest points of superiority over the Confederates. Pope failed also to keep himself well informed of the enemy's movements. The worst breakdown of communications in the war occurred during the Second Manassas campaign. This was a grave and inexcusable fault, and leads Geer to comment that Pope "failed to draw a single correct inference during the course of this campaign." [10]

Perhaps Pope's chief blunder was in fighting at all near Manassas. Taking up a forward position, Pope's duty was to delay the Confederates as long as possible without endangering his army or allowing his communications to be menaced. When these were threatened, or if he saw that a superior enemy force was confronting him, he should have instantly fallen back closer to his base, where reinforcements could reach him more readily. On this point, Randall declares, "It seems impossible to dismiss the suspicion that Pope, taking credit to himself, wanted to win the battle without McClellan's cooperation." [11]

A succinct, if hostile, summary of Pope and his entire campaign is that written by Walker:

The braggart who had begun his campaign with insolent reflections . . . upon the Army of the Potomac and its commander . . . had been kicked, cuffed, hustled about, knocked down, run over, and trodden upon as rarely happens in the history of war. His communications had been cut; his headquarters pillaged; a corps had marched into his rear, and had encamped at its ease upon the railroad by which he received his supplies; he had been beaten or foiled in every attempt he had made to "bag" those defiant intruders; and, in the end, he was glad to find a refuge in the entrenchments of Washington, whence he had sallied forth, six weeks before, breathing out threatenings and slaughter.

[10] B. & L., II, 522; Geer, Campaigns of the Civil War, 135, 147–48.
[11] Ropes, Army under Pope, 168; Randall, Civil War and Reconstruction, 306 n.

As Swinton truly remarks, "It cannot be denied that the estimate of his character held by the officers under his command was not of a kind to elicit that hearty and zealous cooperation needed for the effective conduct of great military operations. [Pope] had the misfortune to be of all men the most *disbelieved*." [12]

Of all the commanders of the Army of the Potomac, only Ambrose E. Burnside was man enough to acknowledge his incompetency to handle such a massive host and to admit the wisdom of Lincoln in removing him from that command in early 1863. Throughout Burnside's campaign, and especially at the battle of Fredericksburg, he failed utterly to secure proper and adequate information of both the terrain and the enemy's position. Therefore, intelligent tactical decisions could not easily be made. Burnside's use of his artillery was skillful on the whole, but his failure to employ his cavalry to better advantage was a serious shortcoming. Throughout the campaign, he showed little imagination in anything. As to why he continued to hurl brigade after brigade at the stone wall when it was obvious to most other officers that only bloody repulse would ensue, the answer lies perhaps in the trait of obstinacy noticed in Burnside's makeup by several perceptive observers. When his force began to suffer a check at any point, he kept stubbornly hammering away as if to win by sheer perseverance alone. It was a characteristic he showed at other times during the course of the war. A newspaper correspondent with the army stated it this way: "Whenever he gets a positive order to GO, he will GO if it breaks his neck." Burnside was not indifferent to his soldiers' lives, but he just seemed to lose all tactical judgment and perception when he could not break through the enemy's lines. As the casualties mounted, he became more and more appalled, lost his ability to think clearly, and could only keep repeating his original orders. Even further, Burnside's command failures were responsible for practically every tactical mistake made during the entire battle by his subordinates. He played right into Lee's hands at almost every

[12] Walker, *Second Corps*, 91–92; Swinton, *Army of the Potomac*, 193.

turn. Palfrey was moved to remark, "There probably never was an occasion since the first body of troops was arrayed, when a general did more precisely what his adversary wished him to do than Burnside did at Fredericksburg." [13]

Meade, usually keen in sizing up the merits and shortcomings of soldiers, gives a brief capsule evaluation of Burnside that is well balanced. "With all my respect, and I may almost say affection, for Burnside," he wrote upon that general's removal, "I cannot shut my eyes to the fact that he was not equal to the command of so large an army. He had some very positive qualifications, such as determination and nerve, but he wanted knowledge and judgment, and was deficient in that enlarged mental capacity which is essential in a commander. Another drawback was a very general opinion among officers and men, brought about by his own assertions, that the command was too much for him. This greatly weakened his position." An analysis of several other deficiencies of Burnside is included in a recent study of the Union side at Fredericksburg, written by Vorin E. Whan:

[Burnside] was slow when he should have been active and too precipitate when the situation called for caution. The last element of leadership which Burnside violated . . . was in the field of supervision. The architect of the battle plan must follow the execution by his subordinates so that the spirit as well as the letter of the plan are complied with. Even more important, the combat leader must be alert to exploit unexpected success, which can only be done if he stays on top of the battle situation. Burnside did not supervise the execution of his plan but stubbornly persisted in the blind execution of a plan which badly required revision early in the day. . . . He could not seem to grasp a situation involving, at most, more than a few thousand troops without getting beyond his depth. Burnside was a very slow thinker and unable to make quick decisions in the heat of battle. He knew very well his lack of ability, and the responsibility of the entire army weighed heavily upon him. This increased his fear of making a mistake to the point that getting the simplest decision from him was almost impossible. Irresolute, yet knowing he had to make the decisions

[13] Louis M. Starr, *Bohemian Brigade: Civil War Newsmen in Action* (New York, 1954), 164; Palfrey, *The Antietam*, 141.

in the end, led Burnside to alternate long periods of inactivity with bursts of unfortunate activity.[14]

Several other commentators are even more harsh in their assessments of Burnside, yet it is difficult to gainsay their value judgments. The historian of the Union Fifth Corps, Colonel William H. Powell, avers that "history points to no parallel where a great commander commenced a movement without a plan of campaign, a movement in opposition to the wishes of his government, against the advice of his immediate subordinates, and contrary to all the principles of warfare." And this is the opinion of historian Carl Russell Fish: "There was no such intention to sacrifice but, if stupidity be culpability, few generals of ancient or modern times rank with Burnside in the guilt of manslaughter." [15]

It is very easy to be distracted from Joseph Hooker and his performance as commander of the Army of the Potomac by the sheer glitter and brilliance of the Chancellorsville campaign itself— and by Lee's admirable generalship. Speaking of Chancellorsville and Hooker's role in it, Dodge declares that it was "one of the best conceived and most fatally mismanaged of the many many unsuccessful advances of the Army of the Potomac." "In looking for the causes of the loss of Chancellorsville," writes Couch, "the primary ones were that Hooker expected Lee to fall back without risking battle. Finding himself mistaken he assumed the defensive, and was outgeneraled and became demoralized by the superior tactical boldness of the enemy." Geer is more blunt when he asserts, "It will be hard to find in the annals of the Civil War a greater series of blunders than those made by the Federal commander during this brief period of eight days!" [16]

[14] Meade, *Life and Letters of Meade,* I, 351; Vorin E. Whan, Jr., "A Tactical Study of the Operations of the Union Army at the Battle of Fredericksburg" (Master's thesis, The Pennsylvania State University, 1958), 225–26.

[15] Powell, *Fifth Corps,* 413; Carl Russell Fish, *The American Civil War* . . . (London, 1937), 281.

[16] Dodge, *Chancellorsville,* 2; B. & L., III, 171; Geer, *Campaigns of the Civil War,* 224.

In essence, of course, Hooker did not possess the requisite qualities of a competent general in command of a great army. He was incapable of sustained mental concentration of a high order. As noted before, he was not drunk during the campaign; but apparently he should have continued in his custom of imbibing his usual quantity of alcohol, which was to him like medicine. In his orders Hooker was often vague and incomprehensible. "His errors," remarks John Bigelow, "were largely due to his interference with his own corps commanders, and not allowing them to do what their own judgment dictated." Meade claims, probably correctly, that the weight of the heavy responsibility of the army command engulfed Hooker, and changed his character for a time. Known for his love of fighting, the General, at the crisis of the battle, absolutely and uncharacteristically refused to fight at all, unless the enemy took the initiative. Despite Lincoln's warning to him to use all his troops in the battle, Hooker left large numbers—Reynolds' and Meade's corps of some 37,500 men—out of the combat altogether. Little can be said, either, for Hooker's handling of his cavalry and artillery.[17]

"It is in war," notes Swinton, "as in life: a single false step often involves an endless train of swift-succeeding misfortune. This false step in the conduct of Hooker was that, having started out to fight an offensive battle, he reduced himself, at the very moment when action was above all imperative, to a perilous defensive." Meade declares that Hooker's "plan was admirably designed, and the early part of it, entrusted to others, was well executed." But then he threw away superior chances, one by one, which even the brilliant attack of Jackson did not seriously impair. However, Hooker was excellent at administration and organization; and for mobilizing an army in camp, and drawing up plans for operations, he had few superiors.[18]

[17] Bigelow, *Chancellorsville*, 481, 483–84; Meade, *Life and Letters of Meade*, I, 374.
[18] Swinton, *Army of the Potomac*, 303; Meade, *Life and Letters of Meade*, I, 379, 380; Livermore, *Story of the Civil War*, I, 114–15.

Perhaps Hooker's gravest shortcoming—and it was fatal in the commander of a large army—was his inability to make war on the map. In other words, he was crippled by his lack of imagination and ability to visualize, direct, and co-ordinate the changing positions and combinations of large bodies of troops by reports unless he was able to see the units with his own eyes. When the enemy did not do what Hooker expected him to do, he could not change his plans and improvise. He was not, as W. R. Livermore says, "a student of the higher branches of military science, and it is doubtful if his intellect was powerful enough to analyze and apply its principles." Corps command was his true level of ability.[19]

Hooker was a man of a very suspicious nature. He never submitted a report of his commandership of the army, and until his death, kept in his sole possession many papers and records of the Army of the Potomac. His own later views of his major battle as an army commander are highly inaccurate, and reveal his own incompetence. "In my opinion," trumpeted Fighting Joe, "there is nothing to regret in regard to Chancellorsville, except to accomplish all I moved to accomplish. . . . When I returned from Chancellorsville, I felt that I had fought no general battle, for the reason that I could not get my men in position to do so." His own confession, in a moment of frankness, to Doubleday and others, shortly after Chancellorsville, sums up the single most important reason for his failure: "For once I lost confidence in Hooker, and that is all there is to it." As Swinton says, "Not the Army of the Potomac was beaten at Chancellorsville, but its commander." To the Confederates, Hooker was known afterwards as "Fallen Joe."[20]

Posterity has not, perhaps, treated George G. Meade fairly. He has been, to a great extent, eclipsed by the very success he scored in the pivotal combat of the Pennsylvania campaign. "There is,"

[19] Livermore, *Story of the Civil War*, I, 114–15. See also Bigelow, *Chancellorsville*, 481–82; Gates, *Ulster Guard*, 394–95.

[20] Dodge, *Chancellorsville*, 4, 253–54; Macartney, *Grant and His Generals*, 154; Swinton, *Army of the Potomac*, 307; Benjamin F. Cook, *History of the Twelfth Massachusetts Volunteers* . . . (Boston, 1882), 95.

declares Walker, "probably no other battle of which men are so prone to think and speak without a conscious reference to the commanding general of the victorious party, as they are regarding Gettysburg." General Henry J. Hunt thinks that, in this campaign, Meade was correct in fighting strictly on the defensive, in not counterattacking at any time, and in his mode of pursuing Lee after the battle. "Rarely has more skill, vigor, or wisdom been shown under such circumstances as he was placed in." In selecting such accomplished subordinates as Reynolds and Hancock, Hunt and Warren, for key tasks of great responsibility, Meade demonstrated the marks of good leadership. This policy was wise in a new commander who had just been abruptly and cruelly placed in charge of an army just a few days before a decisive battle was to be fought. In his handling of his cavalry during the campaign and battle, the Union general outshone Lee; and in his employment of artillery, Meade again showed to better advantage than his able opponent. Gettysburg was the first great battle in which the National army commander and his top generals worked so well together as a team, and the first large-scale combat in which the Federal reserves were thrown forward in battle at precisely the right time.[21]

In the first several days after he assumed command, Meade allowed his army to become too widely scattered. The circular which he issued on the early morning of July 1 should have been in the form of a more positive order. Perhaps a predetermination to fight defensively at Pipe Creek was the reason Meade seemed miffed at Doubleday and Howard for holding on and fighting all day at Gettysburg. This, and the belief that his left wing would certainly fall back to the south from Gettysburg, was probably why Meade himself delayed so long in going forward to the field from Taneytown. But, once he had determined to fight there, the General showed considerable skill and promptness in concentrating his army at Gettysburg by the morning of the second. However, his obsession with his right wing on July 2, and his virtual ignoring of the pos-

[21] *B. & L.*, III, 406; Powell, *Fifth Corps*, 559; Bates, *Battle of Gettysburg*, 184.

sibility of an attack against his left, were unfortunate. He should not have allowed Buford to leave the left flank until actually replaced by another cavalry force. Also, his orders to Sickles should have been more precise. But once he went to the left and saw that Sickles was in danger, Meade's reinforcement of the Third Corps was admirable. The only criticism here can be that he denuded his right too much, and was barely able to stem the Confederate attacks made there at dusk and on the night of the second. On the third, however, Meade's deployment of his infantry, artillery, and cavalry forces was simply superb, and he showed tactical ability superior to Lee's. He was most likely correct in not counterattacking after Pickett's repulse, for he would probably have suffered the same kind of reception that Pickett had met. It is doubtful also whether Meade could have intercepted Lee's retreat to the Potomac, given the earlier start and the more direct roads available to the gray leader. And, despite some opinion to the contrary, it seems to be the concensus that Meade acted wisely in refraining from assaulting Lee's powerful position along the Potomac near Williamsport.[22]

Meade was a sound though by no means a great commander. Samuel Adams Drake thinks that the General "was no genius. He was only a brave, methodical, and conscientious soldier, who, within his limitations, had acted well his part. Under Grant he made an excellent so-called second in command." If Meade had fallen fatally wounded on July 3 at Gettysburg, his reputation would have been secure, and his fame would have exceeded perhaps even that of Grant and Sherman. In a way, it was unfortunate to Meade personally that he remained in command of the army twenty-two months longer. After Gettysburg, and before Grant came East, Meade's failure to accomplish more than he did was perhaps due in part to the absence of such gifted subordinates as Reynolds and Hancock, whose loss could not be made good.[23]

Prominent Confederates held high opinions of "The Old Fox,"

[22] See Bates, *Battle of Gettysburg*, 184–95; Livermore, *Story of the Civil War*, II, 495–98.

[23] Drake, *Battle of Gettysburg*, 165–66; *C.C.W.* (1865), I, 387.

as they called Meade. Jefferson Davis declared, "My idea is that
Meade was the most skillful general in the Federal army. General
Lee once said to me that he could understand the movements of all
the generals in the Federal army easier than those of General
Meade." Said John B. Gordon: "To . . . Meade, history will accord the honor of having handled his army at Gettysburg with un-
questioned ability. The record and results of the battle entitle him
to a high place among Union leaders." According to John Esten
Cooke, "General Lee esteemed the late General Meade very highly
as a soldier, declaring that he was the best officer in the Federal
army, and had 'given him more trouble than any of them.'" Lee
was quoted also as saying, "Meade, in my judgment, had the greatest
ability. I feared him more than any man I ever met upon the field of
battle." Of course, Lee had said, in effect, the same thing about
McClellan and Grant.[24]

The most recent able student of the battle at Gettysburg, Glenn
Tucker, concludes that, "It is true that Meade might have won more
decisively by taking the offensive. He wisely decided, at an hour
when defeat would have meant disaster to the Federal cause, that
a victory in hand, even though it did not destroy his adversary, was
preferable to risking his own badly battered army further, when
there was nothing in the history of Lee's generalship or that of the
Army of Northern Virginia which gave much promise that by a
frontal attack that army could be captured or destroyed. Probably
the preservation of the union [sic] depended a great deal at this
hour on Meade's conservatism. He had the sense to recognize that
after three days of fighting, he possessed, not striking power, but
position." Tucker notes also that "Meade approached many of his
decisions gropingly, owing probably to his brief tenure in command.
In the end, his decisions seemed to be unfailingly correct." [25]

As for Ulysses S. Grant, he remains something of an enigma—

[24] McClure (ed.), *Annals of the War*, 217, 218; Pennypacker, *Meade*,
5; John B. Gordon, *Reminiscences of the Civil War* (New York, 1903),
158.
[25] Tucker, *High Tide at Gettysburg*, 389–90.

inscrutable. "He is a strange character," Sherman once said. "Nothing like it is portrayed by Plutarch or the many who have striven to portray the great men of ancient or modern times. I knew him as a cadet at West Point, as a lieutenant of the Fourth Infantry, as a citizen of St. Louis, and as a growing general all through the bloody Civil War. Yet to me he is a mystery, and I believe he is a mystery to himself." Grant was surprised at the skill of Lee and the fighting qualities of both the Army of the Potomac and its opponent. After coming East, it cannot be shown that his handling of artillery and cavalry was more than mediocre at best. He could—as seen at Vicksburg, at the crossing of the James River, and in the Appomattox pursuit—do difficult things well; but he was occasionally careless in the simpler and more obvious operations. As Swinton asserts, "General Grant's best successes were accomplished only when, departing from his own principle [of hammering continuously on the same line], he manoeuvred as well as attacked." Probably no general could have conquered Lee until the latter's resources and manpower had dwindled to practically nothing. In the great campaign against the Southern soldier from the Rapidan to Appomattox, Grant came out tactically second best in most of the contests, except in the crossing of the James and in the Appomattox chase. But, strategically, Lee was unable to stop the grinding advance of Grant's forces. And, like McClellan before him, Grant had considerable skill in devising sweeping operations on the level of grand strategy, and he was a consummate General-in-Chief.[26]

"The success and fame of generals," comment Nicolay and Hay, "is the joint result of merit and of opportunity; and Grant was, beyond all comparison, the most fortunate of American soldiers." Had he been in command of the Army of the Potomac early in the war, he probably would have suffered the same fate as McClellan and others. "To Grant alone," Colonel A. L. Conger remarks, "appears to have been given the opportunity for the balanced development of that genius through the solving, during his career,

[26] Macartney, *Grant and His Generals,* ix; Swinton, *Army of the Potomac,* 494.

of an orderly sequence of progressively arranged problems," from regimental command to General-in-Chief. Meade's analysis of his superior bears note: "Grant is not a mighty genius, but he is a good soldier, of great force of character, honest and upright, of pure purpose, I think without political aspirations, certainly not influenced by them. His prominent quality is unflinching tenacity of purpose, which blinds him to opposition and obstacles. . . . Grant is not without his faults and weaknesses. Among these is a want of sensibility, and almost too confident and sanguine disposition. . . . Take him all in all, he is . . . the best man the war has yet produced. . . . He has been greatly overrated; but I should be really sorry to see him, through a reaction, underestimated." [27]

As for other opinions of Grant, Nicolay and Hay assert, "When unfriendly criticism has exhausted itself, the fact remains, not to be explained away by any reasoning, subtle or gross, that in this tremendous war he accomplished more with the means given him than any other two on either side. . . . He alone captured three armies." When someone made a disparaging remark to Lee of Grant's ability, the Confederate commander was reported as saying, "Sir, your opinion is a very poor compliment to me. We all thought Richmond, protected as it was by our splendid fortifications and defended by our army of veterans, could not be taken. Yet Grant turned his face to our capital, and never turned it away until we had surrendered. Now, I have carefully searched the military records of both ancient and modern history, and have never found Grant's superior as a general. I doubt if his superior can be found in all history." [28]

Other judgments, however, are less favorable to Grant and more praiseworthy of Marse Robert. Writes Geer, quoting Henderson, "As a commander, Grant can not be compared with General Lee, 'undoubtedly one of the greatest soldiers, if not the greatest, who

[27] Nicolay and Hay, *Abraham Lincoln,* VIII, 336; Conger, *Rise of U. S. Grant,* 347; Meade, *Life and Letters of Meade,* II, 246.

[28] Nicolay and Hay, *Abraham Lincoln,* X, 166; Wilson, *General Grant,* 366–67.

ever spoke the English tongue.'" "In the subtler aspects of the military art Lee always remained [Grant's] superior," avers R. M. Johnston. Sir Frederick Maurice contends that Grant "had not Lee's extraordinary skill in manoeuvre, but he had the vision to see the military problem of the Union as a whole, the imagination to draw his plans on a big scale, the courage to stick to his plans in adversity, and a real understanding of the responsibilities and anxieties of the Government." [29]

In appraising, comparatively, the grasp that these seven commanders of the Army of the Potomac had of civil-military relations, it is of course obvious that the general who came to the top later in the war had many advantages and experiences to profit by that the earlier commanders did not have. Grant undoubtedly had the best appreciation of the political-military relationship. He knew the place of the man in uniform in a republic such as the United States, and seldom overstepped his proper limits. Although not showing sufficient tact in his dealings with his civilian superiors, McClellan was not the worst offender of the principle of civilian supremacy, as Hooker's talk of a military dictatorship showed. Of the seven generals, Grant got along best with the President, and Hooker, followed by McClellan, the worst. Due perhaps to his conservative Democratic leanings, McClellan's relations with the Secretary of War and the Congress were poorer than those of any of the other commanders, although this was scarcely his fault. As to the rapport of the army leaders in the field with the General-in-Chief, McDowell got along fairly well with Scott; Pope worked smoothly with his friend Halleck, while McClellan, Burnside, Hooker, and Meade found it difficult and oftentimes frustrating to deal with Halleck; and Meade got along rather well, all things considered, with Grant.

In the complex field of grand strategy, only two men—McClellan

[29] Geer, *Campaigns of the Civil War*, 345; Johnston, *Leading American Soldiers*, 177; Sir Frederick Maurice, *Statesmen and Soldiers of the Civil War* . . . (Boston, 1926), 97.

and Grant—had the real opportunity, as generals-in-chief, to evolve operations on that level, and both of them were superb in this area of endeavor. As to strategic planning of field operations of their own Army of the Potomac, McClellan and Hooker were the ablest, although both—especially Hooker—showed limitations when it actually came to carrying out these plans in the field. As a tactician, and in the handling of the combined arms of infantry, cavalry, and artillery, Meade was perhaps the superior of the rest, although McClellan was not far behind. Pope and Burnside were the least able in this category. McClellan was certainly the master in the use of artillery, while Meade—though at odds at times with Sheridan —was probably best in directing cavalry operations. In army administration, drilling, and discipline, McClellan—followed by Hooker and Meade—was easily the most talented.

Sea power was a vital contributing factor to Union victory in the Civil War. McClellan and especially Grant excelled in having a grasp of the use and importance of naval power and of joint land-sea operations. McClellan was unquestionably the most popular commander with the soldiers of the Army of the Potomac, but was plagued, later in his war career, with a bad press. Meade established perhaps the best relations and got the most out of his principal subordinates—despite his violent temper—while Pope, Burnside, and Hooker were largely unable to accomplish this. In comprehending the transformation of the conflict from a gentlemanly limited war to a brutal total war, with actions perhaps necessary against the enemy's civilian population and economic resources, Grant and Pope were well ahead of the McClellan-type commander of the early part of the war.

Taking them all in all, and considering the time factor and the increasing weight of manpower and equipment superiorities over the Confederates, it may safely be said that McClellan, Meade, and Grant were, to a greater or lesser extent, competent commanders of the Army of the Potomac, while McDowell, Pope, Burnside, and Hooker were essentially unsuccessful and unsatisfactory. None were by any means perfect; all were earnest and patriotic men; but only the former group of three could be termed adept as lieutenants to Lincoln in the bruising war in the East, where they were pitted against a sublime man of the highest generalship on the opposing side.

Critical Essay
on Selected Authorities

PHYSICAL SURVIVALS

To any student of the commanders of the Army of the Potomac, a comprehension of the arenas in which they fought that army is essential. Fortunately, the battlefields of their major actions are well preserved by the National Park Service, Department of the Interior. The fields of First Bull Run, Antietam, Gettysburg, and Petersburg are quite well developed and marked; while those of the Seven Days, Second Manassas, Fredericksburg, Chancellorsville, the Wilderness, and Spotsylvania Court House are well along toward being further delineated. No authoritative study can be made of these generals' stewardship of the Army of the Potomac without a thorough grasp and appreciation of the terrain difficulties encountered as they moved their armies over the face of the land in the Eastern theater of operations.

MANUSCRIPT COLLECTIONS

Extremely helpful in this present work have been the following manuscript collections, located in the Manuscripts Division, Library of Congress: the papers of Abraham Lincoln (the Robert Todd Lincoln Collection), Edwin M. Stanton, Gideon Welles, George B. McClellan, Montgomery Blair, Ethan Allen Hitchcock, Benjamin F. Wade, Montgomery C. Meigs, Lyman Trumbull, William B. Franklin, Joseph Holt, Fitz John Porter, Zachariah Chandler, Samuel P. Heintzelman, William P. Fessenden, Salmon P. Chase, John G. Nicolay, Charles A. Dana, John Sherman, and Joshua Giddings–George W. Julian.

GOVERNMENT PUBLICATIONS

The massive 128-volume publication of the War Department, *War of the Rebellion: A Compilation of the Official Records of the Union and Confederate Armies* (Washington, 1880–1901), is, of course, indispensable to anyone attempting a study of the Army of the Potomac and its commanders. Herein may be found the official reports and communications of the generals in the field and their military and civilian superiors in Washington, D. C. Beginning with the thirty-sixth book which appeared in this set, serial numbers in arabic were placed on the outside spine of the books; but, in order to harmonize the citations of the first thirty-five books—which were not provided with serial numbers—arabic serial numbers must be *given* to them in order to avoid the long and cumbersome use of series numbers, volume numbers, part numbers, and even supplements. The following table does this:

Roman	Serial Numbers	Roman	Serial Numbers
Vol. I	1	Vol. XIII	19
" II	2	" XIV	20
" III	3	" XV	21
" IV	4	" XVI, Pt. I	22
" V	5	" XVI, Pt. II	23
" VI	6	" XVII, Pt. I	24
" VII	7	" XVII, Pt. II	25
" VIII	8	" XVIII	26
" IX	9	" XIX, Pt. I	27
" X, Pt. I	10	" XIX, Pt. II	28
" X, Pt. II	11	" XX, Pt. I	29
" XI, Pt. I	12	" XX, Pt. II	30
" XI, Pt. II	13	" XXI	31
" XI, Pt. III	14	" XXII, Pt. I	32
" XII, Pt. I	15	" XXII, Pt. II	33
" XII, Pt. II	16	" XXIII, Pt. I	34
" XII, Pt. II, Suppl.	17	" XXIII, Pt. II	35
" XII, Pt. III	18	" XXIV, Pt. I	36

Of considerable value, also, is the verbatim testimony under oath of generals and other important officials which appears in the *Report of the Committee on the Conduct of the War* (Washington, 1863–1866). The debates of the Senate and House in the years 1861–1865 are in the *Congressional Globe.*

NEWSPAPERS

Among the more important newspapers consulted in this present study were the New York *Tribune,* New York *Times, Wilkes' Spirit of the Times,* New York *Independent,* New York *Herald,* Washington *National Intelligencer,* New York *Evening Post,* Detroit *Free Press, Harper's Weekly, Frank Leslie's Illustrated,* Chicago *Tribune,* Philadelphia *Public Ledger,* New York *World,* New York *Sun.*

MAPS

By all odds the finest compilation of Civil War maps is the original edition of the *Atlas to Accompany the Official Records of the Union and Confederate Armies,* which is superior in most ways to the more recent reprint of this work. The maps on Gettysburg by John B. Bachelder, however, and those drawn by the Antietam Battlefield Board, are better than those in the *Atlas* relating to these two engagements. A graphic and useful smaller volume of maps is that published by the Department of Military Art and Engineering at the United States Military Academy: *Civil War Atlas to Accompany Steele's "American Campaigns"* (West Point, 1950). This latter work has more recently come out in a two-volume set, with an accompanying text written by Colonel Vincent J. Esposito.

STATISTICAL AND REFERENCE WORKS

The standard authorities on strengths and casualties in the Civil War are: William F. Fox, *Regimental Losses in the American Civil War* . . . (Albany, 1889), which is a much broader work than its title indicates; Thomas L. Livermore, *Numbers and Losses in the Civil War* . . . (Boston, 1900); and Frederick K. Phisterer, *Statistical Record of the Armies of the United States* (New York, 1883). As to military men, their assignments and appointments, the following three compendiums are invaluable: Francis B. Heitman, *Historical Register and Dictionary of the United States Army* . . . (Washington, 1903); George W. Cullum, *Biographical Register of the Officers and Graduates of the United States Military Academy* . . . (New York, 1868); and Thomas H. S. Hamersly, *Complete Regular Army Register of the United States* . . . (Washington, 1880). The standard and most authoritative collections of Lincoln's writings are: Roy P. Basler (ed.), *The Collected Works of Abraham Lincoln* (New Brunswick, 1953); and James D. Richardson (ed.), *A Compilation of the Messages and Papers of the Presidents* (Washington, 1896–1899). Some useful source material may be found, along with a lot of trivia, in Frank Moore (ed.), *The Rebellion Record* . . . (New York, 1862–1868).

Autobiographies, Memoirs, and Published Correspondence

There is a tremendous amount of information contained in the great number of personal memoirs, autobiographies, diaries, and published correspondence of the Civil War period. Concerning cabinet members, there is the pungent but keen *Diary of Gideon Welles* . . . (Boston, 1911), in three volumes, edited by John T. Morse, Jr.; the excellently edited *Diary of Edward Bates, 1859–1866* (Washington, 1933), by Howard K. Beale; and a modern edition of the diary and letters of Salmon P. Chase. Some of Edwin M. Stanton's correspondence appears in the old and overly eulogistic works, George C. Gorham, *Life and Public Services of Edwin M. Stanton* (Boston, 1899); and Frank Abial Flower, *Edwin McMasters Stanton* . . . (Akron, 1905). Other diaries that have proved of assistance in this present study include: Theodore Calvin Pease and James G. Randall (eds.), *The Diary of Orville Hickman Browning, 1850–1864* (Springfield, 1925); W. A. Croffut (ed.), *Fifty Years in Camp and Field: The Diary of Major-General Ethan Allen Hitchcock, U. S. A.* (New York, 1909); Allan Nevins and Milton Halsey Thomas (eds.), *The Diary of George Templeton Strong* . . . (New York, 1952); George H. Gordon, *A War Diary of Events in the War of the Great Rebellion, 1863–1865* (Boston, 1882); the unpublished manuscript diary, or journal, of Samuel P. Heintzelman, Division of Manuscripts, Library of Congress; and William H. Russell, *My Diary, North and South* (Boston, 1863).

Some of George B. McClellan's correspondence, including the famous letters to his wife, is included in his autobiography, *McClellan's Own Story* . . . (New York, 1887), published after his death by William C. Prime. Also of considerable use in this present work was the two-volume *Life and Letters of George Gordon Meade* (New York, 1913), compiled by his grandson, George Meade. For local color close to the headquarters of Grant and Meade in the overland campaign of 1864–1865, see George R. Agassiz (ed.), *Meade's Headquarters, 1863–65: Letters of Colonel Theodore Lyman* (Boston, 1922). Also consulted were: Jesse Grant Cramer (ed.), *Letters of Ulysses S. Grant to his Father and his Youngest Sister, 1857–1878* (New York, 1912); the two-volume *Cycle of Adams Letters* (Boston, 1920), edited by Worthington C. Ford; Tyler Dennett (ed.), *Lincoln and the Civil War in the Diaries and Letters of John Hay* (New York, 1939); Jesse A. Marshall (ed.), *Private and Official Correspondence of Benjamin F. Butler* . . . (Norwood, Mass., 1917), in five volumes.

Memoirs of principal and lesser military and political figures of the

Civil War period are legion, and must, of course, be used with great caution. Ulysses S. Grant's *Personal Memoirs of Ulysses S. Grant* (New York, 1885–1886), in two volumes, while seemingly open and objective, nonetheless are, in reality, a skillful defense of practically everything that Grant did, and gloss over or remain silent on a number of important incidents. Written on a higher intellectual plane are William T. Sherman's *Memoirs of William T. Sherman* (New York, 1891), in two volumes. Less satisfactory are Philip H. Sheridan's *Personal Memoirs of P. H. Sheridan* (New York, 1888), in two volumes.

Among the more useful recollections of military figures which bear on the seven generals who commanded the Army of the Potomac are: James Harrison Wilson, *Under the Old Flag* (New York, 1912), two volumes; the documented *Military Reminiscences of the Civil War* (New York, 1900), by Jacob D. Cox, in two volumes; the unconvincing *Autobiography of Oliver Otis Howard* (New York, 1907), in two volumes; the terse account by Herman Haupt, *Reminiscences of General Herman Haupt* (Milwaukee, 1901); John Gibbon, *Personal Recollections of the Civil War* (New York, 1928), by an able division commander of the Army of the Potomac; the less helpful book by Erasmus D. Keyes, *Fifty Years' Observation of Men and Events* (New York, 1884); John G. Barnard, *The Peninsular Campaign and its Antecedents* (New York, 1864), by an engineering officer, hostile to McClellan; Regis DeTrobriand, *Four Years with the Army of the Potomac* (Boston, 1889), by another competent division commander; Horace Porter, *Campaigning with Grant* (New York, 1897), a book chock-full of details and local color by one of Grant's staff officers; Allan Pinkerton, *The Spy of the Rebellion* . . . (New York, 1883), in which the secret service chief defends his overly high estimates of Confederate numbers; Adam Badeau, *Military History of Ulysses S. Grant* . . . (New York, 1868–1881), a three-volume effort by one of Grant's staff officers and military secretary, which is much too uncritical and hero-worshipful of Grant; E. D. Townsend, *Anecdotes of the Civil War* . . . (New York, 1884); William Farrar Smith, *From Chattanooga to Petersburg* . . . (Boston, 1893), by the able but tempestuous field leader of the Army of the James; James F. Rusling, *Men and Things I saw in Civil War Days* (New York, 1899); Carl Schurz, *Reminiscences of Carl Schurz* (New York, 1907–1908), the three-volume memoir by a mediocre political general; Joseph E. Johnston, *Narrative of Military Operations* . . . (New York, 1874), by the skillful Confederate opponent of McDowell and McClellan; James Longstreet, *From Manassas to Appomattox* . . . (Philadelphia, 1908), an apologia by Lee's second in command, with frequent comments about Federal generals; and E. P. Alexander, *Military Memoirs of a Confederate* . . . (New York, 1907), by a perspicacious observer who checked his recollections against the records.

For the interplay and ramifications of military and political matters, the present study benefitted from a consultation of the following predominantly political reminiscences: Noah Brooks, *Washington in Lincoln's Time* (New York, 1895); Alexander K. McClure, *Abraham Lincoln and Men of War-Times* . . . (Philadelphia, 1892), by an influential Republican party figure and friend of Lincoln; Charles A. Dana, *Recollections of the Civil War* (New York, 1889), by an assistant secretary of war; Henry Villard, *Memoirs of Henry Villard* . . . (Boston, 1904), by a war correspondent, in two volumes; George W. Julian, *Political Recollections* . . . (Chicago, 1884), by a Radical Republican member of the Committee on the Conduct of the War; William F. G. Shanks, *Personal Recollections of Distinguished Generals* (New York, 1866); Henry J. Raymond, *Life and Public Services of Abraham Lincoln* . . . (New York, 1865), by the editor of the New York *Times;* James R. Gilmore, *Personal Recollections of Abraham Lincoln and the Civil War* (Boston, 1898); Lucius E. Chittenden, *Recollections of President Lincoln and His Administration* (New York, 1891); James G. Blaine, *Twenty Years of Congress, 1860–1880* (Norwich, 1884); Francis B. Carpenter, *Inner Life of Abraham Lincoln* . . . (New York, 1867); Benjamin F. Butler, . . . *Butler's Book* (Boston, 1892).

BIOGRAPHIES

The large number of biographies of Civil War personages which were consulted in this present study will be reduced to those which were of chief value. Helpful throughout, though heavily biased, is the ten-volume *Abraham Lincoln: A History* (New York, 1890), written by Lincoln's private secretaries, John G. Nicolay and John Hay; and the two scholarly and interesting books by T. Harry Williams: *Lincoln and the Radicals* (Madison, 1941), and *Lincoln and His Generals* (New York, 1952), the latter written from the viewpoint of the administration in Washington. On the old "Giant of Three Wars," see the admirable Charles W. Elliott, *Winfield Scott: The Soldier and the Man* (New York, 1937). There is no adequate biography of Cameron, Stanton, Halleck, or McDowell, Burnside, or Pope. Warren W. Hassler, Jr., *General George B. McClellan: Shield of the Union* (Baton Rouge, 1957), is a recent, documented study of that commander's military activities, written in a somewhat sympathetic tenor. The older biographies of McClellan by Peter S. Michie, James H. Campbell, H. J. Eckenrode and Bryan Conrad, and Clarence E. Macartney leave much to be desired. More useful is William Starr Myers, *A Study in Personality: General George Brinton McClellan* (New York, 1934). Much too distorted and eulogistic is Ben: Perley Poore, *Life and Public Services of Ambrose E. Burnside* (Providence, 1882). Walter H. Hebert's *Fighting Joe Hooker* (Indianapolis, 1944), is an adequate biography of that stormy petrel. The two old biographies of Meade, Richard M. Bache, *George Gordon Meade* (Philadelphia, 1897), and Isaac R. Pennypacker, *General Meade* (New York, 1901), are just mediocre. Much better is Freeman Cleaves, *Meade of Gettysburg* (Norman, Okla., 1960). While there is no first-class biography of U. S. Grant during the whole Civil War, the following, while containing weaknesses, are of some merit: Arthur L. Conger, *The Rise of U. S. Grant* (New York, 1931); Louis A. Coolidge, *Ulysses S. Grant* (Boston, 1917); James Grant Wilson, *General Grant* (New York, 1897), too eulogistic; W. E. Woodward, *Meet General Grant* (New York, 1928), popular; J. F. C. Fuller, *Grant and Lee: A Study in Personality and Generalship* (London, 1933), fails to give Lee his due; J. F. C. Fuller, *The Generalship of Ulysses S. Grant* (London, 1929), very favorable to Grant.

GENERAL WORKS AND MONOGRAPHS

Articles by many of the commanders of the Army of the Potomac, as well as by other participants, North and South, appear in the invaluable *Battles and Leaders of the Civil War* (New York, 1884), edited by Robert U. Johnson and Clarence C. Buel, four volumes, although they must be used with caution. An old but still authoritative military and political study is James Ford Rhodes, *History of the United States . . .* (New York, 1896–1904), Vols. III–V. Keen and penetrating analysis of a comprehensive nature is done by John C. Ropes and William R. Livermore in their *Story of the Civil War* (New York, 1894–1913), in four volumes. Also of merit are: Comte de Paris, *History of the Civil War in America* (Philadelphia, 1875), in four volumes, carrying the war up to 1864; James Kendall Hosmer, *The American Civil War* (New York, 1913), two volumes; George Fort Milton, *Conflict: The American Civil War* (New York, 1941), quite readable; William Wood, *Captains of the Civil War* (New Haven, 1921), entertaining; J. G. Randall, *Civil War and Reconstruction* (Boston, 1937), solid and scholarly; W. Birkbeck Wood and James E. Edmonds, *The Civil War in the United States* . . . (New York, 1905), detailed and accurate; Walter Geer, *Campaigns of the Civil War* (New York, 1926), a well-balanced and judicious summary; Fred Albert Shannon, *Organization and Administration of the Union Army* . . . (Cleveland, 1928), two excellent volumes; Margaret Leech, *Reveille in Washington, 1860–1865* (New York, 1941), popularly written but colorful sketches of wartime Washington.

On the Army of the Potomac, two old works are still useful, since they complement each other, and give material and views not found elsewhere: William Swinton, *Campaigns of the Army of the Potomac* . . . (New York, 1866), by the brilliant war correspondent of the New York *Times*, which still wears well and shows remarkable perspective and insight for a book written one year after the war; and J. H. Stine, *History of the Army of the Potomac* (Washington, 1903), which is poorly organized and presupposes advanced knowledge on the part of the reader, but which does contain a great amount of intimate detail.

On the First Bull Run campaign, by all odds the best study is the masterly one by R. M. Johnston, *Bull Run, Its Strategy and Tactics* (Boston, 1913). See also John G. Nicolay, *The Outbreak of Rebellion* (New York, 1881), mediocre; and P. G. T. Beauregard, *A Commentary on the Campaign and Battle of Manassas* . . . (New York, 1891). On the early Shenandoah Valley operations, consult Alexander Kearsey, *A Study of the Strategy and Tactics of the Shenandoah Valley Campaign, 1861–1862* (London, 1930); and Sanford C. Kellogg, *The Shenandoah Valley and Virginia, 1861–1865: A War Study* (New York, 1903).

McClellan's operations are detailed in his *Report on the Organization and Campaigns of the Army of the Potomac* . . . (New York, 1864). On the Peninsula campaign, the two best works are: Alexander S. Webb, *The Peninsula* . . . (New York, 1881); and Theodore F. Dwight (ed.), *Campaigns in Virginia, 1861–1862* (Boston, 1895). The most satisfactory books on Pope's Second Manassas campaign are: John Codman Ropes, *The Army under Pope* (New York, 1881); and George H. Gordon, *History of the Campaigns of the Army of Virginia* . . . (Boston, 1880). The only halfway useful study of McClellan's Maryland campaign is that by Francis Winthrop Palfrey, *The Antietam and Fredericksburg* (New York, 1882). On Fredericksburg, a study soon to appear under the imprint of The Pennsylvania State University Press, by Vorin E. Whan, deals effectively with Burnside and the Union side. Palfrey's book, mentioned above, is helpful, as is G. F. R. Henderson, *The Campaign of Fredericksburg* . . . (London, 1891). A detailed but turgid manuscript study of Fredericksburg, written by John W. McDonald, is deposited at the headquarters building of the Fredericksburg and Spotsylvania National Battlefield Park, Fredericksburg, Va.

One of the finest, most comprehensive studies ever made of an American military campaign is the superb work by John Bigelow, Jr., *The Campaign of Chancellorsville* . . . (New Haven, 1910). Also quite useful are: A. C. Hamlin, *The Battle of Chancellorsville* . . . (Bangor, 1896); Theodore A. Dodge, *The Campaign of Chancellorsville* (Boston, 1881); Abner Doubleday, *Chancellorsville and Gettysburg* (New York, 1882), by a leading participant; and Samuel P. Bates, *The Battle of Chancellorsville* (Meadville, Pa., 1882). On Gettysburg, Glenn Tucker's *High Tide at Gettysburg* . . . (Indianapolis, 1958), is the long-awaited, thorough, one-volume book. Others include: Jesse Bowman Young, *The Battle of Gettysburg* . . . (New York, 1913); Warren W. Hassler, Jr., *The First Day's Battle of Gettysburg* . . . (n.p., 1951); the Doubleday book, mentioned above; John M. Vanderslice, *Gettysburg Then and Now* . . . (New York, 1899); Frank Aretas Haskell, *The Battle of Gettysburg* (Madison, 1908); Comte de Paris, *The Battle of Gettysburg* (Philadelphia, 1886), which is just a reprint of the chapters dealing with Gettysburg from his four-volume work; and Jacob Hoke, *The Great Invasion of 1863* . . . (Dayton, 1887).

Grant's overland campaign to Appomattox is well chronicled in the following studies: Cecil Battine, *The Crisis of the Confederacy* . . . (London, 1905), which includes also Gettysburg; Andrew A. Humphreys, *The Virginia Campaign of '64 and '65* . . . (New York, 1883); Edward Steere, *The Wilderness Campaign* (Harrisburg, 1960), a thorough study; Morris Schaff, *The Battle of the Wilderness* (Boston, 1910), lyrical; G. F. R. Henderson, *The Campaign in the Wilderness* . . . (London, 1908); R. M. Stribling, *Gettysburg Campaign and Campaigns of 1864 and 1865 in Virginia* (Petersburg, 1905). A useful book on the later Valley campaigns is George E. Pond, *The Shenandoah Valley in 1864* (New York, 1883).

Finally, three books which contain brief and somewhat incomplete sketches of prominent National commanders: Gamaliel Bradford, *Union Portraits* (Boston, 1916), well written; Theodore F. Dwight (ed.), *Critical Sketches of Some of the Federal and Confederate Commanders* (Boston, 1895), unbalanced and uneven in merit, with some distortions; and R. M. Johnston, . . . *Leading American Soldiers* . . . (New York, 1907), superficial.

Index